S0-BYL-720

Confession and Absolution

Confession and Absolution

Edited by Martin Dudley and Geoffrey Rowell

THE LITURGICAL PRESS
Collegeville, Minnesota 56321

First published in Great Britain in 1990 by
SPCK
Holy Trinity Church
Marylebone Road
London NW1 4DU

This edition published for the Liturgical Press for marketing in the United States of America, the Philippines, Mexico, Central America (except Belize), and Canada.

ISBN 0–8146–1950-9

Printed in Great Britain

Contents

The Contributors

Perry Butler is Vicar of St Michael and All Angels, Bedford Park, London. He studied history at York and Oxford and trained for the priesthood in Lincoln and at the Venerable English College in Rome. He is the author of *Gladstone: Church, State and Tractarianism* (1982); editor of *Pusey Rediscovered* (1983).

Martin Dudley is Vicar of the new parish of Owlsmoor in the Diocese of Oxford. He studied theology at King's College, London and University College, Cardiff, and has been in parochial ministry for ten years. Co-editor of *Living Stones – a journal of catholic renewal* and a frequent contributor to other journals, his main interest is sacramental theology and its relation to liturgy. He is a member of the Society for Liturgical Study and the Societas Liturgica, and serves on the committee of the Alcuin Club.

John Gaskell, Prebendary of St Paul's, was a 'city gent' until the age of thirty. Now Vicar of St Alban's, Holborn, he has been hearing confessions in central London for twenty-five years. During some of that time he has also been confessor to St Saviour's Priory, Haggerston, and Area Dean of South Camden.

Andrew Greany is Vicar of Hessle, near Hull. Trained at Mirfield, he later served on the staff there as Director of Pastoral Studies, and was for five years Assistant Principal of the St Albans Diocese Ministerial Training Scheme.

Roger Greenacre, Chairman of the Church Union Theological Committee, has been Chancellor of Chichester Cathedral since 1975. He studied at Cambridge, Mirfield and Louvain, and has exercised a pastoral and teaching ministry in London, Ely, Oxford, and Sussex, as well as in France and Belgium. He is a member of the General Synod, of the Anglican-Roman Catholic Committee for England and of the Archbishops' Group on the Episcopate. He is co-author of *The Sacrament of Easter* (1989).

Christine Hall is non-stipendiary parish deacon of St George's, Bickley, in the Diocese of Rochester; she is also a consultant on ministry and a regular teacher and speaker. Her special interests are the theology of the Orthodox Church and the interface between theology and psychology. She is the author of a study on Romanian Orthodoxy and has translated a number of Romanian theological and literary works into English.

John Halliburton is a Canon of St Paul's Cathedral. He is a member of the Church of England Doctrine Commission and was a consultant to the first Anglican-Roman Catholic International Commission. His recent publications include *The Authority of a Bishop* (1987) and *Educating Rachel* (1988).

Brian Horne is a Lecturer in the Department of Christian Doctrine and History at King's College, University of London and Honorary Assistant Priest at Saint Mary's, Bourne Street, London. He is the co-editor of *Seven: An Anglo-American Literary Journal* and the *King's Theological Review*; he is also the author of *A World to Gain: Incarnation and the Hope of Renewal* (1983). He is a member of the Archbishops' Commission on Rural Affairs and the Doctrine Commission of the Church of England.

Jeffrey John is Fellow and Dean of Divinity at Magdalen College, Oxford. After a curacy in South Wales he returned to Oxford to combine the work of a College Chaplain with research and teaching. His main field of interest is the New Testament.

Julienne McLean is a consulting psychologist and psychotherapist in the NHS, in a private hospital in central London, as well as conducting her private practice in north London. She is also a part-time university lecturer in psychology. She has studied in Britain, Australia and the United States, has held various government and university posts, and is the author of numerous publications in the fields of psychology and health. She is presently undertaking a four-year analytical psychology training to qualify as a Jungian Analyst. Her main professional interests lie in the areas of psychosomatic medicine, and the relationship between psychology and religion.

Jill Pinnock read Theology at King's College, London. She has lectured or tutored in liturgy for the Exeter/Truro Ministerial Training Scheme, and at Ripon College Cuddesdon, St Stephen's House, Blackfriars and St Benet's Hall, Oxford. She is Publications Secretary of the Ecumenical Society of the Blessed Virgin Mary, and is an Examining Chaplain to the Bishop of London.

Geoffrey Rowell is Fellow, Chaplain and Tutor in Theology at Keble College, Oxford, and a University Lecturer. He is a member of the Liturgical Commission and is a Canon of Chichester Cathedral. A church historian, he has a special interest in the nineteenth century, and is author of *Hell and the Victorians* (1974), *The Liturgy of Christian Burial* (1977), and *The Vision Glorious: themes and personalities of the Catholic Revival in Anglicanism* (1983), and editor of *Tradition Renewed: the Oxford Movement Conference Papers* (1986). He has a long-standing interest in the Eastern Churches and is a member of the Anglican-Oriental Orthodox International Forum. He is an extra-ordinary confessor to two religious communities.

Preface

The immediate and direct cause of the appearance of this book was a paper presented to the Church Union Theological Committee by Dr Brian Horne, who wanted us to share his concern about the perplexity felt among priests and lay people alike over the theology and practice of the Sacrament of Reconciliation and to engage with him in exploring a way through the uncertainty. As he himself hoped and expected, his paper stimulated a lively debate and provoked no small measure of disagreement. It led us to plan the present volume, which, though the work of individual contributors, not all of them members of our group, is still very much the product of the Committee as a whole, since nearly every chapter has been revised and rewritten in the light of group discussion both at our day meetings at Pusey House, Oxford, and at our residential sessions at Ascot Priory.

An additional incentive in the production of this book has been the comparative lack of attention given in recent theological publication to the Sacrament of Reconciliation. Most of what has been written seems to have come from Roman Catholic writers (notably in the USA) and has largely been centred on the new liturgies of Penance in the Roman rite and on controversies raised by the question of the sacramentality of absolution when given on occasions which preclude individual avowal of sins. We do not wish to suggest that such literature has no interest for Anglicans, but it does have to be recognized that if there is a real crisis with regard to this sacrament and a decline in its use in both the Roman Catholic and Anglican Communions, the background in each Communion has been very different.

Roman Catholics have been questioning the value and necessity of a sacrament previously regarded as obligatory but often administered in a very routine way and with no expectation on the part of either confessor or penitent of spiritual guidance. From having been regarded as being as much of an obligation for the practising Catholic as the reception of Holy Communion it is now in many places being increasingly marginalized; in March 1989 the Bishops of the USA admitted to Pope John Paul II at a special meeting in the Vatican that 19% of practising Catholics – that is, those who regularly attend Sunday mass and contribute financially to the support of the Church – no longer have recourse to this sacrament. Anglicans who have had recourse to this ministry, on the other hand, have always been in a minority and have usually expected 'counsel' as well as 'absolution' –

have often indeed felt more need of the counsel than of the absolution. Common to both traditions has been an increasing sense of the shallowness of the 'laundry list' approach to self-examination and confession found in so many devotional manuals, with their exclusive preoccupation with individual sins and their lack of awareness or concern with the individual's involvement in, and complicity with, the sins of the community. In both traditions also there is now considerable scepticism with regard to the authoritative pronouncements of many confessors on certain moral questions over which there is genuine division. The Roman Catholic debate on contraception and the debate in both traditions on homosexuality have brought this home forcefully to the laity in both our Communions.

The motivation for producing this book must not be sought in the debates on confession or absolution which have taken place in the General Synod of the Church of England and the Convocations of Canterbury and York since 1981. On the other hand, we could not be unaware of those debates or lacking in some sense of responsibility for the continuing search for a solution to some of the problems they have raised. They revealed that there was very widespread appreciation of the value of this ministry among Anglicans of every school of churchmanship; disagreement was concentrated upon the exact nature of what the 1564 Liturgy of John Knox could refer to as 'the promises annexed with the preaching of (God's) Word, and to the power put in the Ministry of his Church', and this found expression in the inability of some Evangelical members of Synod to accept in a proposed *Rite for the Reconciliation of a Penitent* any modern language equivalent of the Prayer Book formula 'I absolve thee . . .' and in the subsequent failure of the proposed rite to acquire the necessary two-thirds majority in the House of Laity. Since then, the Reverend Terence Knight of the Diocese of Portsmouth has been endeavouring with admirable persistence to keep the question on the agenda of General Synod. In 1984 the Synod supported his motion requesting that the matter be referred to the Doctrine Commission. At the Commission's request, a paper was produced by Dr John Macquarrie, and this led Fr Knight to move successfully a further motion in 1987, requesting the House of Bishops to reintroduce the *Rite for the Reconciliation of a Penitent*. The House of Bishops took advice from the Liturgical Commission and accepted that 'ways be sought to re-open consideration of the wider issues in a less technical context in due time, rather than precipitate further controversy . . .'

In 1989 Fr Knight pressed the Archbishop of Canterbury in a question to say whether this amounted to a rejection of the Synod's request. His reply was that the House of Bishops felt unable to support such a re-introduction at present 'simply because we think that there is a better way of getting what we take to be the aims of those who wish what Mr Knight wishes'. At the moment of writing, that is the rather unclear and equivocal state of the question.

While it is our hope that the present volume may be of some small service in this continuing theological debate, a brief perusal of its contents will demonstrate that it is in no sense predominantly theoretical in its approach. Our main reason for writing has been a pastorally rooted experience of, and concern for, the Sacrament of Reconciliation on the part of all our members; we hope that it will help to achieve a wider acceptance of its essential place in the life of the Christian community and a better understanding of its true nature. It was profound conviction inspired by equally profound pastoral experience which enabled two great Christian leaders of our own time to speak movingly of this sacrament.

In his first encyclical *Redemptor Hominis*, Pope John Paul II wrote:

> In faithfully observing the centuries-old practice of the Sacrament of Penance – the practice of individual confession with a personal act of sorrow and the intention to amend and make satisfaction – the Church is therefore defending the human soul's individual right: man's right to a more personal encounter with the crucified forgiving Christ, with Christ saying, through the minister of the sacrament of Reconciliation: 'Your sins are forgiven' (Mark 2.5); 'Go and do not sin again' (John 8.11). As is evident, this is also a right on Christ's part with regard to every human being redeemed by him: his right to meet each one of us in that key moment in the soul's life constituted by the moment of conversion and forgiveness. By guarding the sacrament of Penance, the Church expressly affirms her faith in the mystery of the Redemption as a living and life-giving reality that fits in with man's inward truth, with human guilt and also with the desires of the human conscience. 'Blessed are those who hunger and thirst for righteousness, for they shall be satisfied' (Matt. 5.6). The sacrament of Penance is the means to satisfy man with righteousness that comes from the Redeemer himself.

Earlier, in *The Christian Priest Today* (first published by SPCK in 1972, and still in print), the late Michael Ramsey, 100th Archbishop of Canterbury, could testify:

> Many find that the significance of sacramental confession for them may change through the passing of time. A first confession may be an occasion of vivid realization of the Cross and a decisive turning-

point in spiritual depth. Subsequent confessions in the early years can have a like vividness. Then a time may come when the vividness fades and confession seems to have the staleness of a humdrum discipline. So there comes the tendency to say 'Why bother?', and amidst the intense busyness and tiredness of work to let both self-examination and confession slip. It is, however, when going to confession requires a sheer discipline of the will that a new and creative aspect of it may begin to emerge; the act of will in confessing may enable you to escape vagueness and drift and to regain a true picture of yourself. Then you may find in new ways how the loving kindness of God can hide, as it were, beneath the recesses of your failure, and you are humbled by discovering how God can use you in spite of yourself.

In conclusion, it may be helpful to say something about the Church Union Theological Committee, revived by the Bishop of Chichester, President of the Church Union, in 1979. The 1960s and 1970s had been an exciting but also a confusing epoch and the Church Union, a body which in its nineteenth century heyday could number among its members such leading figures as John Keble, Dr E.B. Pusey, J.M. Neale, T.T. Carter and Lord Halifax, felt that, as the senior of all the organizations which represented the continuing Tractarian tradition within the Church of England, it had a responsibility for gathering together a body of men and women who could be called upon to provide theological guidance for those who thought of themselves as Catholic Anglicans and who were in so many cases confused and bewildered at the speed of change in the life of both Church and Society. To some extent the Catholic Movement had been the victim of its own success; many of the liturgical and sacramental ideas and practices it had pioneered and fostered were now widely adopted throughout the Church of England, but since this had not been accompanied by the same widespread acceptance of either its penitential and ascetic discipline or of its ecclesiological thinking, the Movement itself entered into something of a crisis of identity.

In this situation, the Committee came to perceive its responsibility as a dual one; it has had, in the first place, to respond theologically to specific problems referred to it – often with some urgency – by its parent body, the Church Union, and it has, in the second place, struggled to find time to engage in theological reflection on issues which it has itself identified as being important for those who stand within the Catholic tradition in Anglicanism. For some – both inside and outside that tradition – it may have acquired a rather negative image because it has been obliged to react to proposals and ideas perceived to be destructive of that tradition. We do not apologize for having sometimes to say No; we would however claim that we have consistently tried to be positive, irenic and constructive in our approach. For example, our members have taken part in dialogue with Evangelical Anglicans and the Archbishop of Canterbury felt able to welcome the volume of essays resulting from the first stage of this dialogue, *Stepping Stones* (edited by Christina Baxter and published by Hodder and Stoughton in 1987), in his Foreword as a 'heartening . . . exercise in constructive theology'. Since then we have published the first of a projected series of CUTC papers dealing with the controversial area of Church and Ministry; this publication, the so-called Ascot Statement, *The Household of God* (CLA, London 1988), has been welcomed by a number of leading Evangelicals, including the principal of a theological college who wrote to us: 'I enjoyed reading it and found that it said very positively so many of the things I believe need saying.'

The present volume has arisen, in the way already described, from our determination not to allow our second function of theological reflection on issues we ourselves have identified as important to be crowded out by apparently more urgent demands. It has been a relief to be able to turn aside for a moment from those issues which at present seem to obsess the Church of England and risk destroying its unity and to offer this volume to a public which, though it will include many who will differ from us on other issues, will be able to identify itself with our prayerful concern for the future development of the ministry of confession and absolution and may also, we hope, find what we have written helpful and constructive.

Roger Greenacre
Chichester,
June 1989

1 Introduction: Confession Today

Perry Butler

It seemed sensible, in the discussion leading to this collection of essays, to try and discover something about the actual situation in Anglican parishes today. In most churches, the number of penitents has always been few and there is a general feeling that in churches where the practice was more deeply rooted, numbers have declined. Yet in the last twenty years or so hostility on grounds of churchmanship has largely abated. Among Evangelicals, there has been renewed interest in spirituality, retreats and spiritual direction and, despite hesitations about forms of absolution, many are now more open to the idea of a 'soul friend' and auricular confession as part of spiritual discipline and growth. The ministry of sacramental confession may be talked about more widely in the Church of England, though it is not entirely clear whether more people actually avail themselves of it.

This chapter makes no attempt to answer the many questions that could be asked of Anglican attitudes and practice in a systematic or comprehensive way. It was written as much to satisfy the curiosity of the author as anything else. Nor is it based on sophisticated sampling techniques, simply the impressions and comments of fourteen clergy and slightly fewer laity. Since this group was chosen randomly from among the author's contacts (though with some attention to covering a range of experience, age and geographical spread), it can scarcely be described as representative of the Church of England as a whole. What follows is therefore offered with some diffidence, though with the hope that what has been discovered is sufficiently interesting to deserve a wider audience.

CLERICAL ATTITUDES

All but two of the priests approached considered themselves broadly within the Catholic tradition, though some had come from other traditions within Anglicanism and most did not wish to be thought of as partisan, still less narrow, in churchmanship. One was teaching at an Evangelical theological college after a title in a liberal Evangelical parish. One was a definite conservative Evangelical with experience of the charismatic movement. In all, eleven were in parochial ministry, one a cathedral canon, one a university chaplain and one teaching in a theological college. Several had previous experience of theological college teaching or university chaplaincy work, two had experience of what may be termed 'Anglo-Catholic shrines' with a significant reputation for the ministry of reconciliation. Four were under forty, six between forty and fifty, two between fifty and sixty and two were over sixty.

The older priests agreed that the number of penitents appears to have declined and one was prepared to date this to the upheavals of the 1960s. Inevitably, evidence tends to be impressionistic. Large queues in central London churches at the major festivals seem a thing of the past. The verger at St Stephen's, Gloucester Road could recall preparing sandwiches in the vestry in the 1950s for the two priests manning the confessionals in Holy Week, since the numbers required such long stretches 'in the box'.

This needs to be balanced, however, by the fact that more priests today are probably willing to hear confessions and certainly to advertise the fact. Most cathedrals have developed a not insignificant ministry in this area. Probably more confessions are heard in the context of quiet days, retreats and pilgrimages than was the case in the past. There has also been a growth in prayer groups, often ecumenical, and in Third Orders and Oblates. The development of counselling within the churches has also had its impact – with a clear distinction between counselling and confession becoming blurred.

It is certainly true that to make one's confession was for many people part and parcel of an 'Anglo-Catholic identity'. It was what was expected, part of 'the package'. Now, self-conscious Anglo-Catholicism is a less significant and certainly a less coherent force within the Church of England. Many are regular attenders at 'high churches' without feeling the sort of pressure to become the regular penitent that probably existed thirty or forty years ago or earlier, when Anglo-Catholicism exhibited a more crusading ardour.

It would appear that the sort of confession made has also changed over the years. A more widespread use of the confessional was pioneered by the missionary-minded ritualist priests of the last century. Their understanding tended to be based on contemporary Roman Catholic practice. While their influence has lingered in some places, it has greatly declined. Those priests with long experience agreed that the old style 'confession of devotion' (say, once a month) had all but disappeared. Today, those who make their confession appear to do so because they feel driven to confess a genuine grave sin in a 'one-off encounter' (matrimonial offences often being a significant trigger), or because they have been introduced to the practice as a way of deepening spiritual awareness and see it (as one priest put it) as 'a good sort through!', needed perhaps two or three times a year – almost on the model of servicing a car. In parishes where there has been a tradition of teaching about confession, regularly advertised times and so on, penitents (particularly the more elderly) still appear at major festivals – though in much smaller numbers. Many appear to come quite sincerely, but without any particular expectations, motivated largely by a sense of duty and the feeling that Christmas or Easter wouldn't be quite right without this being done.

All this has meant that, from the priests' point of view, confessions today are often longer and looser than in the past and sometimes more akin to the pastoral interview. While the priests questioned acknowledged this, their reaction to it varied. Some felt that the opportunity provided for more extended spiritual direction and counselling should be grasped within the confessional setting. Others, however, were uneasy and felt that there were dangers that the focus has strayed away from confession of sin and receiving the grace of absolution. 'You can't absolve on the basis of conversation', one commented. 'At some point, there must be a clear and categorical acknowledgement, I was wrong and I must say this to God'. Another was concerned that, nowadays, the emphasis was seen too obviously in therapeutic terms; it was necessary 'to keep always a sense of sacramental encounter'. Most agreed that 'Freudianism' (if it may be so called) had made its impact. People seemed to find it harder to confess specific sins in a concrete way and often tended instead to articulate a vaguer (though probably no less real) sense of 'sinfulness' in their lives or relationships. The more articulate the penitent, the more likely was their confession to reflect the remark of Celia in T. S. Eliot's *The Cocktail Party*,

> It's not the feeling of anything I've ever *done* which I might get away from, or of anything in me I could get rid of – but of emptiness, of failure towards someone, or something, outside myself.[1]

Probably, this change is related to the lack of consensus in moral thinking today, a breakdown of confidence in clear distinctions between right and wrong and more insight into the complexity and ambiguity of 'motive'. It may also reflect a greater awareness of 'social sin' and injustice on a national or world scale which makes people feel that personal transgressions are relatively trivial.

The priests were asked a number of specific questions about their theological understanding of the sacrament.

What made auricular confession sacramental?
Several commented that many Anglicans clearly saw the general absolution given at the Eucharist as being sufficient, except possibly in circumstances of grave sin and an unquiet conscience. Perhaps this is why some lay people have been heard to express a dislike of the use of 'us' in the ASB absolution, trying to turn it, like the form in the Roman rite, into a prayer for forgiveness. All, however, believed that a specific authority to absolve was part of the priestly commission and that this was the understanding of priesthood contained in Anglican formularies, especially the BCP. The priest acted *for* the Church, which had the authority to bind and loose. Those with knowledge of modern Roman Catholic practice in regard to 'general absolution' felt it was muddled. 'Absolution is a particular act reconciling a particular person', one commented. Another believed it was sacramental because 'it is mediated through a person'. This seemed the nub of the matter for all those questioned: Confession was sacramental because it was 'focused', 'specific', 'individual' and 'concrete', to use some of the words given. Three felt that the ecclesial dimensions needed particular prominence in commending the sacrament today. It was sacramental because it restored the Christian, cut off through sin, to the Body of Christ, and most Anglicans had a weak *sensus ecclesiae* and a deep-rooted individualism in religion.

Not surprisingly, the conservative Evangelical felt unable to speak of confession and absolution in sacramental terms. But he had, nevertheless, recommended it to some individuals who felt a lack of assurance about forgiveness. His involvement in charismatic renewal had brought him and others, he believed, to a more sensitive awareness of different practices among Christians. He had come to realize that 'many people are deeply hurt and need forgiveness spoken to them as well as preached at them'. He felt Evangelical suspicion of the practice rested on fears of undermining the truth that Christ is sole mediator between God and man. Another priest, less identified with Evangelicalism, but teaching in an Evangelical theological college, pointed out that Evangelicals still felt that fundamental issues regarding the practice remained, listing the priesthood of all believers, the nature of the ordained ministry, the nature of authority to forgive (in Church/priest or in Scripture as Word of God). He personally felt it was a pity that confessions as such were seldom heard in churches with an Evangelical tradition. While some situations in pastoral counselling were akin to confession, they inevitably lacked 'the dramatic formal quality of the relationship of confessor and penitent'. He perceived that for some, perhaps many, Evangelicals repentance was regarded as a 'once for all event with occasional crises after conversion'.

The conservative Evangelical noted that nothing had been said of the practice in his theological training, to his regret. It would be interesting to know if, when and how sacramental confession is handled in theological training in colleges of different traditions and those less definitely aligned.

How did they understand the role of the priest?

In his book *Hearing Confessions* (1974), Kenneth Ross discussed the priest's role in sections headed (in this order): Judge, Father, Physician and Guide. Interestingly, all the priests in the sample emphasized the priest as 'agent' or 'representative' of the Church or of Christ. One spoke of 'facilitating the encounter with Christ', three others in terms of being a 'channel of God's love'. All emphasized the *pastoral* rather than the *juridical* nature of the role, with three commenting that they felt this was the chief difference between Anglican and Roman Catholic perceptions of the matter. Two commented that a priest might fulfil a useful personal role, as a sort of 'father figure', especially when dealing with younger people. One of these priests in a quite ordinary parish had a high proportion of penitents in the late teenage or early twenties age range.

What did the priests hope for their penitents?

All clearly hoped that pronouncing God's forgiveness would aid spiritual growth. Not surprisingly, some talked of the benefits of 'getting things off your chest', 'mental consolation', 'release' and 'spiritual refreshment'. One spoke of the confessional as providing 'a positive view of sin', correcting the view that it was 'a wrist slapping exercise'. Several mentioned the importance of the seal of the confessional.

All were asked about giving counsel and advice. One saw this primarily as 'a personalized ministry of the Word', though another commented that Anglican priests should realize penitents asked for counsel and not a sermon! All were agreed that, in the Anglican tradition, counsel was expected and that this constituted an important part of the encounter. Not to give counsel was, as one priest put it, 'a prime opportunity missed'. Another felt that where counsel was not asked for he would 'suspect the depth of contrition'.

It was noted that since sacramental confession was a rather 'élite activity' in the Church of England, Anglican penitents might include a high percentage of the introverted, mildly neurotic or self-absorbed. It was, therefore, important to make it clear that confession was not simply an exercise in 'self-assessment' and, in certain cases, it was necessary to gear advice to spiritual deepening, rather than colluding with a desire for what one priest described as 'psychological toning up'. Another suggested that counsel was needed to help penitents pinpoint real weaknesses and avoid scrupulousness.

How did they feel about the 'I absolve you' formula?

All recognized that other forms of absolution would be valid and, apart from the conservative Evangelical who said he would use an ASB absolution, possibly more personalised, none wanted to abandon it. It was felt that most Anglican penitents had come to expect it and valued it. Several based their authority specifically on the Book of Common Prayer, seeing the form as something inherited from Cranmer and the medieval Church. It was felt by most to be psychologically important to the penitent – 'a climactic moment' as one put it. Four used the phrase 'clear cut', or something like it. One said it was 'direct and easy to latch on to'. 'Strong and unambiguous', said another. Three believed it gave a richer and stronger sense of the priest as the personal agent of Christ in his Church. One stressed its importance in a 'one to one encounter': reconciliation was mediated 'one to one'.

The conservative Evangelical apart, none had theological objections to the phrase. Most were distressed that it had been the source of conflict in the Synod and several felt objections (e.g. the comparison of 'I absolve you' with 'I regenerate you', rather than 'I baptise you') should be challenged.

The priest teaching in an Evangelical theological college noted that his training incumbent from a liberal Evangelical background told him to use the formula 'in some cases'. It would be interesting to know whether older Evangelical clergy who heard confessions in a formal sense used 'I absolve you' because it was 'in the Prayer Book', while younger clergy of that tradition were simply less Prayer book orientated and felt that avoiding it was part of the modern Evanglical identity.

How do the clergy understand penance today?

In the traditional understanding of sacramental confession, the notion of satisfaction and giving a penance played an important part.

Making amends was felt to be important, both theologically and sociologically. None of the sample saw penance as the central thrust in their understanding of the sacrament, though, without exception, all continued to give a penance. Two admitted, however, that they felt most traditional penances were 'irrelevant' and another made the cogent point that increasingly there was a smaller reservoir of psalms and collects known by heart today.

Asked why they continued to give a penance, several said that somehow it symbolized the acceptance of being forgiven, 'responding to grace' as one put it. Another felt that it was important not to confuse a penance with reparation, since penances today would rarely reflect the gravity of the offence. One young priest, however, working with students, felt that it was important to link the idea of penance with sacrifice or self-offering in some concrete way. At the very least, as an older priest put it, a penance provides 'an opportunity to recollect'.

An important new emphasis in relation to the sacrament is that of healing. Some of the priests questioned sometimes combined a ministry of laying on of hands or anointing with absolution. This seemed particularly important to penitents who were introverted, angst-ridden or with a low estimation of themselves. Others related this to the 'conscience-consciousness' problem today. Life today appears to make it more difficult to disentangle guilt, anxiety, fear and estrangement from conscious sin. It is often easier to be conscious of these emotions than to confess specific sins or clear transgressions of God's will. Many confessions today, especially of the particularly articulate, tend to consist more of 'I am' than 'I have'. Is this to be viewed negatively (the result of a decline in objective morality) or more positively (as a desire to see the confessional as having a wider scope than confession of sin)? Clearly thought needs to be given to this matter, since a lot of uneasiness was felt. Yet all priests valued sacramental confession for the 'new start' it enabled penitents to make, and many could recall instances when confession had been visibly liberating.

In the past, it was not unusual to urge frequent confession. In this sample, only one priest (in the 40–50 age group) believed a regular communicant should be urged to go to confession as frequently as once a month. One other priest, however, did comment that, since Anglican penitents expected counsel, they might be encouraged to confess fairly frequently so that the counsel given could be brief, to the point and therefore more likely to be acted upon. Generally speaking, most favoured two to four times a year (their own pattern?), pointing out that those Anglicans who went regularly tended to do so at the sacred seasons. Two quoted the old adage that confession was 'medicine, not food'.

Of course, the numbers of penitents in Anglican churches are few and those questioned were asked why they felt this was the case. One felt it was related to the decline of Anglo-Catholic identity, pointing out that where something of the old ethos lingered, penitents were still to be found – even if not in such large numbers. Others felt that the practice was viewed with suspicion as un-Anglican. A Lancashire priest felt this was particularly true in his part of the world and another declared that, among English people, there was a sort of 'tribal feeling against it'. Many felt that there was a lack of teaching about confession and though many Anglicans were aware of it, there was a vague feeling that it was not for the average worshipper. Many, however, felt that preaching about it had little effect – though all made it part of confirmation preparation. Giving the candidates the 'know how' was thought to be important without necessarily putting undue pressure on candidates to make a confession before confirmation.

When, one wonders, did the phrase 'All can, none must, some should', gain currency among Anglicans?

One priest, jokingly, put the small number of Anglican penitents down to 'the endemic pelagianism of the English people'. Yet others did believe a weak or at least vague sense of sin was more prevalent today than in the past. One pointed out that, although the contemporary emphasis was on 'doing your own thing', this seemed to run parallel with a disinclination on many people's part to shoulder individual responsibility.

Two of the sample believed that the growth of the retreat movement and pilgrimages had been beneficial and had opened the door 'for some'. Both priests from the Evangelical tradition felt their constituency was more open to the idea of individual confession within a framework of spiritual guidance, than was once the case. A helpful sociological point was made by two of the priests. The priestly style of Anglican clergy could, they believed, discourage penitents. Parishoners related to a vicar rather differently than to a more detached Roman Catholic priest. Hesitations might be felt in confessing to a man, probably with wife and children, with whom they might enjoy a social relationship. Anyone who has ministered at, say, a central London Church will know how important anonymity is.

Two priests, both in the younger age range, thought that services of penance in Advent and Lent could be useful in sensitizing parishioners to the need for greater self-examination and penitence. Others, however, believed that these were things best explored in prayer and house groups.

LAY ATTITUDES

After surveying clerical opinion, it seemed sensible to attempt a survey of lay attitudes. This proved more difficult, though a number of penitents and lapsed penitents were contacted and eleven replied to a short questionnaire asking, quite simply:

1. If you have lapsed, why?
2. Why did you start in the first place?
3. Why do you continue?

For some, becoming a penitent was linked to adult confirmation and connection with a parish which had a Catholic tradition, though others had held back from confession until prompted by some sort of personal crisis, perhaps in early adulthood during university. The appeal of sacramental confession as part of an overall 'Catholic identity' was clearly felt by some. One elderly woman, now a nun, accepted it as part of a move from Evangelical Anglicanism to an identification with Anglo-Catholicism. It was, she commented, 'the least attractive element, but I realized that that had to be accepted too'. Another woman (late 50s, housewife), had long felt a curiosity about it and 'gathered up the courage' after seeing queues of people at the confessional boxes on a visit to Padua Cathedral. Overall, people talked about initially making their confession in order to deepen their spiritual lives and as a mark of more serious Christian commitment though, interestingly, two commented that they had held back because their local vicar was seen as a personal friend and 'at the time, I felt uncomfortable about confessing to someone so closely associated with my personal and social life' (male, age 24).

Only those who had started confession as a result of a personal crisis talked of the problems of guilt and an uneasy conscience. Others clearly felt confession to be a more rigorous opportunity for self-examination and the opportunity to discuss spiritual concerns with someone else, though this was often in the context of a vague sense of dis-ease and an awareness of definite, though not entirely understood, obstructions in their relationship with God. For some, it had only been as a result of sacramental confession that absolution became a reality. As one woman in her mid-30s put it, 'It became easier to accept in the context of a spoken confession, in the presence of a priest (in contrast to the entirely private 'soul searching' I had done before)'.

Some of those who had lapsed from the practice of sacramental confession had resumed it at a particular point in their lives (e.g. a decision to be ordained deacon). Among those who had lapsed, two reasons were particularly striking: one was the breaking of a personal link with a confessor because either he or the penitent had moved. It was clear, even from those continuing the practice, that having the right person as a confessor was important, mainly because there was a strong expectation of counsel and spiritual direction. When pressed as to why those who had moved away had not bothered to find someone else, a second reason emerged. It was evident that many felt a sense of unreality about the kind of confession they were in the habit of making. Intellectually, people still 'believed' in the sacrament but, as one person put it, 'between the idea and the reality . . . falls the shadow'.

It would seem that this is indeed related to how sin is perceived and its effects taken away. Individual acts of jealousy or cruelty, etc. were not seen by them as necessary to the use of the sacrament. Even among those who had continued the practice, this problem was clearly evident. One elderly woman admitted that she had ceased to go to confession because her sins were 'so petty and pathetic. I almost longed to be able to say that I had robbed a bank, or plotted to murder my charges, or at the very least committed adultery!' She had returned to the practice after a period of great upheaval in her life. Yet now she found 'that individual acts of sin seem to have disappeared into the background. It is not that they are unimportant, but that they have been superseded by a more acute sense of penitence and a realization that most of the good that one endeavours to do, is from selfish motives.'

Why then, do people continue? One teacher (housewife in her mid-30s) spoke for many when she wrote giving her reasons:

> the great release of tension; I can let go and cut the knot of introspection
>
> helps to sort out true/false guilt
>
> helps to mediate acceptance
>
> in confession, I take responsibility and try to work at what I need to confess
>
> absolution comes as a gift
>
> In the past, I suppose I was not free enough to take on board the responsibility . . . now I want to accept my guilt, my responsibility for who I am.

CONCLUSION

The Anglican clergy questioned seemed, overall, to lack a clearly articulated theological rationale for sacramental confession in today's Church – while being able to talk quite interestingly and intelligently from their own experience. For most it was part of their priestly repertoire, used when necessary in pastoral situations that seemed to require it, and practised as much by intuition as anything else. They mostly believed it was firmly anchored in the Anglican tradition, if not much practised. Some newer insights (the ecclesial element and healing, for example) seem to have been gently integrated into their understanding and practice of the sacrament. Most were wary of tampering with tested formularies or well-tried ways.

Its importance in a strategy for deepening the spirituality of a parish varied among them. For some, encouraging penitents by teaching and pulpit exhortation remained important, though most seemed to be philosophic about the numbers of those likely to respond. A few were clearly hopeful that Anglican practice in this area could be revitalized, but most appeared content simply to respond to the situation they encountered, believing that there were more pressing priorities.

Their comments about the sort of confessions they heard, and the comments of the laity about the unreality of confessing sins and vagueness about the concept of sin itself, however, pinpoints a crucial matter: *What exactly is the sacrament of penance for?* As Michael Vasey put it in a recent *News of Liturgy* (September 1988): 'Sacramental confession conflates spiritual guidance and ecclesiastical discipline. This may be legitimate, but clarity of thought requires unpicking the package.'

Clergy today are perhaps more ready than their predecessors to see sacramental confession in ecclesial terms: as 'the reconciliation of a penitent' to the fellowship of the Church. Yet, penitents appear to find it more difficult to confess individual transgressions or to believe that individual sins are necessary to the use of the sacrament. For most of the laity, especially the more articulate, the practice has become a discussion of their spiritual state – with the expectation of some sort of spiritual guidance. Has this come about because of the lack of an agreed consensus in moral theology, which has spawned a breakdown of confidence in what sin is? It would be interesting to know whether such trends are apparent in Roman Catholicism and what the effect of the disaffection of Roman Catholic laity over contraception, for example, has been on confessional practice.

The modern situation has undoubtedly created new problems in the area of sin, confession and forgiveness that demand clearer thinking about the nature of the sacrament, its scope and ultimate purpose. Today's clergy appear to be aware of this, without quite knowing how best to respond. A considered theological response to these difficulties would appear to be necessary and it would seem that this would be valued at the parochial level. Such a response would need, however, to draw upon the aspirations and needs of today's penitents and the insight and experience of those who, in their ministry, seek to pronounce to their people being penitent 'the Absolution and Remission of their sins'.

Notes

1. T.S. Eliot, *The Complete Poems and Plays* (Faber 1969), p.416

PART ONE

The Christian Tradition

2 'Authority given to men': The Doctrinal Basis of Ministerial Absolution in the New Testament

Jeffrey John

INTRODUCTION

Those who oppose the practice of sacramental confession, and those who object in particular to the first-person form of absolution by the priest, 'I absolve you in the name of the Father and of the Son and of the Holy Spirit', are generally scandalized by the priest's apparent arrogation of a power which properly belongs to God alone. It was for this same reason, the Gospel tell us, that the scribes and the Pharisees were scandalized by Jesus' declaration to the paralytic, 'My son, your sins are forgiven': 'They questioned in their hearts, "Why does this man speak thus? It is blasphemy! Who can forgive sins but God alone?' " (Mark 2.7).

Jesus' own authority to forgive was vindicated by the miraculous healing of the paralytic, and the story according to the Gospels of Mark and Luke ends with a description of the bystanders' reaction of amazement and praise. But Matthew's version draws out the wider implications of the story: 'The crowd glorified God, *who had given such authority to men*' (Matt. 9.8).

These words express, as we shall see, the conviction of this evangelist and of other New Testament authors that the power not only to *preach* forgiveness but to *pronounce* it effectually and authoritatively in God's name was not and could not have been restricted to the person and time of Jesus himself. Two of the Gospels describe for us the moment when Jesus handed on this authority to his immediate successors, the apostles; and we can discern the working of this authority in the early Church in several passages of the Epistles. The gift of visible, objective absolution was not given only to be so swiftly withdrawn. It was to remain incarnate, available to all sinners at all times and in all places, through the ministry of his continuing Body on earth, the Church.

This is, of course, a Catholic understanding, but it is not confined to Catholics. In his celebrated discussion of sacramental confession, Max Thurian affirmed as a Protestant:

The power to forgive, like that of healing, since it is the privilege of

> the Son of Man, is also 'given unto men' insofar as they are united with Christ in his Church. The Church, the Body of Christ, which means today the humanity of Jesus at work in this world, retains this power of absolution. It is not a question only of preaching forgiveness, but of actually granting it. The Church has not only a duty to preach the divine mercy in order to arouse faith and the assurance of forgiveness, but also the power effectively to remit sins by the efficacious sign of absolution.[1]

This chapter sets out to examine in detail the scriptural grounds for this assertion.

THE APOSTLE AS EMPOWERED REPRESENTATIVE

Since at least the time of St Jerome it has been recognized that the Christian concept of the apostle had its roots in Judaism. The Greek word *apostolos* translates the Hebrew *shaliach*, having as its basic meaning 'one who is sent'.[2] In an important article written in 1933 Rengstorf[3] first systematically examined the connections between the New Testament idea of apostleship and the Jewish institution of the *shaliach*; and his findings were exploited in an influential and much-contested article on 'The Ministry in the Early Church' published by Gregory Dix in 1946.[4] These may be summarized briefly here.

Rengstorf's evidence showed that the term *shaliach* was used, especially in legal and religious contexts, of a man sent out as an authorized, plenipotentiary delegate. The *shaliach* was understood to represent in his own person the person and rights of the sender, a convention summed up in the dictum frequently quoted in the Talmud, 'The *shaliach* of a man is as the man himself'. He was a fully empowered representative, and the sender was legally obliged to abide by all words and actions of his *shaliach*, provided that they were within the terms of his commission. This institutional usage is attested in the Old Testament, and is probably much older, but it becomes more prominent during and after the intertestamental period, especially in the rabbinic writings.

The *shaliach* could be the envoy of a group or institution as well as of an individual. Thus the sanhedrin at Jerusalem despatched *sh*ᵉ*lochim* to make authoritative liturgical rulings in local synagogues. During his term of office the High Priest was held to act as the *shaliach* of the whole priesthood, and of the nation as a whole on the Day of Atonement. In particular, rabbis despatched to the Diaspora were to be accounted *sh*ᵉ*lochim* in the full technical sense, carrying in their own person the full weight of the central authority in Jerusalem. It is apparently as one such *shaliach* that Paul went to Damascus (Acts 9.1ff.), carrying letters of accreditation which also formed part of the convention. There is also some evidence that the laying on of hands, which was customary in priestly ordination, was originally employed in the commisioning of rabbinic *sh^{e}lochim*, although it seems later to have been abandoned, perhaps in view of the Christian usage.

Though strongly attacked,[5] principally on the ground of the lateness of much of his evidence, Rengstorf's derivation of the Christian idea of the apostle from the *shaliach* idea has more recently regained acceptance,[6] but his thesis cannot be pressed too far. Rengstorf himself emphasized that the derivation was primarily 'conceptual rather than phenomenological', and Barrett (for example) justifiably criticized Dix for going beyond Rengstorf in attempting to derive a complete ecclesiastical system from an only partially analogous Jewish one.[7] It should be emphasized that the *shaliach* is to be compared with the Christian apostle only in this special representative function. *Sh^{e}lochim* were so termed only for the duration of their commission; they were not permanent office-holders, and there is no evidence for an 'apostolic succession' of *sh^{e}lochim* by one *shaliach* handing on his commission to a successor. Nor is there evidence that Jewish missionaries or proselytizers were ever called *sh^{e}lochim*; the institution operates as a convention within the community and does not imply mission beyond its borders. Prophets in general are not termed *shelichim*, except that particular individuals such as Moses, Elijah, Elisha and Ezekiel are said to be *sh^{e}lochim* of God in specific circumstances, when they performed miracles which were normally regarded as restricted to God's operation. In these cases the designation *shaliach* is applied in the rabbinic commentaries in order to make it clear that these men were not violating the divine prerogative, but that God's own power was acting through their agency – a point very relevant to our understanding of Christian apostolic authority to forgive sins.

A number of passages strongly suggest that the *shaliach* concept of the empowered representative is fundamental to the New Testament understanding of the apostle's role. At John 13.16 Jesus addresses his disciples at the Supper: 'Truly, truly I say to you, a servant is not greater than his master; nor is he who is sent greater than he who sent him.' This is expanded at v. 20 with a statement which itself sums up the *shaliach* idea: 'He who receives anyone whom I send receives me; and he who receives me receives him who sent me.'

In Matthew's Gospel, Jesus uses practically the same words in his commissioning of the Twelve, 'He who receives you receives me, and he who receives me receives the one who sent me' (10.40); whereas Luke applies a similar saying in a partly negative form to the sending of the seventy, 'He who hears you hears me, and he who rejects you rejects me, and he who rejects you rejects the one who sent me' (10.16). Probably the very similar saying applied to children at Mark 9.37 derives from the same original saying or sayings, but has been misplaced in this context because of Jesus' custom of referring to his disciples as children: 'Whoever receives one such child in my name receives me; and whoever receives me receives not me but the one who sent me.'

This weight of evidence argues strongly that Jesus himself sent out his apostles having in mind the particular character of the *shaliach* as empowered representative. The authority of the Kingdom embodied in Jesus is conferred upon them at their commissioning, and in his name they wield the same powers of the Kingdom to preach, heal, cast out demons, to confer or withhold *shalom*, 'the peace of God', and to set the limits of the messianic community. It is noteworthy that the apostles are rarely so called in the synoptic Gospels, except in connection with their commissioning and their action away from their Master – a fact which corresponds with the Jewish understanding that the *shaliach* had no function or indeed existence as a *shaliach* when in the presence of the principal, but only when acting on his behalf and in his absence.

The texts quoted above also make clear that the apostles' mission parallels and extends the mission of Jesus himself. Jesus is himself the *shaliach* of the Father; he is explicitly termed an *apostolos* as well as high priest in the Epistle to the Hebrews (3.1). In John's Gospel, although the word *apostolos* is not used, the verbs *apostellein* and *pempein* (used as synonyms) are employed with the same technical significance to define both the relation of the disciples to Jesus after the resurrection and the relation of Jesus while on earth to his Father: 'As thou didst send me into the world, so I have sent them into the world' (17.18). The authority conferred upon the disciples by their 'sending' is the same as the authority conferred on Jesus by the Father. What they enact in fulfilment of their mission will be upheld by Jesus and is pledged to be ratified in heaven. And as it is made clear in John's version of the apostles' commissioning by the resurrected Jesus – a passage to be discussed in detail later – the distinctive sign of this authority will be the power to forgive sins: 'As the Father sent me, so I send you. . . . If you forgive the sins of any, they are forgiven. If you retain the sins of any, they are retained' (John 20.21,23).

THE POWER OF THE KEYS: MATTHEW 16.19 AND 18.18

Matthew's version of the Confession at Caesarea Philippi reports these words of Jesus to Peter:

> And I tell you, you are Peter, and on this rock I will build my church, and the powers of death (lit: the gates of Hades) shall not prevail against it. I will give you the keys of the kingdom of heaven, and whatever you bind on earth shall be bound in heaven, and whatever you loose on earth shall be loosed in heaven (Matt. 16.18–19).

In a second passage, also found only in Matthew, Jesus addresses the same promise to all the disciples, after instructing them how to deal with offences within the Church:

> If your brother sins against you, go and tell him his fault, between you and him alone. If he listens to you, you have gained your brother. But if he does not listen, take one or two others along with you, that every word may be confirmed by evidence of two or three witnesses. If he refuses to listen to them, tell it to the church; and if he refuses to listen even to the church, let him be to you as a Gentile and a tax-collector. Truly I say to you, whatever you bind on earth shall be bound in heaven, and whatever you loose on earth shall be loosed in heaven (Matt. 18.15–18).

In rabbinic literature the terms binding and loosing are regularly used in respect of legal interpretation: to bind something is to declare it to be forbidden, to loose something is to declare it to be permitted. The terms are also applied to the acts of imposing and lifting a ban of excommunication from the synagogue: to bind the offender is to exclude him, to loose him is to readmit him. These meanings are not mutually exclusive in the rabbinic or in the Matthean texts; but the context of 18.18, following the discussion of the circumstances under serves
which a recalcitrant sinner should be expelled, suggests that the second meaning is uppermost.

The same terms appear in the Dead Sea Scrolls, where it is equally clear that admission to the Qumran community by baptism and the Spirit did not preclude the need for a continuing ministry of forgiveness in daily life. Here binding and loosing are the prerogative of the 'supervisor' (*mebaqqer* – etymologically the equivalent of the Christian *episkopos* or bishop):

> He shall have mercy upon them as a father upon his children, and

> shall forgive all that have incurred guilt. As a shepherd with his flock he shall loose all the fetters that bind them [so that no one should be] oppressed and crushed in his congregation.[8]

Again the action of 'loosing' is most readily understood as the lifting of an excommunication (whether formally imposed in an act of 'binding' or following automatically on certain sins).

In all probability these sayings in Matthew's Gospel represent the evangelist's own elaboration on the working of apostolic authority in terms of his own rabbinic background, written to meet the needs of his own subapostolic, Jewish-Christian congregation. Verses 16.19 and 18.18 should be compared with another saying unique to Matthew at 23.13, that the scribes and the Pharisees 'shut (*kleiete* from *kleis*, key) the kingdom of heaven against men'. In Matthew's thinking, the scribes and the Pharisees truly bore the keys of the kingdom in their own day. Thus, in another important saying found only in this Gospel, Jesus is represented as telling the disciples to observe for the time being what they teach: 'The scribes and the Pharisees sit on Moses' seat; so practise and observe whatever they tell you, but not what they do; for they preach, but do not practise. They bind (*dein*, as in 16.19 and 18.18) heavy burdens, hard to bear, and lay them on men's shoulders. . .' (23.2–4).[9]

This is a clear statement of the principle that 'the unworthiness of the ministers hinders not the effect of the sacrament': the scribes' and Pharisees' actions are utterly to be condemned, but their hierarchical authority is upheld by God, and for the moment must be obeyed. The promise of Jesus to Peter and the other apostles in 16.19 and 18.18 is not for now but for the future, when the powers of the Kingdom will be transferred from the Old Israel to the New (cf. Matt. 21.43; 23.28). But when that time has come, after the death and resurrection of Jesus, the pattern and function of the new apostolic hierarchy will be modelled on those of the old. Furthermore, such authority was hardly limited in Matthew's mind to the persons of the Twelve alone. Those who 'sat in the seat of Moses' handed down their authority from generation to generation by the laying on of hands,[10] and it is most unlikely that Matthew's own congregation had direct contact with one of the original apostles. As Goulder remarks, Matthew's readers would simply have assumed a similar handing down of accredited authority within the Church: 'It is inconceivable that Matthew, bred in the rabbinic system of a succession of authority, could have imagined the Church without successors to the apostles; and the care with which apostolic authority is delineated is evidence of the same.'[11]

Matthew's references to 'the keys of the kingdom of heaven' have further reverberations in Scripture. Both the phraseology of 16.19 and its context (the transfer of delegated authority from an unfit to a worthy vicegerent) recall Isaiah 22.15–25, where Shebna, chief steward of King Hezekiah of Judah, is deposed and replaced by Eliakim. Of the latter God says: 'I will place on his shoulder the key of the house of David; he shall open and none shall shut; and he shall shut and none shall open.'

The same passage is the obvious source of Revelation 3.7, where Jesus himself is described as the one 'who holds the key of David, who opens and no one shall shut, who shuts and no one shall open'. The Apocalyptist's application of the text to Jesus need not, however, be incompatible with that of Matthew to Peter and the apostles. Streeter remarked that Matthew in effect depicts Peter in 16.19 as the Church's 'supreme rabbi', which we have seen to be true to the extent that Matthew clearly believed Jesus intended to confer a quasi-rabbinic authority on him and the others.[12] Yet it is also Matthew who alone in the New Testament insists that the title rabbi is rightfully applied only to the Christ (23.8,10), since he is the empowering source of their authority. They are, as it were, derivatively rabbis of the one Rabbi, just as they are derivatively *sh^{e}lochim* of the *shaliach* of the Father.

THE COMMISSION IN JOHN'S GOSPEL, 20.21–23

> Jesus said to them again, 'Peace be with you. As the Father sent me, even so I send you.' And when he had said this, he breathed on them and said to them, 'Receive the Holy Spirit. If you forgive the sins of any, they are forgiven; if you retain the sins of any, they are retained.'

The context of the saying is the appearance of Jesus to 'the disciples' (20.19) on the evening of the day of the resurrection. It has been contended that 'the disciples' here need not be taken to mean the apostles alone (or rather, ten of them, in the absence of Judas and Thomas the Twin), but possibly a wider group of Jesus' followers, and that Jesus is therefore to be understood as commissioning the Church in general and not a hierarchical group with particular powers, as is more evidently the case in Matthew's Gospel. We have already noted that John's Gospel never uses the noun 'apostle', but it does refer to the Twelve, and it counts powerfully against this view that in v. 24 we are specifically told that 'Thomas, one of the Twelve, called the Twin, was not with them when Jesus came'. Furthermore, despite the absence of the noun, the solemn phraseology of 'sending' in v. 21 exactly expresses the *shaliach* idea, and strongly suggests, as we noted, that a formal concept of apostleship is in view here, as in 13.16, 20. In the prayer of Jesus to the Father in the upper room, 17.18, Jesus had prayed, 'As thou didst send me into the world, so I have sent them into the world.' Now comes the moment of their actual sending.

If the author of John's Gospel knew Matthew, or at least a version of the sayings at Matt. 16.19 and 18.18, one can readily understand this episode as John's fulfilment and actualization of the Matthean promises. These, as we saw, were in the future tense, for the time of the Church's inauguration after the resurrection, when the powers of the Kingdom would pass from the Old Israel to the New. In John's Gospel, the time has come. Now, at the 'Johannine Pentecost', as this account is often termed, the risen Christ empowers the apostles by inbreathing them with the Spirit, who was also promised for the time when Jesus' victory and glorification would be accomplished (cf. John 7.39). The reception of the Spirit and the authorisation to forgive are equivalent signs of the new dispensation. Those who are indwelt by the Paraclete will continue Christ's reconciling work in the world.

Even if it is accepted that John had the Twelve (minus two) specifically in mind in this episode, it may of course still be argued that they are representatives of all Christians, and not of a continuing hierarchy with particular powers. The fact that the evangelist avoids describing them as *apostoloi* is itself sometimes taken to imply that his was a radically 'congregational' stance, hostile to any concept of special authority in the Church. The argument cannot be finally closed, but the charge to Peter at 21.15–17 is the clearest evidence against such a view, and there is further evidence in the other Johannine literature of the importance of the apostle's role and of the existence of other authoritative ministries in these churches (cf. Rev. 21.14; the ascription of 2 and 3 John to 'the Elder', and the content of the letters themselves, especially 3 John 9).

More specifically, those who take John 20.23 to be addressed to Christian disciples in general are inevitably unable to understand the terms 'forgiving' and 'retaining' in the same quasi-rabbinic sense of the Matthean sayings. They are forced to interpret the saying in a much more general sense, as being either a command to baptize or withhold baptism for the remission of sins (an assimilation to Jesus' command to baptize in Matthew's resurrection story, 28.19); or else as a command to 'preach the forgiveness of sins' (an assimilation to the command of the risen Christ according to Luke 24.27). The latter view has few supporters, since it fails to account for the fact that the disciples are here plainly authorized to make a personal judgement in specific circumstances, and it is very hard to see what 'retaining' sins might mean in the general context of preaching the gospel. As Brown remarks,[13] Christ is clearly imparting an effective, and not merely declaratory power against sin.

The second alternative remains. Instead of referring to the forgiveness of post-baptismal sins by apostolic authority, might this verse refer to the forgiveness of sins by baptism itself? Proponents of this view have underlined the fact that in patristic exegesis of the verse a baptismal interpretation predominates, but this observation is misleading. Most of the citations are in Cyprian or authors dependent on him, whose exegesis is conditioned by an urgent struggle with Novatianism. Cyprian is naturally concerned to exploit the text (and many others even less relevant to his case) in order to argue that the ministry of valid *baptism* is restricted to the apostles and their successors in the Catholic Church (although nothing he says excludes the verse from applying to post-baptismal absolution also). It is worth noting too that those who would claim Cyprian's baptismal exegesis of John 20.23 as their own invariably reject his more fundamental assumption, that here Jesus was handing down a power and authority strictly limited to the apostles and the Catholic clergy standing in their succession! Furthermore, the earliest patristic commentator, Origen, nowhere mentions baptism in connection with the verse, but relates it to an argument concerning the relative seriousness of sins, and to that judgement of the sinner (presumably *within* the Church) which must be made by those empowered to forgive or retain sins, namely, 'the apostles and those like them, being priests of the great High Priest'.[14]

Within the context of the saying there is no link at all with the idea of baptism. Rather, as Dodd concludes, the natural interpretation is to suppose that the sins to be forgiven or retained are those of Christians who have offended against the Christian law.[15] In this episode there is no doubt that the author of the Gospel has the needs of his contemporary church community in mind. Verse 23 must be related to the Thomas story which follows, and both are directed to an audience that has 'not seen and yet believed'. John's purpose is to reassure Christians that, no less than through Jesus when he was on earth, the grace of God's pardon is available to the Church by the agency of those whom he has inbreathed with his Spirit. We cannot be sure how the ministry of forgiving and retaining sins was realized in the Johannine church, but it seems most likely that, as in Matthew's church and in Qumran and in the synagogue before them, it was essentially a matter of excommunication and restoration, administered by leaders accredited, by whatever means of election or succession, with the same authority as the apostles.

If it is accepted that John 20.23 is dependent on Matt. 16.19 and 18.18, the change in phraseology is easily understood as John's adaptation of the distinctively Jewish vocabulary of binding and loosing to that of forgiving and withholding forgiveness, which would have been much more intelligible to Gentile ears. Reason has already been given for the change in tense and context. Alternatively, if it is doubted that John knew Matthew's Gospel, we may guess with Emerton that an original saying employed the 'opening and shutting' vocabulary of Isaiah 22.22, and that each evangelist translated it independently into his own setting and into a more familiar vocabulary.[16]

'BINDING AND LOOSING' IN THE PAULINE EPISTLES

In the very earliest texts of the New Testament, the Thessalonian correspondence, we find Paul addressing himself to the fact of post-baptismal sin, and the continuing struggle with sin in the congregation is a leading theme in all the subsequent Epistles. At the informal level we find frequent commands to Christians to 'exhort and admonish one another' and to bring back the wanderer into line. At this level the ordinary gospel requirement of mutual forgiveness is an everyday necessity. In cases of graver sin, however, a more formal procedure comes into play; and here the interpretation of apostolic authority to bind and loose sins as meaning chiefly a power, modelled on the rabbinic pattern, to exclude sinners from or reconcile them to the congregation, receives confirmation from Paul's own exercise of his apostolic authority as evidenced in his letters.

In 2 Thess. 3 Paul lays down a provisional excommunication in the case of a man 'living in idleness, not in accord with the tradition you received from us' – perhaps one of those who were alarming the congregation by preaching an imminent Parousia and the abandonment of normal life (2.1–2). If any one of these people will not obey what is now Paul's second warning (3.12,14), the church is to 'note that man, and have nothing to do with him, that he may be ashamed'. Clearly this is not a final excommunication, but a sanction designed to produce repentance and ultimate reconciliation; and so Paul concludes, 'Do not look on him as an enemy, but warn him as a brother.' The imposition of the ban after two or three warnings in the presence of witnesses corresponds exactly to synagogue practice, and also to the procedure laid down in Matt. 18.16–17.

A similar case appears in the Epistle to Titus. Paul (more probably pseudo-Paul) advises Titus to discipline certain individuals who were disturbing the unity of the church in Crete: 'As for a man who is factious, after admonishing him once or twice, have nothing more to do with him . . . he is self-condemned' (Tit. 3.10,11). Here the procedure is the same, though the ban is imposed in harsher terms. The hope of reconcilation after the ban is not mentioned, though the possibility cannot be excluded. It is noteworthy that the command to expel is made to Titus personally (in the singular imperative) and not to the congregation. Just as Titus, acting in Paul's stead, is to appoint presbyters to the local congregations (1.5), so he bears the apostle's authority to impose excommunication.

In 1 Cor. 5 we find the clearest instance of Paul himself exercising the power of binding as a solemn and formal act, in the case of a man having sexual relations with his father's wife (presumably his stepmother). Paul had already written to them that they must not eat or associate with any Christian brother engaged in immorality (5.9,11). Now, Paul himself pronounces sentence:

> Though absent in body I am present in spirit, and as if present, I have already pronounced judgement in the name of the Lord Jesus on the man who has done such a thing. When you are assembled, and my spirit is present, with the power of the Lord Jesus [you are] to deliver this man to Satan for the destruction of the flesh, so that his spirit may be saved in the day of the Lord Jesus (1 Cor. 5.3–5).

The first problem is to understand 'deliverance to Satan for the destruction of the flesh'. Clearly it involves at least an excommunication. This is explicit in v. 2, 'Let him who has done this be removed from among you', and in v. 13, 'Drive out the wicked person from among you' (verse 13 appears to be a loose quotation from Deut. 17.2–7, especially verse 7, which was the scriptural basis for the Jewish practice of excommunication). The primary aim of the expulsion is to cleanse the Body by isolating the infected part, since 'a little leaven leavens the whole lump. Cleanse out the old leaven . . .' (v. 6–7). 'Deliverance to Satan' need of itself mean no more than removal from the realm of God's Spirit and Kingdom within the Body of the Church back into 'the world', which is axiomatically the sphere of Satan's rule. 'For the destruction of the flesh', however, clearly implies more. Many commentators take it to mean that Paul expected the sinner's death to follow automatically on excommunication, just as the condemnation of Peter entails the death of Ananias and Sapphira in Acts 5. Paul reminds the Corinthians at

10.8 that the Israelites' immorality was immediately punished with death. However, the aim of the 'destruction of the flesh' is stated here to be the sinner's ultimate salvation, and it is hard to see how this would be accomplished (within the conditions of Paul's own theology) if he were to die apart from the Body of Christ. Another theory is that 'the destruction of the flesh' means a grave physical illness, which Paul in his own case was able to view as a work of Satan which might be turned to God's purpose (2 Cor. 12.7). In 1 Cor. 11.30 it emerges that Paul still views the sickness or death of a Christian as a matter requiring explanation, and he attributes both in Corinth to sins committed against the Body of Christ. If this interpretation of 'destruction of the flesh' is correct, the sickness may be regarded as a punishment intended to provoke the incestuous man to repentance in this life, leading to readmittance to the Church and thus to salvation in the day of the Lord.

A third, less dramatic possibility remains. 'Destruction of the flesh' may mean no more than 'mortification of the flesh' in the regular Pauline sense of governing one's carnal and sinful lower nature. In this case, although the sin is much more serious, excommunication would operate as in the Thessalonian and Cretan cases, with the intention of bringing home to the offender the gravity of his crime, leading to repentance and the will to conquer the sin 'of the flesh' so that he may be readmitted to the Church. If this occurs, then the offender will be 'saved in the day of the Lord Jesus' in the manner of any Pauline Christian, having put off the old man and put on the new. This interpretation is supported by another, probably post-Pauline text, 1 Tim. 1.20, where 'Paul' refers to his excommunication of the heretical teachers Alexander and Hymenaeus, 'whom I have delivered to Satan in order that they may learn not to blaspheme'. Here being 'delivered to Satan' implies neither death nor illness: the heretics are to be taught a sharp lesson, and the evident hope is that they will reconsider and return.

In considering 1 Cor. 5.3–5 it is important to determine the relation between Paul and the congregation in the exercise of binding the sinner. The excommunication is undoubtedly to be regarded as an act of the whole Church, which has been corporately wounded by the offender's sin. It is an edict put into effect by the whole assembly acting together 'in the power of the Lord Jesus'. The decision and instigation, however, are Paul's own: he has already judged unilaterally (*kekrika* v. 3) in the name of the Lord Jesus. This is clear both from the context, since the burden of Paul's complaint is that the Corinthians themselves have failed to be moved by the scandal, and from the grammatical construction of vv. 3–5. In this latter respect the RSV translation is misleading. Paul does *not* say '[you are] to deliver. . .'; 'deliver' is an active infinitive with its subject implied in Paul's first-person *kekrika* in the previous verse. The grammatical sense is therefore 'I have judged (decided) to deliver . . .' Paul is also at pains to point out that his physical absence makes no difference to his spiritual unity with and authority over the Corinthian congregation. In the realm of the Spirit Paul is present and president in the assembly. Austin Farrer's description of the case can hardly be bettered:

> The ideal pattern is one of united action in which the apostle presides, the elders concur, and the congregation acclaims: it is the action of each and all, every man's share in it according with his place in the 'body' which acts. . . But at Corinth the elders and the congregation are reluctant, if not opposed, and St Paul is absent. He, without waiting for them, declares that his verdict is already in; he has gathered them in a spiritual though not bodily session, and imposed his ban. It is for them to uphold it. Even if they do not, it is upheld in heaven. . .[17]

In 2 Cor. 2.5–11 Paul urges the Corinthians to readmit an expelled sinner to fellowship in the following terms:

> If any one has caused pain, he has caused it not to me, but in some measure – not to put it too severely – to you all. For such a one this punishment by the majority is enough; so you should rather turn to forgive and comfort him, or he may be overwhelmed by excessive sorrow. So I beg you to reaffirm your love for him. For this is why I wrote, that I might test you and know whether you are obedient in everything. Any one whom you forgive, I also forgive. What I have forgiven, if I have forgiven anything, has been for your sake in the presence of Christ, to keep Satan from gaining the advantage over us; for we are not ignorant of his designs.

Most patristic exegetes identify the sinner referred to here with the incestuous man of 1 Cor. 5. The majority of modern commentators find it hard to sustain this view in the light of 2 Cor. 7.11–12, which seems to expand on the above passage, and which refers to 'the one who did the wrong' and 'the one who suffered the wrong' in a way which seems inappropriate to the sin of incest, but rather suggests, as does v. 5 above, that the man had committed a personal injury against Paul or one of his associates.[18] But whether or not the two men should be identified, this passage is clearly significant because it affords an example of the readmission of a sinner described in terms which correspond very closely to the excommunication. The reconciliation seems to be viewed as a rescue from Satan's clutches, just as the condemnation was seen as projecting him back under Satan's rule. We note the same understanding that a sin committed by an individual is, by virtue of the mystical fellowship of the Body, a sin committed against the whole Church (2.5); and the corollary, that the act of reconciliation, like the act of condemnation, must therefore be the act of the whole Church (2.6,8). Again the apostle's personal forgiveness 'in the presence of Christ' is supposed to parallel the forgiveness of the whole congregation; and again it is quite clearly he who is taking the initiative (2.10).

1 Timothy may also afford us a glimpse of the rite with which an excommunicated sinner was restored to the fellowship of the Church. The author admonishes Timothy, 'Do not be hasty in the laying on of hands, nor participate in another man's sin; keep yourself pure' (1 Tim. 5.22). The patristic and traditional exegesis of this verse takes 'the laying on of hands' to refer to ordination, but this does not suit the context. It is much more likely that the readmission of a penitent is in view here; with the implication that if Timothy (who like Titus bears an apostolic authority delegated from Paul) reconciles the offender to the Church without properly ensuring that he is penitent and willing to amend, then he himself will be an accomplice in the sin. This interpretation is corroborated by Eusebius' statement that the laying on of hands at the reconciliation of an excommunicate heretic was already 'ancient custom'; and also by the similar practice of the synagogue, from which it was probably derived at the earliest stage as an integral part of disciplinary procedure.[19]

Finally we should note that at the close of 1 Cor. 5 Paul supplies a list of specimen sins which ought to entail the removal of the sinner from the *koinōnia* of the Church: 'I wrote to you not to associate with any one who bears the name of brother if he is guilty of immorality or greed, or is an idolater, reviler, drunkard or robber –not even to eat with such a one.' The list is obviously not meant to be exhaustive, and it could be supplemented from similar lists of sins elsewhere in the Epistles, but no doubt these are what Paul perceived to be the main problems in Corinth. Paul nowhere addresses the problem of assessing the relative seriousness of possible sins within these categories, but since his aim is to spur the Corinthian church into taking action, he clearly has in mind cases like that of the incestuous man where the sin is both sufficiently serious and publicly well known for it to be a scandal to the congregation, and so to demand sanction.

THE UNPARDONABLE SIN

According to Mark 3.28–30, Jesus excluded one sin from all possibility of forgiveness: ' "Truly I say to you, all sins will be forgiven the sons of men, and whatever blasphemies they utter; but whoever blasphemes against the Holy Spirit never has forgiveness, but is guilty of an eternal sin" – for they had said, "He has an unclean spirit." ' The content and context of Matthew's version of this saying are essentially the same. Both however are different in Luke's version (Luke 12.10): 'And every one who speaks a word against the Son of Man will be forgiven; but he who blasphemes against the Holy Spirit will not be forgiven.' It is widely agreed that the version of Mark and Matthew is likely to be original. Confusion could easily have arisen from a misunderstanding of the Aramaic term 'son of man', meaning simply 'man' or 'humanity' in general, as it would have been used in the original saying. Luke or someone before him has taken it to apply to the Son of Man, Jesus. The meaning of the saying in Mark and Matthew is readily supplied by the context. It is spoken as a retort to the Pharisees who have seen the working of God's Spirit in Christ and called it the power of Beelzebub. The 'unpardonable sin' is thus a radical rejection of the revelation of God's grace in Christ: 'a perversion of spirit which, in defiance of moral values, elects to call light darkness'.[20] It is not 'the unpardonable sin' in the sense of being one sin among other less serious sins. Rather, it is unforgivable in that it consists in precisely that attitude of mind which never would acknowledge its own sinfulness or accept God's forgiveness.

Luke's understanding of his own version of the saying is less clear. Here the context is Jesus' prediction of the future persecution of the disciples. The immediately preceding verse gives warning that 'everyone who acknowledges me before men, the Son of Man will acknowledge before the angels of God; but he who denies me will be denied before the angels of God.' Patristic exegesis of this verse, almost uniformly from Origen on, interprets the saying in terms of a contrast between pre- and post-baptismal sin. On this view, the 'blasphemy against the Son of Man' is the sin of the heathen before baptism. This is of course sin; but it may be forgiven, as all sin may be forgiven, in baptism. After baptism, however, the Holy Spirit dwells in the believer, and sin takes on a more serious aspect; post-baptismal sins are against the Holy Spirit, and are therefore unforgivable. On this understanding then, blasphemy against the Holy Spirit means post-baptismal sin, for which there is no remission. However, the notion that all post-baptismal sin is unforgivable, although it appears in the later history of the Church, cannot seriously be attributed to St Luke, who includes teaching on the need for mutual forgiveness which is clearly directed to members of the church community and not only, if at all, to those outside (e.g. 6.37; 6.41–2; 11.4; 17.4). All sins committed by a Christian must, in a sense, 'grieve' the indwelling Spirit, as St Paul testifies, but clearly Luke, no less than Paul, believes such sin is normally forgivable. Most plausibly, Luke identified the ultimate 'blasphemer against the Holy Spirit' with the man of the previous verse, who under trial before rulers and authorities in time of persecution fails to testify in the Spirit (12.11,12), but rather denies Jesus before men and so will himself be denied before the angels. For the New Testament authors in general, but supremely for Luke, the author of Pentecost, the Holy Spirit is 'the characteristically Christian possession, the absolutely constitutive factor of the life of the Church'.[21] To remove oneself from the Church by denying Christ is to remove oneself from the sphere of the Spirit's operation, to empty oneself of his life. For Luke, then, the sin against the Spirit would be apostasy from the Church. A saying originally directed against opponents outside the community has been redeployed to warn Christians within the later Church to stand fast in time of persecution.

There is good reason to take other New Testament references to unpardonable sin in this sense also. The sternest are in the Epistle to the Hebrews:

> It is impossible to restore again to repentance those who have once been enlightened, who have tasted the heavenly gift, and have become partakers of the Holy Spirit, and have tasted the goodness of the word of God and the powers of the age to come, if they then commit apostasy (*parapiptein*, fall away), since they then crucify the Son of God on their own account and hold him up to contempt (Heb. 6.4–6).
>
> If we sin deliberately after receiving the knowledge of the truth, there no longer remains a sacrifice for sin, but a fearful prospect of judgement, and a fury of fire which will consume the adversaries. A man who has violated the law of Moses dies without mercy at the testimony of two or three witnesses. How much worse punishment do you think will be deserved by the man who has spurned the Son of God, and profaned the blood of the convenant by which he was sanctified, and outraged the Spirit of grace? (Heb. 10.26–9).

Apostasy is explicitly under attack in the first passage, and almost certainly in the second. Warning and threat against falling away provide a refrain throughout the Epistle (2.1–3; 3.12; 4.1,14; 6.6; 10.39; 13.9). Evidently the church has lost members, probably under pressure of present persecution and the expectation of worse to come (12.3–11). Time is short before the Parousia, which also helps account for this author's insistence on the impossibility of reconciling the lapsed (1.2; 4.1; 10.25,37). For obvious reasons the Epistle to the Hebrews provided excellent ammunition for the Novatianists. One passage, however, is often taken to extend the unforgivable sin beyond apostasy:

> See to it that no one fail to obtain the grace of God; that no 'root of bitterness' spring up and cause trouble, and by it the many become defiled; that no one be immoral or irreligious like Esau, who sold his birthright for a single meal. For you know that afterward, when he desired to inherit the blessing, he was rejected, for he found no chance to repent (*metanoias topon ouch heuren*), though he sought it with tears (Heb. 12.15–17).

Here as in 1 Cor. 5 sexual sin seems to be in view. (Many rabbinic commentaries elaborate on the legendary immorality of Esau, amplifying the mention of his relations with Hittite women in Gen. 26.34.) Here too the ground of excommunication is the charge of defiling the community: the phrase 'root of bitterness' had become proverbial for an infectiously evil individual (from Deut. 29.18, cf. 1 Macc. 1.10). In particular, v. 17, the example of Esau, appears to imply the impossibility of repentance as in the case of the apostate, but in fact this interpretation is much more doubtful than it at first appears. The phrase *metanoias topon ouch heuren* might equally be translated 'he found no opportunity of getting a change of mind' – that is, a change of mind on the part of Isaac his father, who had given the birthright to Jacob by mistake.[22] The translation is the more satisfactory since of course Esau did repent, so that it makes little sense to speak of his seeking an opportunity to repent of his folly. What he sought was an opportunity to alter its consequences, and this he did not find, although he sought it 'with tears'. It is also hard to view Esau as a symbol of final rejection, since he still inherited the not inconsiderable blessing of the younger son, as the author to the Hebrews himself recalls at 11.20. We do not, therefore, have in this passage any clear doctrine of the impossibility of repentance for post-baptismal sin, but rather a warning to keep away from it, or even to desist from it, in the short time that remains. If the reference to the 'root of bitterness' implies, as seems likely, an injunction to weed out notorious sinners by excommunication, we are not able to assume that this would have been an irreversible measure, any more than in the Pauline letters. Furthermore, the author's frequent exhortations in this Epistle to greater moral effort, his admonition not to become *hardened* to sin (3.14), and in particular his reassurances that our High Priest can sympathize with our weaknesses and temptations (2.18; 4.15) all suggest a writer who was perfectly well acquainted with the whole range of congregational lapses, but who under pressure of persecution was adamant against any possibility of readmitting the apostate.

In the first Epistle of John the problem of post-baptismal sin produces a paradox. The author holds emphatically to the view, also expressed by Paul, that in principle sin is impossible for Christians, since the old personality has been stripped off in baptism and the new put on: 'No one born of God commits sin, for God's nature abides in him, and he cannot sin because he is born of God . . . whoever does not do right is not of God (1 John 3.9,10).' The same unequivocal teaching appears again at 3.6 and 3.18. Conditioned by a strongly dualistic outlook, the author's conviction is that on becoming a Christian a man is transferred from the realm of sin and darkness to the realm of righteousness, truth and light. Because he views these as sharply distinct realities, any evidence that the transfer is imperfect or incomplete is hard for him to assimilate. Yet at the same time it is clear that like the author to the Hebrews, he has been forced to acknowledge and come to terms with the fact of post-baptismal sin:

> If we say we have no sin, we deceive ourselves, and the truth is not in us. If we confess our sins, he is faithful and just, and will forgive our sins and cleanse us from all unrighteousness. If we say we have not sinned, we make him a liar, and his word is not in us. My little children, I am writing this to you so that you may not sin; but if any one does sin, we have an advocate with the Father, Jesus Christ the righteous, and he is the expiation for our sins (1 John 2.1–2).

One way in which forgiveness may be sought for a Christian's sin is given in ch. 5, along with a partial solution to the author's theological dilemma. He draws on a distinction which was well known in Judaism and in later Catholic moral theology between venial sin, for which forgiveness may be sought by intercessory prayer, and mortal sin, *hamartia pros thanaton*, sin unto death, where apparently prayer will not avail:

> If anyone sees his brother committing what is not a mortal sin, he will ask, and God will give him life for those whose sin is not mortal. There is a sin which is mortal; I do not say that one is to pray for that. All wrongdoing is sin, but there is sin which is not mortal (5.16–17).

Unfortunately the Epistle offers no criteria for distinguishing mortal and venial sins. In orthodox Jewish practice and in the Qumran community it was essentially a distinction between deliberate and inadvertent sin, i.e. a distinction made with reference to motive rather than to the gravity of the sin itself, on the basis of a distinction made in the Old Testament between 'sins of the high hand' for which the punishment was death, and 'unwitting sins' for which punishment might be remitted (Lev. 4.2ff; Num. 15.22–31).[23] Possibly this distinction was in the writer's mind, but his phraseology suggests he is thinking of the relative seriousness of sins rather than questions of motive. The only particular sin which he seems to have in view, and which indeed is a leading theme in this Epistle, is that of false teaching leading to apostasy (2.18–27; 4.1–6). Here again apostasy appears as the ultimate blasphemy and negation of Christ, the distinguishing sin of the antichrist: 'Many antichrists have come; therefore we know it is the last hour. They went out from us, but they were not of us; for if they had been of us, they would have continued with us' (2.18–19).

The writer's last word is 'keep yourselves from idols' – evidently the false worship of those who, having abandoned the true God and eternal life, have returned to the world which is in the power of the Evil One (5.21,19; 2.15–17). Since the Church is the sole sphere of 'life' in Johannine vocabulary, separation from it is all the more appropriately termed 'sin unto death'. It also accords with this interpretation that the 'sin unto death' is clearly one which is readily recognizable to other Christians, since they will know not to bother to pray about it! We may, then, very reasonably conclude that apostasy was the mortal and unpardonable sin for this author, as it was for the authors of the Epistle to the Hebrews and of Luke's Gospel.

CONFESSION AND PRAYER FOR FORGIVENESS

What is the practical meaning of the injunction of 1 John 1.8–10 (quoted above) that we may not say we have no sin, but that we should confess (*homologein*) our sins in order to obtain Christ's forgiveness? Catholic commentators have sometimes argued that the verse implies a formal or liturgical practice of confession, but there is nothing in the text either to support this view or to exclude it. The context of 1.8ff. seems to be polemical, apparently aimed at a group who were in actual fact claiming to 'have no sin'. The claim to have achieved sinlessness (or, more precisely, to have achieved a state of perfection in which the concept of sin was irrelevant) is characteristic of Gnosticism, and it is widely supposed that the author was combating an early form of this heresy. (Verses. 4.2 and 5.6ff. are plainly aimed at a heresy denying that 'Jesus Christ has come in the flesh' – a second pillar of Gnostic teaching.) This being so, *homologein* need imply no more than to admit or acknowledge one's sin in an interior or theoretical sense, as opposed to 'saying we have no sin'.

A more plausible argument in favour of taking *homologein* in a more active sense is the command to pray for a sinful brother's forgiveness in 5.16 (also quoted above). This presupposes a knowledge of the brother's sin and evidence of his repentance, which in turn suggests that there was a practice of opening one's sins to a brother or brethren, whether this was done privately or publicly, formally or informally. It is worth noting that this author has no qualms in speaking of one Christian's prayers as *effectively* gaining forgiveness for another; it is clearly not felt to subtract in any way from the role of Christ as Advocate and expiation for sin (2.1,2). Here, however, we seem to be at the level of everyday prayer and mutual forgiveness in the ordinary life of the congregation; there is no sign of a hierarchical power of 'binding and loosing', or of any formal procedure of warning such as we have noted elsewhere. One may compare Gal. 6.1–2, where Paul seems to have in mind a similar informal practice of mutual exhortation and strengthening in the context of everyday temptations and lapses (though this might be felt to be the special task of more experienced, 'spiritual' Christians): 'Brethren, if a man is overtaken in any trespass, you who are spiritual should restore him in a spirit of gentleness. Look to yourself, lest you too be tempted. Bear one another's burdens, and so fulfil the law of Christ.' The *Didache* enjoins a confession of sins in church before praying, and in particular before participating in the weekly Eucharist (cf. 1 Cor. 11.28).[24] Unfortunately, here as in 1 John there is insufficient evidence in the text to determine with certainty whether the confession was made publicly before the rest of the congregation or privately in a personal prayer of confession. If, as we may guess, it was more than an act of private prayer, we may wonder whether any form of absolution or formal prayer for forgiveness followed the confession. Since the reader is told to make confession 'so that [your] sacrifice may be a pure one', it is evidently supposed that God's forgiveness is assured, but this may be subjective faith in the efficacy of prayer, and not dependent on a formal declaration.

In the Epistle of James, however, we have an unmistakable reference to prayer for forgiveness as a formal and effectual act by designated ministers:

> Is any among you sick (*kakopathei*)? Let him call for the elders (*presbuteroi*) of the church, and let them pray over him, anointing him in the name of the Lord; and the prayer of faith will save (*sōsei*) the sick man (*ton kamnonta*) and the Lord will raise (*egerei*) him up; and if he has committed sins, he will be forgiven. Therefore confess your sins to one another, and pray for one another, that you may be healed (*iathēte*) (James 5.13–16).

The words used for 'sick' (*kakopathei*; *kamnōn*) imply serious illness, as does the use of the verb *sōzein*, to heal or to save (from death). Noting the ambiguity of the word *sōzein*, which might imply physical or spiritual saving, and also of the verb *egeirein*, which might imply either a rising from one's sick-bed or a resurrection, the Council of Trent found in this text the grounds for administering the sacrament of *extreme* unction in expectation of death, as a guarantee of resurrection and salvation *post mortem*. It is quite clear, however, that the Epistle primarily envisages physical healing from grave illness, though the alternative understanding cannot be excluded from the writer's intention.

The sick person is told to summon 'the elders, *presbuteroi*, of the church'. Their role in this passage evidently attaches to their office as presbyters: there is no mention of lay charismatic healers in the Church, whose ministry was among those listed by Paul (1 Cor. 12.28). These presbyters perform an essentially apostolic function, mediating, of course, the healing and forgiveness of Christ himself. In the Gospels Jesus imparts to the apostles in particular the mission and ministry of healing; and in Mark's version of the sending of the Twelve we find the only other reference in the New Testament to anointing as part of this activity: 'they anointed with oil many that were sick and healed them' (6.13). We know, of course, from Acts and the Epistles that missionary apostles left officials termed 'bishops' or 'presbyters' in charge of local churches, though the precise nature and function of these ministries is disputed, and no doubt varied in any case from church to church. Here, however, since the presbyters in particular are to be summoned, we may conclude that in James' church at least they were supposed to have inherited the apostolic mission to anoint, heal and forgive as a function of their office.

Once again a direct connection between sickness and sin is presupposed. Physical healing is the first concern here, but 'if he has committed sins' – meaning probably, if there are sins which are the hidden cause of this sickness – these will also be forgiven in the process of healing. Presumably such sins would have been confessed to the presbyters prior to the anointing, according to the direction of v. 16, 'confess your sins'. The absolution of the sin is simultaneous with the healing of its physical effects; and both are guaranteed by the authoritative ministry of the presbyters.[25]

Verse 16, however, though clearly linked to the preceding, seems to have a more general application: 'Confess your sins to one another and pray for one another so that you may be healed'. Here a neutral word is used for 'healing' (*iaomai*) which is regularly applied to the forgiveness of sins and need not imply physical sickness at all. The confession and prayer envisaged by this verse recall the more general kind of shared confession and praying about sin enjoined in Galatians, 1 John and the *Didache*. All the evidence we have seen suggests that formal, apostolic powers of 'binding and loosing' were brought into play only in cases of the gravest sin meriting excommunication, or, as in James, in cases of grave sickness. Everyday matters of sin and disorder were probably dealt with by informal confession and prayer within the congregation or between groups of Christians. As 'James' himself remarks, 'we all frequently stumble'; the role of the presbyters was to deal with more serious concerns.

CONCLUSION

We have seen that the New Testament very plainly teaches that Jesus delegated his own authority to forgive sins, the use of which so scandalized the Pharisees, 'to men' – that is, in the first instance, to his apostles. Such authority was already implied in the concept of the apostle, deriving from the Jewish convention of the *shaliach*, as a plenipotentiary delegate whose decisions, if made within the terms of his commission, are guaranteed to be upheld by the sender. It was perhaps the author of Matthew's Gospel who first drew out and highlighted this aspect of the apostle's role, by expressing it in terms of 'binding and loosing' borrowed from the practice of the synagogue. The rules set out in Matt. 18 about the prior warning to be given before imposing excommunication – rules also deriving from the synagogue – make it practically certain that for Matthew 'binding and loosing' primarily meant the acts of excluding and readmitting an offender. The terms could also refer to rabbinic judgements pronouncing any doubtful matter or action legal or illegal, and this second meaning need not be excluded. In Matthew's view the hierarchy of the New Israel is closely patterned on that of the Old. The apostles are 'Christian rabbis', and we may safely assume that Matthew's church at least depended on a quasi-rabbinic succession of apostolic authority.

The story of the apostles' empowering to forgive or retain sins in John 20 is probably dependent on Matthew, and represents this author's translation of the saying about 'binding and loosing' into a post-resurrection context and a more familiar vocabulary. There is no reason to interpret the text as a command to baptize, and little reason to doubt that this author, like Matthew, wrote with a view to explaining the origins of a theory and practice of authoritative absolution which still obtained in his own day.

The Pauline epistles show us the practical working of apostolic authority to 'forgive or retain' sins from the earliest recorded stage of the Church's existence. Paul himself (as well as Timothy and Titus in the Pastorals) is found to exercise individual authority to excommunicate and reconcile sinners. Again the synagogue rule about due warning appears. The episode of the incestuous man in 1 Cor. 5 shows that, since sin was held to be an offence against the whole Church as well as against God, the whole Church could be regarded as the agent of reconciliation. Nevertheless the apostle is able to act unilaterally to exclude the offender, and to demand that the church submit to his decision. Paul names numerous categories of sin which should entail excommunication, but nowhere implies that any sin is incapable of forgiveness.

The unforgivable 'sin against the Spirit' condemned by Jesus in the Gospels of Mark and Matthew evidently refers to the perverse attitude of the Pharisees who, when faced with the power of God in Christ, blasphemously ascribed it to Satan. It consists in that spiritual state which would in any case refuse repentance and exclude all possibility of forgiveness. In the Gospel of Luke, however, the 'sin against the Spirit' is the sin of denying Christ by apostasy from the Church, and apostasy is also the unpardonable sin attacked in the Epistle to the Hebrews, and the 'mortal' sin mentioned in 1 John.

Throughout the New Testament there are numerous references to the need for mutual forgiveness in the everyday life of the Church. Several epistles enjoin confession and prayer for forgiveness of an apparently informal kind among Christians, which by the time of the writing of the *Didache* appears to have gained a more formal character as a prelude to church worship, although it was not, as far as we can tell, associated with ministerial absolution.

Apart from Timothy and Titus, who are better described as special apostolic delegates than as proto-bishops, the Epistle of James provides the best evidence within the New Testament that the apostles' authority to heal and forgive sins was handed on to local presbyters or bishops. James lays down that in a case of serious sickness, the presbyters (priests) of the church are to be summoned, who will pray over the sufferer and anoint him with oil (after the manner of the apostles in Mark's Gospel); this will achieve the double effect of healing and forgiveness. Since the same Epistle also urges a general and seemingly informal confession of sins 'to one another', we may conclude that presbyteral authority was brought in only in cases of grave sickness or sin, just as Paul's apostolic authority was deployed only in the most serious cases.

To sum up: although the application of ministerial absolution varied, as we shall see in the following chapters, at different times and places in the Church's later history, here is very ample evidence that the doctrinal basis of the practice is firmly grounded in the New Testament. The writers of the texts which we have been considering did not and could not have supposed that the authority to forgive was limited to Jesus himself. Equally they did not and could not have supposed that it was delegated to the apostles, but then died with them. The Gospels which authorize men to bind or loose, forgive or retain sins were addressed to churches in which the apostles' authority must already have passed in succession to a second or third generation of empowered ministers; and in the Epistles we see direct evidence, scant but sure, of this post-apostolic ministry in operation.

Notes

1. M. Thurian, *Confession* (London 1985), p.50.
2. Jerome notes (*Commentary on Galatians* 1.1) that 'even today apostles are sent out by the patriarchs of the Jews. The word apostle, that is, "one sent", is properly a Hebrew term, pronounced *Slias* . . .' – evidently Jerome's rendering of *shaliach*.
3. K. H. Rengstorf, '*Apostolos*', in *The Theological Dictionary of the New Testament* (ET Grand Rapids 1964), pp.407–47.
4. G. Dix, 'The Ministry in the Early Church', in *The Apostolic Ministry* (London 1946), pp.183–304.
5. See esp. G. Klein, *Die Zwölf Apostel, Ursprung und Gehalt einer Idee*, FRLANT NF 59 (1961) and W. Schmithals, *The Office of Apostle in the Early Church* (ET London 1971), pp.96–110.
6. See esp. G. Schille, *Die Urchristliche Kollegialmission*, Zürich, 1967; J.

Roloff, *Apostolat-Verkündigung-Kirche*, Gütersloh 1965; F. Agnew, 'On the Origin of the Term "Apostle" ', in *CBQ* 38 (1976), pp.49–53.

7. C. K. Barrett, *The Signs of an Apostle* (London 1969), pp.11–15.
8. CD XIII. 9–10.
9. See S. Westerholm, *Jesus and Scribal Authority* (Lund 1978), esp. pp.126f.
10. Westerholm gives a useful summary of evidence for the laying on of hands in rabbinic practice: op. cit., pp.37–9.
11. M. Goulder, *Midrash and Lection in Matthew* (London 1974), p.389 n25.
12. 'He is the supreme rabbi in whom resides the final interpretation (the power "to bind and to loose") of the New Law given to the New Israel ("my [i.e. the Messiah's] Church") by Christ,' B. H. Streeter, *The Four Gospels: A Study of Origins* (Oxford 1936), p.515.
13. R. E. Brown, *The Gospel according to John* (London 1966), vol.ii, p.1044.
14. Origen, *De Oratione* 28.9.
15. C. H. Dodd, *Historical Tradition in the Fourth Gospel* (Cambridge 1963), p.348 n2.
16. J. A. Emerton, 'Binding and Loosing – Forgiving and Retaining' in *JTS* 13 (1962), pp.325–31.
17. A. Farrer, 'The Ministry in the New Testament', in *The Apostolic Ministry*, op. cit., p.176.
18. See Lampe's review of the arguments in 'Church Discipline and the Epistles to the Corinthians', in *Christian History and Interpretation: Studies Presented to John Knox*, ed. W. R. Farmer (Cambridge 1967), pp.337–61. Lampe himself concludes that the readmitted sinner quite probably *is* the incestuous man of 1 Cor., and notes that 'Paul and his communities did not regard any moral offender, however grave his sin might be, as standing outside the scope of pastoral discipline and beyond repentance and restoration'. (pp.354f.).
19. Eusebius, *Ecclesiastical History*, VII.2 See note 10 above and: P. Galtier, 'La Réconciliation des Pécheurs dans la première Épître à Timothée', *RechSR* 39 (1951), pp.317–20; O. Dibelius and H. Conzelmann, *The Pastoral Epistles* (ET Philadelphia 1972), pp.70f. and 80f.
20. V. Taylor, *The Gospel according to St Mark* (London 1952), p.244.
21. C. K. Barrett, *The Holy Spirit and the Gospel Tradition* (London 1947), p.106.
22. So H. W. Montefiore, *The Epistle to the Hebrews* (London 1964), pp.225f.
23. cf. J. L. Houlden, *The Johannine Epistles* (London 1973), pp.134f.
24. *Didache*, 4 and 14.
25. cf. S. Laws, *A Commentary on the Epistle of James* (London 1979), pp.229f.

3 'A Godly Discipline': Penance in the Early Church

John Halliburton

Instructing the catechumens one Sunday morning at the turn of the fourth century on the articles of the Creed, St Augustine explained quite simply that there are 'three ways in which sins are forgiven in the Church – by baptism, by prayer and by the humiliation of the greater penance'.[1] The sun shone, the flies buzzed and the catechumens blinked. The bishop could not have put it more plainly. Baptism was still the great divide between the old life and the new, between the misspent youth and Christian adulthood. In their eyes, the bishop who spoke to them was at least honest if not something of a hero. In his youth, as he had openly admitted, he had erred (in his own opinion) more effectively than most. But in his early thirties, he had come to recognize the wastage and futility of his current life style (despite the brilliance of his teaching career) and had chosen the Christian religion as the prime inspiration of a useful and creative life. Guilt strikes early in adolescence. The sense of having hurt parents, trampled on those we believed we loved, wasted the most opportune moments of our early life, can leave the young adult confused and drifting, wondering what further disasters lie ahead. A new commitment at this stage, coupled with the sense of being chosen, sorted out, put on the right course by a God who actually believes in you is undoubtedly a salutary experience. The feeling that the past is the past, that everything lies ahead, that the nagging complaints of previous inadequacy are of no consequence can act like a spring to future achievement. That, at least, is what Augustine himself confessed.[2]

The road to baptism in the early Church, however, was far from smooth. The parish clergy did not stand at the door welcoming newcomers and saying 'I hope to see you again next Sunday'. Once the faithful were in their place in church, the doors were barred to all but those who had seriously proposed themselves (or had been proposed) as potential Christians and were prepared to undergo the rigorous two and sometimes three year training for baptism. Standards of belief and conduct were high. 'No Christian is an evildoer,' explained Athenagoras to the pagan authorities in the second century. 'If he were, his membership would be mere sham.'[3] 'In baptism', wrote Clement of Alexandria not many years later, 'we are rid of the faults which like a cloud . . . obstructed the work of the Divine Spirit.'[4] Every precaution was taken to ensure that not only was no stone left unturned in the teaching of Christian doctrine but that every escape route back to paganism and its associations was firmly closed. Sometimes this meant a change of profession. Hippolytus, Bishop at Rome in the third century, gives a list of callings forbidden to the would-be Christian. Brothel keepers and prostitutes, gladiators and soldiers on active service, actors, astrologers, necromancers and concubines, those who manufacture idols or earn their living from the revenue of a pagan priesthood, even teachers (no doubt having to instruct children in the pagan myths) – all are barred from even enrolling as catechumens until an alternative mode of livelihood has been found.[5] In the fourth century Theodore, Bishop of Mopsuestia warns his candidates that renouncing Satan means giving up the reading of classical authors and abandoning 'the theatre, the circus, the racecourse, the contests of athletes, vulgar songs, water-organs and dancing.'[6] Not much left, one might say, but the early Church had to recognize that the lure of the pagan world was very strong. Some no doubt would want to resort to a 'belt and braces' prescription and hang their corn-dolly next to their palm cross. Nothing, however, would damage the Christian cause more seriously than the sight of Christians making merry at the festivals of the Prince of this World when they had openly given their loyalty to the King of the age to come. 'Already,' writes St Cyril of Jerusalem, 'you are at the entrance hall of the King's house . . . your names have been given in and the roll-call made for service.'[7] There could be no turning back. Daily therefore were the catechumens taught, daily were they exorcised until the last vestiges of affection for the old life had been thoroughly purged. The washing and anointing when it came was once and for all and could never be repeated. The filth of sin and the darkness of ignorance were by a single act removed. The early light of Sunday morning saw the newly baptized walk out into a world in whose pagan ceremonies and common distractions they no longer shared nor even wanted to. Their sins were forgiven and the risen life called.[8]

'And what did Our Lord say to the woman taken in adultery?' says the priest in *Dr Zhivago* to the penitent Lara. 'Go and sin no more,' replies Lara. 'And did she?' says the priest. 'Nobody knows.' Many a neophyte, taking off the white garment on Low Sunday and facing ordinary life on a cold Monday morning must have wondered whether there was perhaps a touch of unreality, a hint of idealism in the notion that once cleansed from sin in baptism, a return to the old life was basically unthinkable. Certainly new Christians were powerfully supported by the fellowship to which they now belonged, its services, sermons and sacraments. In fairness too, they had all been taught that no one is perfect, that Christians do sin and acquire bad habits and that it is for this reason that they pray daily, 'Forgive us our trespasses'. 'It is not as if,' writes Augustine, 'we were given an impossible rule to live here altogether free from sin. Nobody,' (he goes on) passes this life without committing some lesser or more pardonable sins. Baptism was appointed for the remission of all sins of whatever kind; but for the lesser sins, prayer was appointed. . . . We are once washed or cleansed from sin by baptism, we are daily cleansed from sin by prayer.'[9]

But he adds a warning. There are some sins which are not purged by prayer, sins 'for which it will be necessary to separate you from the body of Christ, – which God forbid!'[10] The catechumens swallow hard. They know perfectly well that with them in church on Sunday is a group known as the 'penitents', who like them are dismissed by the bishop before the Prayers of the Faithful and do not receive communion. 'You see them doing penance, don't you?', says Augustine. In other words, 'Let that be a warning to you'. Because there are some sins which reveal an attitude of mind that makes a mockery of church membership and destructs the life of grace. Those who commit them require a new conversion, literally a change of heart which is not achieved in a matter of moments or even days. The murderer needs to back track over the years of hatred, anger and resentment that fuelled the destruction of another's life as well as his own trustworthiness and place in society. The adulterer, though he may have physically forsaken the woman for whom he deserted his wife needs a season to rebuild the marriage relationship he so rashly compromised. And (perhaps worst of all) the man or woman who has unobtrusively given up Christianity and lapsed into a conventional paganism or even chosen some *ersatz* version of church life from the extensive variety available stands in need of a solid period of re-instruction before true Christian conviction is reawakened. It was quite clear to Augustine and to the Church of his day that those found guilty of these three so-called 'captial'[11] sins (and of offences related to them)[12] should (a) cease forthwith to communicate (both *in sacris* and socially) with the rest of the Church and (b) be exhorted to penitence and to the Church's discipline of penance. For Augustine, the sacraments are the incarnation of charity; therefore to receive communion, having stolen your neighbour's wife or murdered his friend, or having joined a rival sect is an act which clearly contradicts all that the sacraments of the Church stand for. For those who have broken charity so blatantly, a clear declaration of intent to renew and restore the relationships they have damaged is essential before they may even contemplate participating fully in the common life of the Body of Christ. For a time they must be content to remain excommunicate. Then, after a period of penance, as the wounds heal and relationships are restored, they may, if the church community and its leaders think fit, look forward to being received back once more into the fellowship of the Church and to peace with God.

It is often said that this very public discipline of the early Church, this routine of public acknowledgement of the need for penance, public excommunication, public penance and public reconciliation is the direct ancestor of our more private and certainly less spectacular modern arrangements for the quieting of conscience and the confession and absolution of sin. Where once the penitent stood weeping at the door of the church, dressed in sackcloth and ashes, now he kneels in the side aisle waiting for his turn in the confessional. Where once penance was awarded for the space of anything from two to twenty years, now it is apparently reduced to the promise (just before absolution) to recite a devotion before leaving the church. Where once absolution was a public act of reconciliation in the sight of the whole congregation, now it is a formula pronounced in secret for the private benefit of the penitent's peace of mind and peace with God. Indeed it could be said that just as the private Mass is as authentically the Christian Eucharist as the great solemn liturgies (though virtually deprived of any demonstrable social or community dimension) so the modern practice of private penance is but the ancient liturgy of penance 'writ small' on a microcosmic scale.

We are not always convinced. Going to confession in the church today feels nothing like what one imagines the experience of penance to have been in the early Church. To begin with most go into the confessional today with what Augustine and his contemporaries would call 'light' or 'venial' sins on their conscience; whereas no one in the early Church went anywhere near the Church's penitential system unless they were dragged there on account of their public behaviour or were kept awake by the remembrance of grave or mortal sin. Similarly no one with only venial sins on his conscience really feels 'excommunicate'; and absolution, even if it is for mortal sin, does not nowadays feel like being welcomed back into a community that did not even know we had left it! So in many ways, for us to be told that what was once public has now 'gone private' is not always particularly enlightening.

A closer examination of the penitential system of the patristic period, however, reveals that the paternity charge laid against it stick more closely than at first might be apparent. Take for example th ancient distinction between mortal and venial sin. This is not medieval or scholastic invention. Already in the New Testamen period, sin is looked upon as depriving the Christian of life, stifling hi enterprise, thwarting his purpose;[13] and although the reference in John[14] to a 'sin unto death' and a 'sin not unto death' cannot probabl be read as referring precisely to 'mortal' and 'venial' sin, there can b no doubt that in the apostolic age, there were some sins which alread severed from communion (e.g. apostasy) and were thought of a depriving the Christian of baptismal grace.[15] It was these tha required 'the greater penance' (*paenitentia major*). Murder, adulter and idolatry were the so-called 'capital sins' which incurred instan excommunication; and though the patristic lists seem to extend to wider variety of human frailty, nevertheless the sins commented on a requiring the discipline of penance seem to fall into the categories o 'offences against the person', denial of one's faith and sexua irregularity.[16] Lesser sins, light sins, pardonable or venial sins, wer forgiven daily in private and sometimes in liturgical prayer.[17] Hence i is reasonable to say that the majority of Christians in this early perio were never subject to the Church's public penitential discipline. Th Canon Law, however, of the Western Church today states that al Christians should make confession of their sins at least once a year an at Easter, though they are encouraged pastorally to make use of th sacrament more frequently.[18] Therefore (we could argue) the disci pline has changed; we are not like the Church of the Fathers in thi respect. Until we realize that even today, we are not *obliged* to mak any confession at all *unless* we have committed mortal sin and could, i we chose, behave like St Catherine of Genoa, attending the confes sional once a year and assuring the priest that our conscience was clea of any grave offences.[19] Even Cranmer was inclined to direct peopl towards the sacrament of penance if their conscience was troubled b any 'weighty' (i.e. *gravis-mortalis*) matter, allowing those with onl lesser sins on their conscience to make their peace with God i prayer.[20] There is therefore a continuity in principle in this matte between the patristic Church and that of our own day. Nobody has t go to confession unless the sin is recognizably grave, and threaten their whole status as a Christian. Penance, in other words, serve primarily those whose actions have led them 'into a far country',[2 who are at odds with Church, home and community and stand in nee of pastoral care and reconciliation.

Second, there is the actual *confession of sin*. Nowadays performe privately in the presence of a priest or bishop, in the patristic period it is almost certain that there was never a corresponding self-accusation by the penitent in the face of the whole congregation. Those who write of 'public confession' in the early Church normally fail to distinguish between the terms '*exhomologesis*'[22] and '*confessio*'. The former certainly means 'confession' but in the contexts in which it is used refers to the public act of enrolling as a penitent and doing one's penance for all to see.[23] That is what is meant by public confession. It does *not* refer to another and separate exercise, (called by e.g. Cyprian *confessio*), namely the detailing of problems of conscience in private to the bishop or to a clergyman appointed by him. Cyprian gives two cases of this. The first concerns those who did not actually betray the faith in persecution but thought seriously of doing so. Troubled in conscience, they went immediately to the '*sacerdotes*' (presumably the presbyters appointed by the bishop) and asked their advice (*apud sacerdotes Dei confitentes*).[24] The recommendation was that though no open crime had been committed they should do penance of an appropriate length. The second concerned the virgins who were accused of breaking their vow and of sleeping 'adulterously' with a deacon and other members of the male sex.[25] Here Cyprian orders a private enquiry (enlisting if necessary the help of a midwife) before deciding whether penance is necessary or not. If the virgins are intact, then they may immediately return to communion; if not they must do penance of the same length as any adulteress. But the enquiry is private and confidential; only the penance is public.

This system eventually led to the appointment of presbyters specially commissioned to conduct private interviews and to recommend a suitable length of penance (as Socrates records was the case in the time of Theodosius the Great).[26] This was of particular benefit to those whose offence was liable to punishment by the civil law as well as by ecclesiastical censure. In such cases, the Church generally chose to protect its members from public exposure, as the penalties were usually severe. Basil, for example, writes in one of his canonical letters: 'Women who have committed adultery and have confessed through piety or were in any way whatever convicted, our fathers did not command to be denounced publicly, lest we give cause for their being convicted and put to death.'[27] But private confession (not always in detail), or at least the open acknowledgement that grave sin had been committed, was the rule. Once more the ancient practice seems closest to our modern discipline in the encounter between the penitent and the bishop or presbyter where sin was identified and penance discussed. Here already is the pastoral relationship which grew into the great tradition of spiritual care in the generations that followed.

Third, *the liturgy of penance*. There is no one text that describes a pattern that could be considered common to the whole of Christendom in the patristic period. Nevertheless, such fragments as we have make it possible to establish the following main features of the penitential liturgy.

(a) *An act of excommunication*

This is normally *voluntary* on the part of the penitent who having acknowledged his fault to the bishop or presbyters then simply accepted his place in the ranks of the penitents and did not receive communion until his penance had been worked. Occasionally constraint had to be used in the case of those unwilling to recognize that their fault was grave and/or public knowledge.[28]

In addition (in Syria at least) there was a formal liturgical act of excommunication, held when the greater part of the penance had been performed. The penitent stood outside the church and was then summoned in by the bishop, the clergy and the congregation. He was examined as to how satisfactorily he had done his penitential exercises and whether he was ready for readmission. He was then ceremonially led out of the church and formally ostracized by the congregation. There he remained for a period of two to seven weeks, during which the bishop would visit him and ask if he had truly repented, giving him counsel and spiritual guidance. At the end of this period, he was ready for the formal act of reconciliation.[29]

(b) *The setting of a penance*

The author of Hebrews' rather pessimistic view that it is 'impossible to renew unto repentance those who were once enlightened'[30] (sc. baptized) might at first suggest that the early Church held out little hope for those who after baptism had fallen into serious sin. This rigorist view continued to emerge in the ensuing centuries, with parties like the Novatianists maintaining that to lapse in time of persecution warranted permanent exclusion from the Christian assembly.[31] Most churches, however, offered a second chance (though in the West at least, one only), as is explained, for example in the second century Roman text known as *The Shepherd of Hermas*.[32] In which case, penitents had to be enrolled, penance needed to be set and a decision made about its length. Though presbyters were often involved in this process, it was ultimately the bishop who decided when the penance would start and when it would end. Clearly in the interests of justice, the penance had to some extent to fit the crime.

Basil in the fourth century, recalling 'the tradition of the fathers' provides his fellow bishops with a catalogue of crime and punishment:[33] wilful murder – 20 years; unintentional killing – 10 years; adultery – 15 years; fornication – 7 years; grave robbers – 10 years; marriage within forbidden degrees – 15 years; readers sleeping with their fiancées – one year; sleeping with other women – suspension from the order. At the same time the bishop reserved the right to shorten penances at his discretion. Cyprian in the third century is twice recorded as urging the (presumably) early reconciliation of the sick who are in danger of death.[34] While Basil holds the view that a penance well done can be a penance halved (or at least reduced).[35] This suggests that there was a continuing pastoral contact between the local church and the penitent during the time set for penance; so that the season of excommunication was not, as it were, a sentence to be fulfilled but an opportunity for a thorough examination of life and the rediscovery of its opportunities and potential.[36] Confessors today might well suggest as much for those at odds with their church, themselves, their families even. Our present discipline presumes that an immediate return to communion is not always for the best; those honest enough to stay away from church because they cannot reconcile their lifestyle with what they believe to be the demands of the Gospel need to be respected. And a time of regular pastoral care from the church, a time for reconstruction and planning for the future might well make the eventual return to communion both more lasting and more joyful.

(c) *The penitent in church*

Not all those excommunicate joined the ranks of the penitents. Anyone accused before the church and refusing the call to repentance is not only excommunicated but, according to Basil of Caesarea, totally ostracized. 'Let it be proclaimed to the entire district,' he writes, 'that he must not be received in any of the ordinary relations of life, so that by our not associating with him, he may become entirely food for the devil.'[37] This 'delivering to Satan' is a practice well known from the apostolic age onwards[38] – not in itself a final condemnation (since the accused's redemption is still hoped for) – but a firm decision to place the offender well out of court and to have him nowhere near the church until genuine signs of repentance appear.

Those voluntarily excommunicating themselves or immediately showing signs of repentance however may continue a relationship with the worshipping community and take their place in church among the ranks of the penitents. By the fourth century in Asia

Minor, there were four classes of penitents: those who stood at the door of the church, weeping for their sins, those just inside called the 'hearers', those admitted as penitents and those allowed to stand with the rest of the congregation but dismissed before the prayers of the church.[39] Not all scholars are convinced that this pattern obtained universally,[40] but it is probably the case that most churches arranged for the penitent to keep their association with the church to which they sought readmission by some kind of Sunday attendance. Liturgies of this period provide for the dismissal of the penitents with prayer,[41] as they include prayers for the dismissal of the catechumens, energumens etc.; and this association of penitents and catechumens serves also to underline the theology of penance as a 'second baptism',[42] the penitent being prepared in church for this time of readmission to communion as the catechumen prepares for baptism and first communion.[43] Since moreover the penitents needed to be known to the regular congregation who would be present and would give their approval to their restoration,[44] it seems likely that they preserved many of their original associations with the Christian community. In the Syrian churches, the bishop himself visited the penitents during the time of their excommunication which in itself may well be an indication of a general pattern of pastoral care for the fallen.[45]

(d) *Actual penance and liturgical penance*

Rather as the period of instruction for baptism is stated as being either two or three years and ends with a formal 'giving in of the name' at the beginning of Lent and a fairly intensive six week catechizing;[46] so penance (which may last anything up to twenty years) seems in some places also to have an end in the liturgical excommunication (mentioned above) followed by a shorter period (maximum seven weeks) leading up to the act of reconciliation. This is certainly the case in the Syrian church in the third century.[47] In Africa, Tertullian writes of the custom of Christians who, realizing their need for penance, begin the actual penitential exercises privately *before* asking liturgically for admission to the *ianua paenitentiae*[48] (a practice also attested by Cyprian).[49] Both these witnesses give the sense that when the penitent actually asks to be enrolled publicly, the day of his reconciliation is not infinitely distant, even though the period for his appearing on the penitents' bench may be longer in some places than in others. Understandably the church had to be satisfied that the penitent was ripe for reinstatement before allowing him to embark on the very public course of *exhomologesis* which involved the prayer, concern and indeed judgement of the whole congregation.

It is precisely at this point that we seem to be a long way from modern practice. Nowadays, penance (i.e. the 'set' penance) is related more to the notion of satisfaction than to a period of reflection, withdrawal and self examination. Provided we confess, and receive absolution, we are not barred from communion, however heinous the crime. Yet the wise confessor will know that the man, for example who has become entangled in an extra-marital relationship will not in a moment of time suddenly become a faithful and devoted husband. He must decide that he wants to change his pattern of life; he must prove or give some surety that he can; and he must then embark on a thorough preparation for a return to the lifestyle he has decided he wants to pursue and believes to be right. 'Time for true repentance' is not an empty or merely pious phrase. A change of heart is not achieved miraculously overnight and therefore even in our contemporary penitential system, we still have to think in terms of the penitent being guided over what may be a fairly lengthy period of spiritual growth and development – not necessarily excommunicate – but at least coming to a realization of their need for a genuine reconversion. In all this we are likely also to need not only the counsel of our spiritual guides but also the moral support and commonsense of our fellow Christians. Finding our way home may be much more of a community activity than we realize, and a discovery that through the sheer down-to-earth humanity of the church, friends, family, sometimes strangers – the Good Shepherd comes out to seek and to save that which was lost.

(e) *Restoration to communion*

(i) The minister of the rite

In the patristic period, it is invariably the bishop who presides at the public reconciliation of penitents. Presbyters are not normally authorized to perform this rite and it is important not to confuse the role of presbyters in counselling those troubled in conscience, letting them know whether they needed to do penance and sometimes determining the length of penance;[50] and the role of the ordained minister in the laying on of hands with prayer on the penitent and readmitting them to communion.[51] Presbyters certainly joined with the bishop in this act of reconciliation;[52] but only in emergency may they act in place of the bishop. Cyprian has no qualms about recommending this. His concern is for the lapsed, some of whom are seriously ill. Presbyters or deacons, he writes may in such cases supervise their repentance and reconciliation but he does also require testimony to their good intentions from the martyrs who are prepared to stand surety for them.[53]

Already then, there is an involvement of more than the church leader alone in the act of reconciliation. When the bishop presides over the rite in church, he does so with the clergy (who also lay on hands)[54] and in the face of the congregation whose judgement about the penitent is in no way to be disregarded. Cyprian on one occasion has to remonstrate quite angrily with a church which 'gave the peace' to a fallen presbyter without the lay people having been consulted.[55] The penitent has to have his 'life inspected'[56] to the satisfaction of all which is not simply a concession to democracy but a further illustration of the ecclesial dimension of the primitive rite.

(ii) The laying on of hands

In this period, the laying on of hands accompanies a variety of rites and prayers. Hands are laid on by the bishop in the final act of initiation (corresponding to our modern rite of confirmation); hands are laid on for commissioning to the ordained ministry; hands are laid on for healing and for blessing.[57] Baptism in the early church was universally (in orthodox circles) considered unrepeatable. Therefore the laying on of hands in penance cannot be a 'repeat' of the final laying on of hands in initiation, though it is considered (in Syria at least) that both rites convey the gift of the Spirit[58] (which of course matches the theology that repentance and reconciliation re-open the soul to the lifegiving Spirit of God). Neither has the laying on of hands in penance any connection with a commissioning of a particular kind of service. There may however be some association between the choice of such a rite for penance and the church's development of the healing ministry. St James after all does connect the forgiveness of sins with the ministry of the elders of the church in praying for and anointing the sick. Sin and sickness are closely associated in both Jewish and early Christian thought; and when Origen, for example, applies the text of Jas.5.14ff to penance and interpolates into it a laying on of hands, then one has to ask what theology of penance is here implied.[59] If the penitent of Alexandria are prayed over by clergy and people, have hands laid on them by the ordained ministry and are then anointed with oil, what are they meant to understand? Origen to begin with presumes that the grave sin of the penitent has severed him from the life of grace;[60] his penance is like a second catechumenate; his reconciliation a 'rejoining' of the community which lives by the life of God himself.[61] If he believes St James to be writing about penance, then quite clearly he sees the rite of his own day – prayer, laying on of hands and anointing – as a restoration of the life of God to the penitent, a true healing, a new opening to the life of the Spirit. There is no need to confuse this rite with that of initiation of the laying on of hands on the sick, the energumens or on the catechumens. As it has developed in his own day, the rite of penance simply signifies what it effects.

(iii) The words of reconciliation

With such an emphasis in the early Church on the community aspect of reconciliation, it might easily be assumed that whatever words were spoken on such an occasion were a simple declaration by the local church of the penitent's renewed acceptance in the assembly. Not quite the place, we might say, for a formula such as 'Ego te absolvo'. But we must not presume too much. There is in fact very little information about what was actually said by the bishop as he laid on hands. Tertullian does not refer directly to such a rite and Cyprian only tells us that the bishop and clergy together perform the reconciliation.[62] In the East, however, the Syriac Didascalia goes into some detail.[63] The penitent stands in the presence of the whole community, the whole community offer prayer for him, the bishop lays on hands and he is reinstated once more to his rightful place in the church. But this is much more than a family gathering welcoming back the prodigal. According to the text (here summarized by Rahner), the bishop in this act 'represents Almighty God and according to Matt. 18.18 has the power to forgive sins. . . . The bishop undertakes the lifting of personal guilt "in God's place". It is through the bishop that the Redeemer says to the sinner, "Your sins are forgiven" and the bishop grants the *aphesis* of sins.'[64] In the last resort, it is peace with God that the penitent is seeking; only God can forgive sin, and therefore what the penitent really wants is a direct assurance of such forgiveness and the loosing that leads to new life. This seems almost certainly the theology that was eventually to find expression in the declaratory formulae of absolution normally used in the Church today. Much as we may protest about the lack of a social dimension to our modern penitential discipline, much as we may feel we have recovered some of this in the authorized liturgies of penance, one aspect we throw out at our peril is the sense that forgiveness is offered to us by God in Christ, and that something in the rite of penance must express this divinely and authoritatively given fact. We are not the authors of our own peace, nor indeed is the community that restores us; and without the divine initiative, without our first being loosed and then restored, it is unlikely that any effective reconciliation would take place at all.

If then the penitential discipline of the early Church is to be honoured as the progenitor of our contemporary rites, then there remains one feature which might still question its (or our?) pedigree. In the patristic age, the biship pronounced the absolution much as he (or more usually the parish priest) does now. But in the early Church you could only be absolved *once*: whereas now, even for mortal sins, there is no limit to the number of times we may return. The rule of a once only reconciliation is attested by several authorities. Hermas in second-century Rome is the first to mention this in the literature that survives,[65] though it has to be taken into account that Hermas himself was expecting the return of Christ in judgement rather sooner than the Church of a century or so later. The picture he gives of the Church as a tower in the process of being constructed implies a date of completion; and the stones waiting to be built into the structure, which, he says, represent the penitents, can therefore win only one permanent place in the tower and are not constantly to be taken out and used again. During the years of persecution, it was unlikely that the Church would welcome back those who regularly lapsed. It has to be remembered also that church penance was only normally imposed for the three capital sins; and that common sense would dictate that the Church for the sake of the individual's good and for her own reputation would say that such sins in the future were to be avoided at all costs. Therefore the penitent need not expect the church to organize penance for repeated offences. In the East there are some signs of a yielding to this absolute rule of a 'once only' reconciliation. Neither *Apostolic Constitutions* nor the *Didascalia Apostolorum* mention the traditional rule; they do not seem particularly concerned to stress the three capital sins, and in the former, there is a hint that a 'second stumble' may be as treatable as the 'first'.[66] It is not, however, the evidence concerning a second reconciliation that is important, but the theology. There is in fact nothing in the theology of either east or west to suggest that God will forgive us any less frequently than the times we are supposed to forgive our brother. We have much to learn from the insistence that grave sins need careful repentance and preparation for a new way of life and should not be repeated. But we have also much to value from a system which from the beginning appealed to the troubled conscience and grew into the very available pastoral ministry that we know today.

Notes

1. Augustine, *De symbolo ad catechumenos*, 8.16.
2. i.e. in the *Confessions*, *passim*.
3. Athenagoras, Suppl., 2.3.
4. Clement of Alexandria, *Paedagogus*.
5. Hippolytus, *Apostolic Tradition*, ed. Botte, 16.
6. Theodore of Mopsuestia, *Catechetical Lectures* III, tr. A. Mingana (Woodbrooke Studies, Cambridge 1933), pp.37ff.
7. Cyril of Jerusalem, *Cathechetical Lectures*, the *Procatechesis*.
8. On this see E. J. Yarnold, *The Awe-Inspiring Rites of Initiation*, London 1972.
9. op.cit., 7.15.
10. op.cit., loc.cit.
11. Murder, adultery and apostasy; in Roman law, adultery and murder were punishable by death. Hence only those not openly indicted of these offences did penance (in some cases the penance had to be secret for fear of civil consequences). Apostasy was a major cause of excommunication.
12. On sins which required the greater penance, see K. Rahner, *Theological Investigations*, vol. XV (London 1983), pp.129–30; 146–7; 218–19.
13. Rom. 6.23.
14. 1 John 5. 16.
15. On the subject of sin and spiritual death see Rahner, op.cit., pp.23ff. and on Origen, ibid. pp.254ff.
16. See, for example, the sins and penances listed in the 'canonical' letters of St Basil, *Epp*. 188, 199 and 217.
17. cf. Basil, *Ep*. 207: 'When day begins to dawn all in common as of one voice and one heart intone the psalm of confession (*psalmous exhomologéseós*) to the Lord, each one forming his own expression of repentance (*metanoias*).'
18. By the Fourth Lateran Council, 1215. See also H. Davis SJ, *Moral and Pastoral Theology*, vol.iii, p.345 n2.
19. cf. Friedrich von Hügel, *The Mystical Element of Religion* (London 1923²), vol.i, p.120; and St Thomas Aquinas, *Summa Theologiae* III supplem. quaest.6, art. 3.
20. BCP Office for the Visitation of the Sick; cf. the first longer exhortation in the service of Holy Communion.
21. Luke 15.13.
22. The Greek word is normally transliterated in the Latin authors.
23. Cyprian, *The Lapsed*, tr. M. Bevenot, London 1957 (Ancient Christian Writers No. 66).
24. Cyprian, *De Lapsis*, 28.
25. Cyprian, *Ep*. 4.
26. Socrates, *Historia Ecclesiae*, 5.19.1.
27. *Ep*., 199.34.

28. cf. Tertullian, *De oratione*, 7: 'Exomologesis est petitio veniae quia qui petit veniam delictum confitetur.'
29. *Didascalia Apostolorum*, II.16. 1–2; cf. Rahner, op.cit., pp.231ff.
30. Heb. 6.6.
31. Epiphanius *Adv. Haereses*, 59.1. Their position was bitterly resisted by Dionysius of Alexandria *apud* Eusebius, *H.E.* 6.42.5.; cf. ibid., 6.46.1.; and Athanasius, *ad Serap.*, 4.13; Chrysostom, *Hom.*9.3. *in Hebr.*; and Theodore of Mopsuestia, *Hom. in Hebr.*, 12.12.
32. *Mand.* IV.iii. 1–6; cf. IV i. 8; and *Vis.* III.vii.5.
33. In the canonical epistles, 188, 199 and 217.
34. Cyprian, *Ep.* 18.1; and *Ep.* 19.
35. Basil, *Ep.* 217.74: 'He who has been entrusted with loosing and binding, if he should become more merciful in diminishing the time of punishment on seeing the magnitude of the sinner's penance, shall not be worthy of condemnation since the story in Scripture makes known to us that those who do penance with greater labour quickly obtain the mercy of God.'
36. The *Didascalia Apostolorum* relates that the bishop visits the penitent during the time of excommunication to enquire about his progress and to give spiritual guidance. See II.21.2; and II.40.2.
37. Basil, *Ep.* 288.
38. 1 Cor. 5.5; cf. 1 Tim. 1.20.
39. Basil, *Ep.*, 199.22.
40. See H. B. Swete, *The Forgiveness of Sins* (London 1916), p.107 and n3.
41. Brightman, *Liturgies Eastern and Western* (Oxford 1896), i.pp.3, 9.
42. Though obviously not a repetition of baptism.
43. cf. Rahner, op.cit., p.155.
44. cf. Cyprian, *Ep.*, 17.2. '. . . inspecta vita ejus qui facit paenitentiam'. As Rahner writes (op.cit., p.155) 'The procedure may be imagined along the lines of the examinations before baptism, when the catechumen and his witnesses are questioned by the bishop and his clergy about the life of the candidate during the time of preparation for baptism.'
45. cf. n36 above.
46. As described e.g. in Theodore of Mopsuestia, *Catechetical Lecture* II, ed. and tr. Mingana, ed.cit., p.25.
47. See above, p.46; and Rahner, op.cit. pp.231ff.
48. Tertullian, *De Paenitentia*, 10.1; and Rahner, op.cit., p.132.
49. *Ep.*, 16.2.
50. As e.g. in Cyprian, *De lapsis*, 28.
51. e.g. *Ep.*, 15.1.
52. e.g. *Ep.*, 17.2.
53. *Ep.*, 18.1.
54. *Ep.*, 15.1.
55. *Ep.*, 64.
56. *Ep.*, 17.2; cf. n44 above.
57. On the significance of the laying on of hands see E. Lohse, *Die Ordination*

im Spätjudentum und im Neuen Testament, Göttingen 1951; and J. Coppens, *L'imposition des mains et les rites connexes*, Paris 1925.

58. *Didascalia Apostolorum*, II.41.2: 'per impositionem manus . . . accipiunt (in penance) Spiritus Sancti.'
59. *Hom. in Lev.*, 2.4.
60. *Hom. in Luc.*10.4 (on the Prodigal Son. Origen is of the opinion that the person in grave sin has lost the ring, the robe and indeed his sonship).
61. e.g. *in Ezek. Hom.*, 3.8.
62. *Ep.*, 15.1, etc.
63. II.18.2; cf. II.20.9; and II.18.1.
64. Rahner, op.cit., p.238.
65. Hermas, *Mand.*IV; and *Vis.*III.
66. *Ap. Const.*, II.40.1.

4 The Sacrament of Penance in Catholic Teaching and Practice

Martin Dudley

This chapter surveys the history and theology of penance over a period of more than a thousand years, from the influence of the Desert Fathers on Western monasticism and penitential practice until the reforms of the Second Vatican Council and what has followed from them. It is divided into five sections:

1. The birth of private confession
2. Scholastic theology from Abelard to the Reformation
3. Tridentine theology and practice
4. Preparing for reform: penance in the theology of Karl Rahner
5. Vatican II and the future of penance

THE BIRTH OF PRIVATE CONFESSION

The period from the end of the patristic age until the emergence of Scholasticism is one of the most exciting and worst documented periods in the history of the Church and of theology. It parallels the ultimate collapse of the Roman Empire and the emergence of new political units, including Charlemagne's attempt to retrieve the glory of Rome. Care must be taken in building a picture of Catholic devotion and teaching both for the Middle Ages in general and for this period in particular. It was a time in which traditions met and clashed. Two kinds of humanity, in Focillon's words, were at grips. One had advanced through a long and glorious era of civilization; the other had remained attached to the most primitive systems of social and cultural life. The work of bringing these opposing traditions into equilibrium went on most obscurely; it is not for nothing that these are called the Dark Ages. At one point, in the remarkable flowering of Charlemagne's sprawling rural empire, with Alcuin as a guiding light, it looked as if a new order would emerge, but it was weighed down by 'an inert mass of more primitive ideas, which were indeed to remain a permanent stratum in the profound life of the Middle Ages'.[1]

One factor shaped the religious life of these ages more clearly than any other: monasticism. The monastic life as a significant feature of Christianity made its appearance simultaneously and spontaneously almost everywhere at the end of the third or beginning of the fourth century. It has its roots in various pre-monastic developments and more generally 'in a very widespread movement of asceticism that was as old as the Church itself'.[2] Monasticism spread rapidly throughout the Eastern Empire, but came more slowly and sporadically to the West, like plant seeds blown in the wind. Dom David Knowles thinks that Athanasius, friend and biographer of Antony of Egypt, was the most effective proselytizing agent. Jerome, Ambrose and Augustine played their parts as well, and monasticism spread along the northern shores of the Mediterranean and into Gaul, and on to the Celtic regions of the British Isles.[3] Monasticism gave institutional form to practices and aspirations inherent in the life of every Christian and buttressed them with particular norms and structures of authority. So the monk was to be separated from the world, given to prayer, liturgical and private, and to poverty, and obedience both to the authority of Christ and to its embodiment in the religious superior. Essential to this life was 'an intense awareness of the need of "conversion", *metanoia*, inherent in every life in Christ'.[4] 'It was usually expressed in self-accusation inspiring a constantly renewed effort with a view to mortifying 'sinful flesh', and not only avoiding sin, but repressing inclination to sin. This accounts for the importance given to confession and penance. The life of a monk is a life of penance.'[5] The influence of the monastic life of penance contributed to the growth of the practice in medieval Christendom. It paralleled the spread and growth of monasticism. Monasticism demonstrated in a practical way that spiritual perfection and detachment from sin are ultimately one and the same thing and that the path to sanctity is the only sure path away from sin. As the monastery stood as a model of the Church, so the methods used to reconcile the erring monk to his community stood as a model for penance and reconciliation for the Christian and the Church. The most frequently used method was to require a particular quantity and severity of penitential behaviour, a tariff appropriate to the sin. Tariff penance appears to have emerged from Celtic monasteries and to have spread spontaneously, meeting the need caused by the disuse of public penance.

Public penance belonged to the Roman tradition. Private penance was the produce of a most un-Roman form of Christianity. Here Latin Christianity and its culture encounters Focillon's inert mass, a much less hopeful version of the Gospel, the religion of the phlegmatic north. As the remnants of the classical culture decayed, its values also dissolved. Penance was now less about divine grace and the promise of redemption than about fear and not least fear of sudden death and terrible punishment. The separate category of public penitents disappeared and the whole community of the faithful were cast as penitents, hence the general reception of ashes at the start of Lent. At first these were reserved for the public penitents, but between the eighth and tenth centuries it became general. Public and private penance had been advanced together from about the time of the Council of Chalons, 813, with the axiom: public penance for public sins; private penance for secret sins. But with the shift towards the private administration of penance as often as might be necessary for the forgiveness of sin, greater emphasis was placed on the need for confession. Whilst confession was insisted upon before communion when grave sins had been committed, it was left to the individual to judge when it was necessary. The Venerable Bede (673–735) says that 'sins cannot be forgiven without confession of amendment', and that 'if then the sick are in sins, and shall confess them to the presbyters of the Church, and shall with complete sincerity do all that is necessary to quit and make amends for the same, they shall be forgiven them.'[6] In the same place, his commentary on James, Bede encourages confession of daily and light sins to fellow Christians so that they may be forgiven by their daily prayer, thus inaugurating the medieval practice of lay confession.

The monastic understanding of penance stresses woundedness and healing rather than guilt and expiation. Although the priest continues to be referred to as a judge imposing sentence, the preferred metaphor was that of the physician discerning and prescribing the remedy. In 798 or thereabouts, Alcuin of York, *c.* 735–804, wrote a letter which is concerned with penance and uses phrases and identifies issues that will be repeated and developed in early scholastic theology. He affirms the power of binding and loosing which priests have received from Christ and exhorts sinners to confess to them: 'The ministry of the physician' (i.e. the priest as physician of souls) 'will come to an end, if the sick do not lay bare their wounds.' He continues:

> If you say: It is good to confess to the Lord, yet it is good for you to have a witness to this confession. . . are you ashamed to show to a man for your salvation's sake what you are not ashamed to perpetrate with a man unto your perdition? Will you have your companion aware of your iniquity and be unwilling to have a priest of Christ assist you in your reconciliation? Through an enemy you fell, and will you not rise through a friend? . . .
>
> How does a priest reconcile one whom he does not know to be a sinner? . . . And so the remedies and prescriptions against all the

> wounds of our sins which are established in the churches and in authoritative writings are useless . . . unless the festering ulcers of our crimes are revealed to those who have been appointed in the Church of Christ to heal them.[7]

Both Alcuin and Theodulf of Orleans, his contemporary, call penance a second baptism, and the medical analogy, with the necessity of the sick person laying bare the wound, is found in Bede, Alcuin, and Rabanus Maurus, as later in Abelard and Aquinas.

Pastoral considerations led to confession being made obligatory on all at fixed times, quite apart from the gravity of the sins committed, as shown by Chrodegang of Metz who, about 760, required his canons and the poor supported by the Church to confess twice a year, at the beginning of Lent and in the autumn.[8] Theodulf of Orleans says that 'one week before the beginning of Lent confessions are to be made to priests'.[9] Often more was demanded, perhaps three times a year, but this regulation was very difficult to enforce. Despite the stress on confession, Poschmann observes that satisfaction remained the most important factor in the performance of penance; it was the real efficient cause of the forgiveness of sins. Confession was the means by which the priest was enabled to determine the penance appropriate to the quantity of sins.[10] But with the decline of severe penances, the humiliation involved in making confession was itself seen as penitential and of expiatory value. The process by which private sacramental penance emerged as a procedure complete in itself, involving contrition, confession, imposition of penance, and absolution, took about six hundred years. It was complete by the end of the first Christian millennium and so became the subject matter of theological reflection.

SCHOLASTIC THEOLOGY FROM ABELARD TO THE REFORMATION

Alger of Liège, who flourished 1100–21, already counted penance as a sacrament (according to his understanding of the nature of a sacrament). The Oxford theologian Robert Pullen (d. 1146), who was made cardinal in 1143–4 and used his influence as Chancellor of the Holy Roman Church against Abelard, wrote a book of *Sentences*, soon superseded by the *Sentences* of Peter Lombard, in which he set out his theology and expressly proved that penance is a sacrament. It was also taught as such in the *Sententiae Divinitatis*, in Simon Magister and by the Glossators of Gratian's *Decretum*. On the basis of the ancient tradition there was never any doubt, from the twelfth century onwards, that penance was a sacrament necessary and obligatory for the mortal sinner, though the theoretical explanations given for this necessity varied.

Peter Abelard

We begin this section with Abelard's teaching on penance and reconciliation as it is set out in the *Ethics*, teaching which exercised a predominant influence for more than a century. D. E. Luscombe, who prepared the edition and translation for the Oxford Medieval Texts, suggests that it was in circulation at least among Abelard's disciples in 1138–9. (References, given here in curved brackets, are to this text, Oxford University Press, 1971.) Master Peter begins with an extensive discussion of the nature of sin in which, with all the appearance of originality, he teaches that sin is consent to evil and contempt of God. He then turns to the reconciliation of the sinner to God. Here we find already the parts of penance as they will be expressed in the Tridentine teaching, contrition or repentance, confession, and satisfaction (cf. Aquinas, *ST* 3a, 90, 1–2; Trent XIVth Session, ND 1615–34). Repentance is defined as 'the sorrow of the mind over what it has done wrong' (77). This sorrow occurs for one of two reasons: because of the love of God, when it is fruitful, or because of fear, when it is not fruitful. Unfruitful repentance is vividly illustrated by examples that range from Judas, who repented not 'on account of the fault of a sin as on account of the vileness of him who felt himself damned in everyone's judgement', to Abelard's own contemporaries who, buying Masses in an attempt to save their souls – 'one denarius for a Mass and five solidi for Masses and all the hours for thirty years and sixty for once a year' – yet would not pay back those from whom they had stolen. Wholesome repentance, he says, proceeds from the love of God 'with the result that we are sorry to have offended or to have shown contempt of God because he is good rather than because he is just', and he later quotes St Gregory the Great's axiom: 'Repentance is weeping for what one has done and not doing what one weeps for' (91).[11] Would it be unreasonable to think that he had his relationship with Heloise in mind when he pointed to the contrast between our fear of men, which leads us to hide our sins, and our fear of God which, by contrast, seems not to inhibit us? He also contrasts carnal desire, which makes us do and endure many things, and spiritual desire, which makes us do and endure very little: 'Would that we would do or endure as much for God to whom we owe all as for our wife or children or any mistress!' (87).

Repentance, then, is truly fruitful when sorrow for sin and

contrition of mind proceed from love of God. The fruit of this repentance, Abelard says quite clearly, is that 'sin does not remain' (89). 'In this sigh we are instantly reconciled to God and we gain pardon for the preceding sin.' Abelard cites Ezek. 33.12, 'In what hour soever the sinner shall sigh, he shall be saved', and says that the truly penitent sinner 'is worthy of pardon without delay, and that eternal punishment in which the condemnation of sin consists, is not owing to him'. This pardon is effective even if confession and satisfaction are 'prevented by some necessity'. It relieves eternal punishment but not other punishments and the deceased, who has not made satisfaction, may be 'detained for purgatory, not damnatory, punishments in the future' (89). Whatever the case, as far as God shall determine, Abelard says, satisfaction must be made for faults, if it has been deferred or prevented.

As sin is contempt against God, it is not possible to repent of one sin, for example, of murder, and not of another, say fornication, which one has not yet stopped committing. Abelard says, 'As long as one contempt remains there can be no means be said to be a repentance to which the love of God is urging us.' Repentance, which is inspired by God, makes it unnecessary for him to inflict the punishment that should be rendered for sin (93).

Only a very small section of the *Ethics* is devoted to confession. When he comes to deal with it, he begins from James 5.16, and recommends confession by the faithful to each other, that they might be helped by the prayers of those to whom they confess and because 'in the humility of confession a large part of satisfaction is performed and we obtain a greater indulgence in the relaxation of our penance' (99). The last reason is that priests 'to whom have been committed the souls of those who confess' have to impose satisfactions (penance) so that those who have used their own judgement wrongly and proudly may be corrected in obedience to the judgement of another. Here again Abelard speaks with passion, the fruit of experience:

> 'For we are not ignorant,' says the Apostle, 'of Satan's devices', and we must not here pass over his wickedness by which he impels us to sin and draws us back from confession. In fact, in inciting us to sin he divests us of fear as well as of shame, so that now nothing remains which may call us back from sin. For there are many things we dare not do for fear of punishment; we are ashamed to undertake many things because of damage to our reputation, even though we could do it with impunity. So anyone unimpeded by these two tethers, as it were, will become strongly inclined to commit any kind of sin. By

this means the same things which he earlier took away from him so that he should commit sin, he later restores to him to call him away from confession. Then he is afraid or is ashamed to confess; when first he should have done so, he was not afraid nor was he ashamed. He fears lest by perhaps becoming known through confession he, who did not fear to be punished by God, be punished by men. He is ashamed that men should know what he is not ashamed to commit before God. But he who seeks medicine for a wound, however foul it is, however smelly, must show it to a doctor so that an effective cure may be applied. The priest in fact occupies the place of a doctor and he, as we have said, must establish the satisfaction (99, 101).

Abelard therefore places the stress on judgement and satisfaction as the reasons for confession to a priest, with no mention of absolution, and argues that 'sometimes by a wholesome dispensation confession can be avoided' (101). He points to St Ambrose's exegesis of Luke 22.62 and to Peter making satisfaction 'by weeping rather than by confessing'. But Abelard uses the question of forgiveness without confession as an occasion to criticize corrupt clergy, especially prelates, and those who do not know the right satisfaction to impose, differentiating those whose fault is negligence, who 'preach well although they live badly', and those in the blindness of ignorance, who might thereby put the salvation of others at risk. He requires of those to whom the power to bind and to loose is given a blameless and worthy life and maintains that this power was not conferred by the Lord on all bishops but only on those 'who imitate Peter . . . in the dignity of his merits' (119). And the bishop is to be a fair and just judge, because his judgement must not vary from 'divine fairness' and reflects it in readmitting to ecclesiastical fellowship one who has been reconciled with God through contrition and confession.

Hugh of Saint-Victor

The writings of Hugh (d. 1142) and Peter Lombard (*c.* 1100–1160; the *Sentences* date from *c.* 1155–8) take account of Abelard's teaching. Hugh's book *On the Sacraments of the Christian Faith* (English version by Roy Deferrari, *Hugh of St Victor on the Sacraments of the Christian Faith*, The Medieval Academy of America, Cambridge, Mass., 1951; page or chapter references in curved brackets) is the first great *summa* of theology. He begins his theology of penance in Part XIV with a chapter on confession, reversing Abelard's order, and seeks to justify the necessity of confession from Scripture whilst acknowledging that there is not an explicit precept for men to confess their sins (403). He swiftly moves from James 5.16 to the need of those who have sins to confess to those who have power to forgive sins, for those who do not confess their sins cannot be saved (404). Here he makes a distinction which he finds in Bede. Daily and slight sins are to be confessed to one another, that we may be saved by the prayers of others. But more serious guilt and blame is to be confessed to the priest. Hugh takes issue with Abelard's stress on tears washing away shameful sins and refuses to see in this passage any ground for qualifying the necessity to confess sin. Rather his axiom is: first there should be weeping, afterwards confessing, that the humility of confession may aid the tears of contrition.

Next (XIV, 2), Hugh treats of exterior and interior penance, the former an affliction of the flesh, the latter in the contribution of the heart. Through exterior penance the blame of a small deed may be punished and interior penance amends the depraved will. He also distinguishes penance and the fruits of penance. Penance is grief for a sin committed; but only when we give satisfaction, punishing and correcting evil, do we have the fruits, with the caveat that 'if the affliction in the correction is less than the delight was in the sin, the fruit of your penance is not worthy' (406). How do we know if our penance is worthy? First Hugh says we cannot know and so we should do more rather than less, then he qualifies this, and necessarily so if repentant sinners are not to live in real fear of purgatory punishment to come, by saying that, for the consolation of the sinner, 'a method and a measure of exterior penance have been laid down'. In the next chapter (XIV, 3) Hugh makes it clear, as Abelard did (p. 109, 'So when priests who do not know these canonical rules have been unwise, with the result that they impose less satisfaction than they should, penitents thereby incur a great disadvantage since, having wrongly trusted in them, they are later punished with heavier penalties for that for which they could have made satisfaction here by means of lighter penalties'), that satisfaction must be made. 'For even after death', says Hugh, 'there is a certain fire called purgatorial, where they are purged and cleansed who began to correct themselves in this world but did not complete the task. . . Nevertheless, it is safer in every respect that you should strive both to begin and complete it here, so that nothing may remain for you to suffer or to do there. It is hard to feel those torments even for a little' (407–8).

Without wishing to encourage leaving repentance to the last moment, to the death bed 'when pain binds the limbs and grief oppresses the sense', Hugh of St Victor says that forgiveness is promised to those who then repent truly, for it is better late than never, and the person goes forth 'in firm hope with the pledge of good devotion' (XIV, 5; p. 412). Chapters 6 and 7 are concerned with the will, and the sufficiency of good will alone, if the opportunity for implementing the will is not given. That implementation is the work of the will. God, teaches Hugh, weighs the will, whilst man judges the work. The will and hidden works are reserved for divine judgement, but it is God's will that evils be judged and punished in the world 'lest, if the judgement of these should be reserved for the future, all judgement be exercised not for correction but for damnation. So, God has established men as judges to examine, punish and correct evils. Hugh points to the existence of penitential books containing antidotes of spiritual medicine (416).

Hugh takes issue with Abelard in chapter 8, 'On the remission of sins and whether priests who are men can forgive sins', and sets out the latter's case for sins being forgiven by God in the contrition of the heart before the confession of the mouth. Hugh replies that a man is bound in two ways: by obduracy of mind, and by the debt of future damnation. The first bond is removed by contrition; the second is only loosed by absolution. Hugh has in effect, even if not formally, introduced into theology the distinction between guilt, *cúlpa* and punishment, *poena*. But Hugh's theory of the effect of absolution was untenable. As Peter Lombard showed, the forgiveness of eternal punishment cannot be separated from the forgiveness of guilt. Whilst Richard of St Victor tried to save and modify his master's position, it was not taken up outside the Victorine School.

Peter Lombard

The Master of the Sentences, Peter Lombard, 'was not an original thinker, but had all the qualities of an excellent teacher of theology: clearness, order, equilibrium, faithfulness to the tradition of the Church'.[12] Eugene Fairweather called him 'relatively unimaginative'.[13] So, as might be expected, he added little to the scholastic theology of penance, but because his book is brief, accurate, and clear, and because it incorporated many of the basic ideas of Hugh, of Abelard, of the anonymous *Summa sententiarum*, and of the canonists Ivo of Chartres and Gratian, it became a widely circulated textbook. Commentaries were written on it by Aquinas, Bonaventure, Albert the Great, Duns Scotus, and Ockham, and it was the basis of theological teaching until superseded after the Reformation by the *Summa Theologiae* of St Thomas Aquinas.

The Lombard follows Jerome in calling penance 'a second plank after shipwreck', the means by which the erring can be renewed after baptism, by which we raise ourselves again after a fall (IX, d. XIV, c.1). He notes that scholastic theology has, so far, raised a number of questions on which 'even learned men are found to have different views, since the tradition handed on by the doctors . . . is varied and all but contradictory' (d. XVII, c.1). The main questions are these:

1. Whether through confession of the heart alone sin is forgiven anyone, without satisfaction and oral confession?
2. Whether it is enough for one to confess to God alone without the priest?
3. Whether confession made to a layman who is a believer is of profit?

Master Peter's own answer is clear and this is his main contribution to the theology of penance. As Thomas Tentler writes:

> For although the *Sentences* follows Abelard's lead in exalting contrition, and although it became a source for all future theologians who would do the same, even at the expense of sacerdotal power, Peter Lombard nevertheless decided that it was necessary to salvation to confess to a priest if one had the chance. The service Peter Lombard performs for confession is profound. For in the midst of the theology of contrition, confession to a priest is upheld, if not logically, at least emphatically.[14]

This was the Lombard's unequivocal teaching. 'It is certain that it is not enough to confess to God alone without confession and the judgement of the priest, nor is he truly humble and penitent who does not desire to seek the priest's judgement' (d. XVII, c.5). So, what does the priest do? Peter Lombard teaches, against Hugh, that only God, and not the priest, remits the debt of eternal punishment, just as it is God who quickens the soul. Yet the power of remitting and retaining sins was granted to priests. He says: 'Surely we can say and believe that God alone remits and retains sins; and yet, he has granted to the Church the power of binding and loosing. But he looses or binds in one way, the Church in another' (d. XVIII, c.5). Peter cites the raising of Lazarus, quickened by Christ, loosed by the disciples, and the leper, restored to health by the Lord but sent to the priests for judgement that he might be shown to be clean, 'because even if a person is loosed before God, he is not held to be loosed in the eyes of the Church except by the priest's judgement' (d. XVIII, c.6).

St Thomas Aquinas

It is in Aquinas that the scholastic doctrine of penance reaches it culminating point and its close. 'By the power of his systematic thought he united the personal and the ecclesiastical factors in penance to form an organic unitary principle, with the aim of thereby securing for absolution a causal significance in the remission of guilt.'[15] How does he achieve this? The thought of St Thomas, writes Thomas Tentler, is at once a cautious and yet fundamental departure from the contritionist thinking of Peter Lombard. He remains loyal to the basic contritionist position whose foremost proponent was Abelard, a teaching expressed in Hugh, Alain de Lille, Gratian, and the Lombard, but he explains the priest's absolution in such a way that it is not just formally necessary but actually indispensable to justification, even for the perfectly contrite sinner. 'For the priest's words, "I absolve you", were, in the language of St Thomas's scholasticism, the form of the sacrament. Pronounced in the indicative mood, the absolution works to cause grace . . .'[16]

The texts of Aquinas on penance include the relatively youthful *Commentary on the Sentences* (1252–6), the *Summa Contra Gentiles* (1259–64), the *Summa Theologiae* (IIIa, 84–90; September 1272–December 1273); commentaries on relevant texts of Scripture, some questions from the *De veritate* (q.24 a.14–15; q.27,28); *De malo* (q.2 a.11,12; q.3 a.14); *De virtutibus* (q.2 a.1–3); *De potentia* (q.3), which treat individual questions in greater detail; *Quaestiones de quodlibet*, 1. qu.5, 6; and the *Opusculum de formula absolutionis* (probably 1269) in which Thomas advocates the indicative form against the master general, John of Vercelli, who required the use of the deprecatory form. Unfortunately, Aquinas never completed the questions on penance in the *Summa*. The remaining headings, after question 90, were 'the recipients of this sacrament', 'the power of the ministers belonging to the keys', 'the solemn rite of this sacrament'. They are treated in the *Supplementum*, a fourteenth-century compilation taken from the *Commentary on the Sentences*, but this is not of great help. The *Commentary* was written when Aquinas was twenty-five. Poschmann asks: 'How indeed could he have examined and solved at the age of twenty-five, when he wrote down in the greatest haste the *Commentary on the Sentences*, all the complicated individual problems? Had he been permitted to complete the *Summa* he would undoubtedly have clarified a number of points.'[17]

As we have already noted, Aquinas is first of all a 'contritionist'. He affirms that the parts of penance are contrition, confession, and satisfaction (3a. 90,2). Contrition is the intention of making amends, and he states quite plainly that a priest may not absolve a penitent in whom he does not see signs of contrition. (*De forma absol.* 2.7; 3.8) But Aquinas does not lay down rigorous and over-rigorous conditions for contrition, the conditions which are almost out of reach for average Christians. He teaches that the motive for contrition is love of God without specifying the further motivation of that love and he warns against meticulous weighing of motives (*IV Sent.* d.17 q.2 a.3 sol. 1 ad 4). The basic and significant teaching is clear however, there is no justification without conversion and no true conversion without a turning to God.

At the same time as he stresses this, Aquinas insists on the principle of the authoritative power of the Church to forgive sins. Poschmann points to his categorical demand for the indicative form of absolution as evidence of this. Aquinas claimed that it had always been used, though that was not the case, but it quickly prevailed (p. 174). It is difficult to know when the deprecative and optative formulas for reconciliation found in the *Gelasian Sacramentary* and the *Pontificale* were first introduced. The eleventh-century *Sacramentary of Arezzo* has a deprecative formula, referring to sins, and an indicative formula relating primarily to penalties imposed by the Church. As late as the thirteenth century, the deprecative formula or prayer for absolution is regarded as the sacramental formula. Bonaventure speaks of the confessor in two roles, mediating God to man and man to God, mouthpiece of the sinner and mouthpiece of God. And so

> to signify this twofold role, in the formula of absolution a prayer precedes which is deprecative in form, and then there is added an absolution, which is indicative in form. Now the prayer asks for grace, but the absolution supposes grace. For the priest would never absolve anyone whom he does not presume to have been reconciled by God (*On the Sentences*, 4, d.18, p.1, a.2, q.1).

The Angelic Doctor specifically deals with the necessity of the formula '*Ego te absolvo*'. For him, it is axiomatic and of the faith that penance is a sacrament. In 3a. 84, 1 resp., he quotes Gregory the Great (though the quotation actually comes from Isidore of Seville via Gratian's *Decretum*) defining a sacrament as a ceremony 'in which the action is so performed that we take it to signify the sanctity it bestows'. In penance what the penitent sinner does and says 'signifies that his heart has turned away from sin' and the priest likewise 'signifies the work of God forgiving'. Hence penance is a sacrament (though this is not all that Aquinas would put into a definition, as he shows, e.g., in

3a. 64, 2). In sacraments that use material objects, these are applied 'by a minister of the Church, who stands in Christ's place (*qui gerit personam Christi*), to signify that the excellence of the power working in the sacrament is from him.' In penance, internally prompted human acts supply matter, 'yet the minister furnishes the complement of the sacrament by absolving the penitent' (3a, 84, 1 ad 2) and this absolution is the form of the sacrament. Now, as the sacraments effect what they signify (3a. 62, 1 ad 1), 'the form of the sacrament should signify what the sacrament accomplishes in regard to the matter of the sacrament'. Penance accomplishes the forgiveness of sin and, as this is signified by the priest when he says '*Ego te absolvo*', it is the most suitable form for this sacrament (3a, 84, 3 resp.). Other forms, asking for God's forgiveness, may preface the absolution 'in order that the effect of the sacrament may not be blocked', but they are not sufficient for the absolution because they do not signify that absolution is being granted (3a, 84, 3 ad 1). For Aquinas only the formula 'Ego te absolvo' shows that the penitent has been absolved not only symbolically but also in fact.

Penance and Reform

John Wycliff (*c.* 1330–84) held a theology of the forgiveness of sins quite different from that of the medieval Church. He did not believe that either penance or confession was necessary. But he held that confession was good and useful, if it was voluntary and made to a suitable person. He saw no scriptural basis for compulsory confession to a priest, who might, in his reckoning, be a most unsuitable person. Wycliff's theology was created in the fact of a decline of real belief in absolution by confession and penance. The form had not yet been abandoned, but the laity had ceased to feel the spirit of that sacrament. The husk was still left, the kernel was gone. The system had become, in fact, a superstition.

So what were the Reformers' criticisms? To make our reply, we can now benefit from the detailed research of a number of scholars on the state of penance at the time of the Reformation. The most notable of these, already cited, is Thomas N. Tentler's *Sin and Confession on the Eve of the Reformation*. Francis Oakley says that 'the seriousness with which theologians and canonists took that sacrament in the late Middle Ages can be gauged by the impressive number of "aids" they wrote to help confessors discharge their responsibilities, both the simpler and more "popular" sort and the more formidable and encyclopaedic *summae*.'[18] These *summae* conveyed to confessors the teachings and laws of the Church relevant to penance. Two trends are found in them. The first places the emphasis on the role of priestly absolution rather than on contrition, thus following Scotist teaching. The second, as Tentler has shown, was the attempt by the ecclesiastical authorities to develop consciences by a process of socialization, so that norms of conduct would be maintained not by legal sanctions but by the internal sanction of guilt. Of course, we cannot tell how successful the second trend was, but Oakley says that 'given the stirrings of reform evident in the late fourteenth and fifteenth centuries, it seems permissible to suspect that by the eve of the Reformation the process of socialization they were seeking to sponsor was shaping the conscience of more and more of the faithful.'[19] Tentler challenges the usual picture of the medieval Church:

> The most traditional picture of the Reformation emphasizes the immorality or inadequacy of the clergy. But the massive attempt to instruct clergy and laity on the proper way to confess indicates – as any biography of Luther must show – that the Church may not have been doing too badly, but rather too well.[20]

The Reformers were not primarily critical of excesses, nor of the lechery, ignorance, unworthiness, or scarcity of confessors. We know there to have been problems in the administration of penance. St Bonaventure, Giovanni di Fidanza, in his treatise *Quare Fratres Minores Praedicent*, c. 1260, says that

> there are other cases which sometimes make even honest persons fear confession to their own priests; because vicars are unstable and often changed, wherefore men dare not reveal secrets to them, since they must so often have unknown confessors. Again because many of them are so vicious that an honest woman fears to lose her reputation if she whisper secretly with them. Again, because many of them are unknown, and men fear that they are apostates, or hindered in their priestly office, or perchance with no priestly Orders at all. . .[21]

Friar Salimbene relates stories of the confessional, including a not uncharacteristic one of a certain woman not only invited, but forced to sin by a priest to whom she had come for confession. One such story, though told by a bishop, within whose experience it happened, and repeated by Pope Alexander IV to St Bonaventure, cannot, says Coulton, 'be reproduced here even in summary'![22] But the criticisms of the Reformers were directed less at abuses than at the theory and practice of sacramental confession as it was taught by Catholic bishops and theologians and practised by priests and penitents. They complained:

1. That confession tormented rather than consoled. Full, unconditional forgiveness of sin and assurance of salvation were utterly foreign concepts to the medieval theology and religious practice criticized by Luther, himself a victim of this torment.

2. That confession could not be commanded but could only be made by the freely willed choice of the penitent. Both Luther and Calvin approve of free confession 'in order to obtain consolation and counsel'.

3. That a complete confession is neither necessary nor even possible. A confessional manual of 1504 obliged the penitent not only to confess all sins of commission and omission but also to narrate the exact circumstances of each: with what persons and where, at what time, how often, why and in what matter, and the consequences to others of one's sinful acts.[23] By contrast, the Augsburg Confession, 1530, says, in Article XI, that Lutherans teach 'that private confession is to be retained in the churches, although it is not necessary to enumerate in confession all sins. For this is impossible according to the psalm: Who understands his sins?'

4. Confession is not a necessary sequel to contrition; all that is needed is belief in the promise of forgiveness, for that belief constitutes forgiveness itself. Absolution is still pronounced 'by God's command' but the Augsburg Confession teaches that 'God requires faith that we may believe in that absolution as his voice sounding from heaven, and that that faith truly arrives at and receives the remission of sins'. The stress is placed on faith and Christ's merits, not on satisfaction (Article XXV).

John Calvin writes at length on the question of confession in his Exhortation to the Emperor Charles V entitled *The Necessity of Reforming the Church*.[24] His position is clear and may speak for itself.

> The case is the same with confession. For they enumerate the advantages which follow from it. We on the contrary are equally prepared to point out not a few dangers which are justly to be feared, and to refer to numerous most grievous evils which have actually flowed from it. . . The perpetual rule of Christ is that conscience should not be brought into bondage. Besides, the law on which our opponents insist is one which can only torture souls and ultimately destroy them. For it requires every individual to confess all his sins once a year to his own priest; if this be not done, it leaves him no hope of pardon. Those who have made a serious attempt

. . . have found it impossible thus to do even a hundredth part of it. Being unable to extricate themselves by any remedy, they were driven to despair. Those again, who desired to satisfy God in a most careless manner, found this confession a most suitable cloak for hypocrisy. For, thinking that they obtained an acquittal at the bar of God as soon as they had disgorged their sins into the ear of a priest, they were bold to sin more freely, since they were disburdened in such an expeditious way . . .

Our opponents cannot show that the necessity of confession was imposed earlier than Innocent III. For twelve hundred years this tyranny, for which they contend with us so keenly, was unknown to the Christian world. . . To this cruel torturing of consciences has been added the blasphemous presumption of making it essential to the remission of sin. For they pretend that none obtain pardon from God but those who are disposed to confess. What is this, I ask, but for men to prescribe by their own hand the mode in which a sinner is reconciled to God, and to withhold the pardon, which God offers simply, until a condition which they have added shall have been fulfilled? On the other hand, the people were possessed with this most pernicious superstition: that as soon as they had disburdened themselves of their sins, by pouring them into the ear of a priest, they were completely freed from guilt. This opinion many abused by a more unrestrained indulgence in sin, while even those who were more influenced by the fear of God paid greater regard to the priest than to Christ.[25]

RIDENTINE THEOLOGY AND PRACTICE

he Council Fathers considered Penance in October and November 551, and issued a decree and canons. This is their teaching in ummary.[26]

Penance is a sacrament, given by God, 'a life-giving remedy . . . hereby the benefit of Christ's death is applied to those who have llen after baptism.' Penance had always been a necessary virtue eeded by all who were strained by mortal sin, yet before the coming f Christ it was not also a sacrament and is now dependent upon aptism. The Fathers quote John 20.22f for the institution of the acrament by Christ, with the power to forgive sins 'given to the postles and their lawful successors' (ND 1617).

The second chapter is concerned with the difference between aptism and penance. Penance is a 'tribunal'; the penitent is 'in the ole of the accused', freed 'by the sentence of the priest'. Whilst in aptism we put on Christ and, in being made a new creature, receive full and integral remission of all sins, penance, as a means of renewa after mortal sin, requires 'many tears and labours' and has been callec 'a laborious kind of baptism'. The Council teaches that it is 'necessary for salvation for those who have fallen after baptism. . . .' (ND 1619) and it is available as often as necessary. It is, as the second canon affirms, 'a second plank after shipwreck' (ND 1642).

The third chapter teaches with St Thomas that the form of the sacrament is 'Ego te absolvo', to which other words may laudably be added. The 'quasi-matter' is the penitent's own acts, contrition confession, and satisfaction, required 'for the integrity of the sacrament and for the full and complete forgiveness of sins' (ND 1620). The reality and effect of the sacrament is reconciliation with God.

Contrition is defined in the fourth chapter as 'the sorrow of the sou and the detestation of the sin committed, together with the resolve no to sin any more'. It is necessary; it prepares for the forgiveness of sins 'if it is joined with trust in the divine mercy and the intention to fulfi whatever else is required for the right reception of this sacrament (ND 1622). Contrition can be perfect and reconcile a man at once to God, though the desire of the sacrament must be included. Imperfec contrition, called attrition, is also 'a gift of God and a prompting of the Holy Spirit' which helps prepare for penance (ND 1624).

The fifth chapter is concerned with the necessity of confession. I teaches that penance 'is by divine law necessary to all who have faller after baptism' and that confession is an integral part of it, for withou it the priest cannot exercise judgement or impose specific penances (ND 1625). All mortal sins must be confessed 'after a diligent self examination'. Venial sins, however, 'may be omitted without guil and can be expiated by many other remedies'. Sins which are no brought to mind by careful self-examination but are forgotten, are nevertheless included in the confession and forgiven.

In chapter six the Council condemns the idea that all the faithfu have the power to forgive sins and teaches that this power is conferrec only on priests and bishops and that 'even priests who are in mortal sir exercise the office of forgiving sins as ministers of Christ through the powers of the Holy Spirit conferred in ordination' (ND 1627). It goes on to say that in penance the priest pronounces sentence as a judge anc that faith without penance effects no remission of sins (ND 1628) Chapter seven is concerned with questions of jurisdiction and o reserved sins.

The last two chapters are concerned with satisfaction as a part o penance and chapter eight states that satisfactory penances serve to 'detach penitents from sin; they act like a bridle to keep them in check, and make them more cautious and vigilant in future'. It is said that they heal after-effects of sin, destroy evil habits, avert future punishments, and conform us to Christ 'who made satisfaction for our sins'. The Council teaches that the worthy fruits of penance have their efficacy from Christ, by Christ they are offered to the Father, and through him they are accepted by the Father (ND 1632). And so priests must 'impose salutary and proportionate satisfactions'. Finally, the Council teaches that temporal afflictions imposed by God, rightly accepted, also work for the expiation of sin.

Poschmann concludes that the Council makes no significant steps forward but remains within the bounds of theology up to its time. Its importance for the development of doctrine was its sanctioning of St Thomas teaching that the sacrament is the efficient cause of the forgiveness of sins. It also swept aside the theory of the declarative character of absolution. But it offered no real solution to the chief problem at which theology was labouring throughout this scholastic period, the relation of the subjective and personal factor to the objective and ecclesiastical one in the production of the forgiveness of sins.[27] The bare bones of the Council's decrees and canons were fleshed out in the Roman Catechism and, because it details the teaching that the priests are to give to the faithful and explains how the sacrament is to be administered, it is a clearer statement of the Tridentine theology and practice.[28] The Catechism first sets out the various meanings of penance. Faith must precede penance and inward penance, the response of the faithful heart to sin, will lead to outward penance, whose purpose is the removal of doubt about forgiveness.

> For the mind should be in the greatest suspense as to the sincerity of inward penance, because in pronouncing on what he himself does, every man has reason to have doubts respecting his own judgement. To calm this our solicitude, the Lord therefore instituted the sacrament of penance, in which we cherish a well-founded confidence, that, through the absolution of the priest, our sins are forgiven us; and our consciences, on account of the faith which is justly reposed in the virtue of the sacraments, are rendered more tranquil; for the voice of the priest, legitimately pardoning our sins, is to be heard even as that of Christ the Lord, who said to the paralytic: 'Son, be of good cheer; thy sins are forgiven thee' (X).

The Catechism repeats the Council's scholastic teaching on the form and matter of penance. In practice, it instructs the penitent to cast himself down 'with a lowly and humbled spirit at the feet of the priest' and reminds him that 'in the priest, who sits as his legitimate judge, he should venerate the person and power of Christ the Lord' (XVII).[29] But its tone is pastoral, comforting and reassuring. The advantages of penance are clearly stated: 'it restores us to the favour of God, and unites us with him in the closest friendship.'

> After this reconciliation with God, pious men, who approach this sacrament, holily and devoutly, sometimes experience the greatest peace and tranquillity of conscience, accompanied with the highest spiritual delight. For there is no crime, however grievous, however revolting, which the sacrament of penance does not remit, not once only, but often and repeatedly (XVIII).

Essential to the Tridentine model is integral confession. It is defined as 'a sacramental accusation of one's self, made with a view of obtaining pardon by virtue of the keys' (XXXVIII). Confession to be efficacious, must possess integrity and completeness. All mortal sins, even if 'buried in the darkest secrecy', must be revealed to the priest 'for it often happens that such secret sins inflict deeper wounds on the soul, than those that men commit openly and publicly' (XLVI). And the circumstances of the sins are to be mentioned, so that their true gravity can be established.

> Has he had illicit intercourse with a woman? He must state whether the female was free from marriage restriction, married, or a relative, or a person consecrated to God by vow. These are circumstances which alter the species of the sins; so that the first is called by theologians, simple fornication; the second adultery; the third, incest; and the fourth, sacrilege (XLVII).

Lest the penitent get carried away with his description, the Catechism also calls for prudence and modesty! This is not an occasion to boast of one's sins.[30]

The sacrament also requires satisfaction. Sensitive to the criticism of 'the enemies of the Catholic Church', the Catechism explains that, in this context, satisfaction signifies 'that compensation by which a man makes some reparation to God for the sins that he has committed' (LIX). The essential words are 'some reparation'. Question LX affirms the full satisfaction made by Christ, 'full and abundant, commensurate and adequate to the character of all crimes committed in this world', and continues 'There is another sort of satisfaction, which is called canonical, . . .' and that is the penance imposed by the priest 'the performance of which has commonly been called "satisfaction". The merit of penance depends altogether on the merit of

Christ's passion' (LXVII) and 'our satisfaction does not obscure the satisfaction and merit of Christ' (title of Question LXVIII).[31]

There were two tasks after Trent. The first was controversial and theologians largely directed their teaching against the Reformers. The dogma had been settled by the Council and theologians were concerned with secondary issues. The Jansenist controversy, for all its importance, was ultimately about a secondary issue. The second was the recommendation of the Council's theology and practice to Catholics. Penance was to be vigorously revived. Philip Neri, the Apostle of Rome, and Carlo Borromeo, Cardinal-Nephew and Archbishop of Milan, were among its greatest and most active advocates. Most writing about penance was concerned with its administration and was moral theology rather than dogmatics or else it was in writings on spirituality. Francis de Sales calls on Philothea not to remain long in a state of sin when the remedy of confession is readily to hand. 'If we have yielded to sin,' we should 'hasten in horror to cleanse ourselves as soon as possible out of respect; for God's eyes are upon us.'[32] He counsels her to go to confession weekly 'even though you may not have any mortal sins on your conscience, for confession not only absolves venial sins but also strengthens you to avoid falling into the same sins again'. And he reminds of the need for contrition: 'It is an abuse to confess any kind of sin, mortal or venial, unless you will to be freed from it, for that is the very purpose of confession.' De Sales lays down the method of confessing. The penitent is to be specific in confessing the act, the motive and the duration of the sin, simply and openly. 'By accusing yourself in this way,' he says, 'you not only make known your sins but also your evil inclinations, customs and habits, and the very roots of your sin, enabling your confessor to understand your heart better and apply the best remedies.'[33] This approach was instrumental in bringing confession and direction together so that most spiritual directors were also confessors, but it also meant that most direction was based on a view of the penitent as sinner rather than as a whole person. This helped to shape a distinctive Counter-Reformation spirituality. Spiritual direction, especially of those souls who were not particularly advanced, was concerned with sin and avoiding it. Jean Grou (1731–1803), a Jesuit and renowned director, did not find a distinction between spiritual director and confessor appropriate anymore than one between the physician who cures an illness and one who prescribes a remedy for preserving health.

The confessor hears the admission of our sins, and absolves us from the guilt of them. He tells us what we are to do, that we may avoid sin for the future. He also gives good advice that we may advance in virtue. The tribunal of reconciliation, then, includes confession and direction, and it is as essential for it to preserve us from failings as it is to absolve us from them. *Nevertheless, by fault of the penitents as well as of that of the confessors, there have always been few confessors who are good directors at the same time.*[34]

The confessional-based spirituality was beginning to show signs of strain.

PREPARING FOR REFORM: PENANCE IN THE THEOLOGY OF KARL RAHNER

The pattern of theological writing which developed after Trent – restatement of dogma, instructions to penitents, instructions to confessors – continued until the Second Vatican Council. In the theological manuals, e.g. Tanquerey, Hurter, Perrone, Pohle-Preuss, the *Sacrae Theologiae Summa* of the Spanish Jesuits etc., the pattern was fairly standard: the power of the Church to forgive sins; penance as a sacrament; contrition, confession and satisfaction; effects of the sacrament; necessity of the sacrament; the minister and recipient. Devotional manuals assumed regular confession and provided forms for the examination of conscience. Manuals of moral theology, e.g. Noldlin, Prümmer, etc., stated the practical rules drawn from the dogma and dealt with questions of jurisdiction, reserved sins, errors in and misuse of the sacrament, and ecclesiastical punishment. However, outside of the manuals, a new historico-dogmatic approach was yielding rich fruit.

Before the First World War the Catholic theology of penance was largely concerned with controversy with Protestants. This controversial approach, in which penance, penitential discipline and confession were seen as *a*, if not *the*, distinguishing feature of Catholicism, gradually gave way to a more historical approach. Between the wars theologians, like Karl Rahner – 'this serenely objective and incomparable master of historico-theological hermeneutics' – were involved in more fundamental historical and dogmatic studies.[35] Rahner points especially to the pioneering work of Poschmann in his *Paenitentia secunda* [1940] and the preparatory essays that he published from 1908 onwards, which was thoroughly consolidated in his later writings, particularly 'Buβe und Letzte ölung' in the *Handbuch der Dogmengeschichte*.[36] We may also note the work of his fellow Jesuit, the liturgist Joseph Jungmann.[37]

Karl Rahner's own writings on penance took their origin from his formation as a Jesuit. Repentance and baptism appear in the themes of the first week of the *Spiritual Exercises* of St Ignatius Loyola and, whereas Hugo Rahner concentrated on baptism, Karl made a thorough study of the history of Christian penance. His first important article was in the form of a *quaestiones disputatae* on 'The meaning of frequent confession of devotion', published in 1934.[38] Then came 'Sin as loss of grace in early Church literature' in 1936. In the late 1940s and into the 50s Rahner published a number of historical studies and dealt with the penitential teaching of the *Shepherd* of Hermas, Irenaeus, Tertullian, Cyprian, the *Didascalia Apostolorum*, and Origen (with 475 footnotes!). These have now been revised and collected in *Theological Investigations* 15, which also has an extensive bibliography. The lessons of the historical research were swiftly applied. In 1953 there appeared 'Guilt and its remission' (TI 2), followed by two enormously influential articles (in 1954) 'Problems concerning confession' (TI 3) and 'Forgotten truths concerning the Sacrament of Penance (TI 2). In 1958, volume 2 of the new edition of the *Lexikon für Theologie und Kirche* carried his '*Bußdisziplin, altkirchliche*' (*LThK* 2.805–815) and '*Bußsakrament*' [*LThK* 2.826–38). The latter appears in English in *Sacramentum Mundi*, vol. 4.385–99 (with bibliography; Burns & Oates 1969) and in the *Encyclopedia of Theology* (Burns & Oates 1975, pp. 1187–1204).

Rahner's great gift, to which Taft testifies, was the bringing together of the historical and the dogmatic. Whereas Denzinger's *Enchiridion Symbolorum* and the Roman theological manuals tended to be ahistorical, even when Rahner edited the former, he recognized in the history of dogma a history of remembering and of forgetting. He became a reminder, a retriever of 'lost' truths. Historical studies were the springboard. From it Rahner made crucial contributions to the development of theology in general and to the theology of penance in particular. Rahner's basic thesis was that the theory and practice of penance would in future tend towards a theologically fuller and also more personal accomplishment of the sacrament.[39] He looked for a reduction in the legalistic and, as he termed them, magical tendencies in the practice of confession. One area for reform was the approach to the sacrament as an *opus operatum*. Rahner pointed to the basic axioms of sacramental theology and made it clear that the efficacy of the sacrament is measured and limited by the disposition of the penitent. Personal growth is an important aspect of the regular reception of the sacrament and 'one good confession is better than three routine confessions'.[40]

Every sin committed within the Church has an essential ecclesial character. This was another truth often overlooked and restated by Rahner. Related to it is penance as a liturgical celebration, but one which has become impoverished. The liturgy should help a person 'accomplish out of the depths of his being what takes place sacramentally'.[41] And here the ecclesial dimension must be stressed (which the emphasis on absolution does not do). Sin is not merely a temporary misfortune that happens to someone who remains fundamentally good, for sin is the rejection of the validity of God's order (so penance, as a virtue, is the painful acknowledgement of the inviolable validity of that order) and where we are concerned with the sin of the baptized, the Church cannot treat it as a matter of indifference. Even venial sins damage the Church and lower her standards. The person who commits mortal sin is no longer a productive living member of the organism. The Church's response is a 'binding' of the unmasked sinner, who, though having the appearance of being alive, is really dead. 'Binding' includes exclusion from the Eucharist, but with the intention of obliging the sinner, now cut off from the Body, to confess and be 'loosed'.

Confession of devotion was much encouraged in Catholic spirituality, but it raised important questions. If the sacrament existed for the forgiveness of mortal sin, what value had it in regard to venial sin? Venial sins are not forgiven by the sacrament. They are forgiven by examination of conscience and contrition, by almsgiving, and especially by the Eucharist. Rahner replied that frequent confession of devotion obviously had its uses – it was an affirmation of divine grace, promoted better examination of conscience, and required submission to an external and objective control – but it had one major feature. If everyone ceased to confess when they had only committed venial sins, then anyone going to confession would, simply by going, declare that they were guilty of mortal sin. This, thought Rahner, would involve a *de facto* return to a form of public penance which had already been shown to be unsound from a pastoral point of view. Its most obvious feature is the way that, because public penance has a stigma attached to it, real sinners put off their reconciliation with the Church until the moment of their death.[42]

Rahner's post-conciliar writing on penance involves a working out of his theological anthropology with regard to sin, guilt and forgiveness. The paper on guilt and its remission written in the 1950s is a prelude to this, but the idea of man as a being threatened radically by guilt is an essential feature of his fundamental theology as set out in *Foundations of Christian Faith*. It would be impossible to elaborate this complex theological system here and we must be content with observing that in the divine self-communication God addresses the word of forgiveness to man. Man's ultimate guilt comes not from the breaking of this or that commandment but from the freely willed and divinely permitted 'no' to God, which is also a rejection of all humanity and of the person himself in his freedom. This is the true meaning of mortal sin, the sin that is, in reality and in eternity, life-denying.

> But if we have really understood what guilt means . . . then we long to hear the word of forgiveness from God. This word is never experienced as something to be taken for granted, but rather as a miracle of his grace and of his love. Forgiveness is the greatest and the most incomprehensible miracle of God's love because God communicates himself in it, and does this to a person who in something which only appears to be a mere banality of everyday life has managed to do the monstrous thing of saying 'No' to God.[43]

This word of forgiveness is received from and in the Church, the community whose centre is Jesus Christ, the crucified and risen one, who 'entered into solidarity with sinners in love, and accepted God's word of forgiveness for us'. The Church is the basic sacrament of this word of God's forgiveness. The word of forgiveness is addressed to the individual person by the Church in a normative way for that person's whole life in the sacrament of baptism. But the baptized remain sinners after baptism and can fall into new and serious sin. When a sinner 'repents and confesses serious guilt or the poverty of his life to the Church in its representative, or if in certain circumstances he brings them before God and his Christ in the common confession of a community', then this word of forgiveness 'which always builds upon the word which was spoken in baptism' is again addressed to the individual by the Church in a special way. In this understanding of forgiveness and penance, which contains so many echoes of patristic and early scholastic writing, Rahner demonstrates that neither the free 'No' to God, which is, as he says, so commonplace and treated as so minor a matter, nor the word of forgiveness and the sacraments in which it is addressed to an individual, i.e. baptism and penance, are subsidiary matters. They are central to the Christian faith, though many who welcome the celebration of Easter joy in the Church's life find it hard to accept that guilt, and therefore the cross, are also an essential part of the mystery of salvation. And it is this difficulty which faced, and still faces, the Catholic Church after Vatican II. In pointing to it, Rahner continued his ministry as a reminder, a retriever of lost truths.

VATICAN II AND THE FUTURE OF PENANCE

Is penance justified today? Is not penance punishment? Is it not sadness, mortification, renunciation, frustration? Why must the Christian religion present itself under this aspect, an unattractive one? How can we preach to modern man, straining towards the conquest and enjoyment of life, a penitential practice that is beyond his every conception, every aspiration, and practical possibility? These were the questions addressed by Pope Paul VI on Ash Wednesday, 1975. He recognized the contemporary call for a gospel of joy. People asked him, why not make membership of the Church easy and pleasant, widening and smoothing the way that characterizes its course and ensures its goal? The Pope sympathized with this view, but maintained that the greatest error would be 'to take away the cross from the centre of Christian faith and life', for not only does Jesus himself bear the cross, but his followers must bear it with him. Why is this?

> Because man is a being that is spiritually and morally sick: he needs the medicine of penance, that is, he needs to atone. The development and operation of his natural faculties are not regular and orderly. His behaviour, as a result of original sin, easily goes wrong. Left to himself he acts contrary to duty and generates disorderly states of mind. What will be necessary for the healthy man, for the 'new' man according to the Christian conception, is 'conversion', that is, a change of spirit, which we call repentance, which prepares for faith and grace, and demands from us willpower, contrition, effort, perseverance; it calls for twofold repentance, sacramental and moral.[44]

It was this sort of fundamental conviction, deliberately referred back to Aquinas and to Trent's teaching on justification, and expressing the traditional Catholic teaching that had shaped the mind of the Second Vatican Council when it decided that 'the rite and formulae of penance are to be revised so that they more clearly express both the nature and effect of the sacrament'. These brief words by which penance was included in the process of liturgical reform did not commit the Fathers to any particular theology or practice of penance and they seemed quite unsure as to what should be done. Jungmann observed in his commentary on the Constitution on the Liturgy that 'time will teach what can be done'.[45] In 1978, five years after the promulgation of the new rites, Godfrey Diekmann pointed to the avalanche of books, learned articles and pastoral material on penance; research had been truly massive but consensus about its meaning had not been forthcoming: I do not know of a single theologian in the field who is entirely satisfied with the new rite. Conflicting interpretations of the historical and theological facts which surround the development of penance in the Christian church have made such a consensus nearly impossible.[46] The problem for those who prepared the new rites was that they had to produce something. They could not simply wait in the hope that consensus would emerge and so they proceeded on the basis of the norms for reform set down in the Constitution. They tried to provide an enriched liturgical celebration but were limited in what they could achieve by the dogmatic parameters received from Scholasticism and canonized at Trent.

The New Rites

The Introduction to the new rites has six sections, five concerned with penance as such and a sixth devoted to adaptations of the rites according to various regions and circumstances.[47] The first 'The Mystery of Reconciliation in the History of Salvation', provides the context for penance. It is the will of God that men and women should be freed from slavery to sin and the Father has shown his mercy 'by reconciling the world to himself in Christ and by making peace for all things on earth and in heaven by the blood of Christ on the cross'. Jesus not only called for repentance, he also welcomed sinners and was the means of their reconciliation to the Father. The Apostles were empowered to forgive or retain sins, and they were to preach repentance and forgiveness. In particular, Peter received 'the keys' and was the first to preach repentance and baptism for the forgiveness of sins on the day of Pentecost. Since that day 'the Church has never failed to call men from sin to conversion and by the celebration of penance to show the victory of Christ over sin'.

The second section, 'The Reconciliation of Penitents in the Church's Life', begins by repeating Vatican II's teaching that the Church includes sinners and is at the same time both holy and always in need of purification. 'The people of God accomplishes and perfects this continual repentance in many different ways.' Both baptism and penance, 'the water of baptism, the tears of penance', are the means of forgiveness. Between them is the Mass, the sacrifice of the new covenant instituted by Christ on the night of his betrayal 'for the forgiveness of sins'. To these are added the Church's own unspecified difficulties by which she shares in the suffering of Christ, works of charity and mercy, penitential services and 'the penitential aspects of the eucharistic celebration'.

The Introduction refers to but does not explain the role of the Mass in forgiveness. Diekmann sees an unanswered question here: if communion can itself forgive sin, then is confession before communion necessary? The Introduction's notes refer to the instruction *Eucharisticum mysterium* 35:

> The Eucharist is also presented to the faithful 'as a medicine by which we are freed from our daily faults and preserved from mortal sin'; they should be shown how to make use of the penitential parts of the Mass. 'The precept "let a man examine himself" should be called to mind for those who wish to receive communion. The custom of the Church declares this to be necessary, so that no one who is conscious of having committed mortal sin, even if he believes himself to be contrite, should approach the holy Eucharist without first making sacramental confession.'

There is nothing new here, simply two quotations from the decrees of the Council of Trent put together, and the question remains unanswered. Rahner wanted to remove the idea that confession is the necessary preparation for the Eucharist and that the Eucharist is the reward for confession. In part this has been achieved by the new Mass. The Mass as celebrated after Trent lacked a communal penitential rite such as that introduced in the Missal of Paul VI. That rite made it possible for people to express repentance within the context of community worship and for many people it came to fulfil the function that had previously belonged to confession before communion.

The sacrament of penance itself is the subject of the rest of the Introduction. Its parts are listed in the traditional way: contrition, confession, act of penance [satisfaction], absolution, together with the requirement that the faithful 'must confess to a priest each and every grave sin' and an encouragement to frequent and careful celebration as 'a remedy for venial sins'. But the traditional teaching is set into a new context, one which reflects and expresses the faith and confidence of the Church. The second section is concluded with these words:'The celebration of this sacrament is thus always an act in which the Church proclaims its faith, gives thanks to God for the freedom with which Christ has made us free, and offers its life as a spiritual sacrifice in praise of God's glory, as it hastens to meet the Lord Jesus.'

Sections three, four and five deal with ministries and celebrations. It is upon the whole Church, as a priestly people, that Christ laid the ministry of reconciliation with a duty not only to call sinners to repentance, but also to help them and intercede for them and enable them to obtain the forgiving mercy of God. The Church exercises the ministry of the sacrament through bishops and priests. This ministry includes the preaching that calls the faithful to conversion as well as the declaration and granting of the forgiveness of sins. The penitent 'celebrates *with* the priest the liturgy by which the Church continually renews itself'.[48] This liturgy takes three sacramental forms and one non-sacramental.

1. The reconciliation of individual penitents. (As this is the normative text it is given in *Liturgies*, p. 194ff. below, together with a brief commentary.)
2. The reconciliation of several penitents with individual confession and absolution.
3. The reconciliation of penitents with general confession and absolution.
4. Penitential celebrations, which are 'very helpful in promoting conversion of life and purification of heart' but which are not to be confused with celebrations of the sacrament of penance.[49]

Despite the multiple provision, the reconciliation of the individual penitent by individual, integral confession and absolution remains the 'only ordinary way for the faithful to reconcile themselves with God and the Church'.[50] Where there are several penitents, the second rite can be used to provide a celebration of the word as a fitting preparation for individual confession. General absolution is only to be given when there are insufficient confessors available to hear individual confessions properly and then it can only be given with the permission of the diocesan bishop after consultation with other members of the episcopal conference. General absolution of grave sins must be complemented by individual confession within a year (s. 34). General absolution given at a penitential celebration (rite 4) is not sacramental and cannot be considered a substitute for individual confession.

The Form of the Absolution

It is the question of the form of absolution which has, in the end, controlled the current development of the rite. Bishops and priests, according to the Introduction (s.9a), exercise a sacramental ministry when 'in the name of Christ and by the power of the Holy Spirit they declare and grant the forgiveness of sins'. Section 6b refers to the priest 'acting in the person of Christ' and pronouncing his decision of forgiveness or retention of sins 'in accord with the power of the keys'. In 6d, 'the sign of absolution' is described as the means by which God grants pardon to the sinner for 'God uses visible signs to give salvation and to renew the broken covenant'. There can be no doubt that the priest is not merely an agent who dispenses forgiveness. Confession involves an encounter between the penitent and the Church, between the penitent and Christ. This encounter is mediated by the priest both in his person and in virtue of his office. He has to judge personally whether forgiveness should be granted and he has to declare it. He has to ask whether the penitent has fulfilled the precondition of truly contrite confession, a willingness to open his heart to the minister of God, and so make a spiritual judgement. When he has made that judgement and if it is affirmative then he both grants and declares forgiveness.

At first, there were a number of proposed variants from which the minister would be free to choose, variants that expressed differing views of what the priest is doing in absolution. They are given by Dallen, who sets out their history, as follows:[51]

Original Form	*Revised Form*
By his self-giving our Lord Jesus Christ has set the whole world free and given his disciples power to forgive sins. By the grace of the Holy Spirit and my ministry may he absolve you from your sins and restore you to complete unity with the Church. He lives and reigns forever and ever.	Our Lord Jesus Christ has offered himself for us to the Father in sacrifice and given his Church power to forgive sins. By the grace of the Holy Spirit may he absolve you from your sins and restore you to complete peace with the Church. He lives-and reigns forever and ever.
Our Lord Jesus Christ, who redeemed the world by his passion and resurrection, by the grace of the Holy Spirit absolves you from your sins and fully restores you to peace with Church. He lives and reigns forever and ever.	Our Lord Jesus Christ, who redeemed the world by his passion and resurrection, by the grace of the Holy Spirit through my ministry forgives your sins and restores you to the full life of the Church. He lives and reigns forever and ever.
May our Lord Jesus Christ absolve you and by his authority I absolve you from your sins in the name of the Father and of the Son and of the Holy Spirit.	Our Lord Jesus Christ forgives your sins by my ministry and fully restores you to the Church's peace. He lives and reigns with the Father and the Holy Spirit forever and ever.
We ask you, Lord, to grant your servant the fitting fruit of penitence so that by obtaining pardon for what he/she has done he/she may be restored blameless to your holy Church, from whose wholeness he/she has strayed by sinning. [We ask this] through Christ our Lord.	

The alternatives were ultimately abandoned, apparently because of the Congregation for the Doctrine of the Faith's commitment to the explicit Tridentine formula, and one revised version of the third form was accepted:

> In the name of our Lord Jesus
> Christ and in the power of the
> Holy Spirit I absolve you from
> your sins and restore you
> completely to peace with the Church.

But there was still some way to go and the final rite had a composite version:

Deus, Pater misericordiam, qui per mortem et resurrectionem Filii sui mundum sibi reconciliavit et Spiritum Sanctum effudit in remissionem peccatorum, per ministerium Ecclesiae indulgentiam tibi tribuat et pacem. Et ego te absolvo a peccatis tuis in nomine Patris, et Filii, + et Spiritus Sancti.	God, the Father of mercies, through the death and resurrection of his Son has reconciled the world to himself and sent the Holy Spirit among us for the forgiveness of sins; through the ministry of the Church may God give you pardon and peace, and I absolve you from your sins in the name of the Father, and of the Son, + and of the Holy Spirit.

(Latin text from Neuner-Dupuis, 1671.)

Hamelin notes the trinitarian nature of the formula. Crichton thinks that it should have placed a greater emphasis on the mediation of Christ in the act of forgiveness. Dallen would have preferred a beginning such as 'Blessed be God, the Father of mercies!' or else that the prayer (as he takes it to be) should have been addressed directly to God. He notes that the element of proclamation is strong and the priest should 'proclaim it as a prayer – clearly, slowly, and reverently, like the eucharistic prayer'.[52] So is it prayer, declaration or proclamation?

In the Post-Synodal Apostolic Exhortation *Reconciliatio et Paenitentia*, Pope John Paul II says that in the absolution the confessor is acting as 'judge and healer, a figure of God the Father welcoming and forgiving the one who returns'.[53] Whilst the new Rite requires the priest to extend his hands, or at least his right hand, over the penitent's head, the Pope speaks of the imposition of the hand, *and* the sign of the cross (indicated in the prayer), which, with the sacramental formula 'I absolve you . . .'

> . . . show that *at this moment* the contrite and converted sinner comes into contact with the power and mercy of God. It is the

> moment at which, in response to the penitent, the Trinity becomes present in order to blot out sin and restore innocence. And the saving power of the Passion, Death and Resurrection of Jesus is also imparted to the penitent as the 'mercy stronger than sin and offence'. . . God is always the one who is principally offended by sin – '*tibi soli peccavi!*' – and God alone can forgive. Hence the absolution that the priest, the minister of forgiveness, though himself a sinner, grants to the penitent, is the effective sign of the intervention of the Father in every absolution and the sign of the 'resurrection' from 'spiritual death' which is renewed each time the Sacrament of Penance is administered. Only faith can give us the certainty that *at that moment* every sin is forgotten and blotted out by the mysterious intervention of the Saviour.[54]

The Pope has here developed the trinitarian structure of the prayer and given a new dimension to the doctrine of the priest acting *in persona Christi* (= figure of the Father], as well as stating quite explicitly that the formula defined by Trent remains normative. Clearly, the 'I absolve you . . .' formula is not negotiable, at least for the present.

The Future of Penance in Roman Catholicism

Although the official line seems to be the maintenance and promotion of individual integral confession and absolution, liturgists are still seeking ways to celebrate liturgically the painful experience of reconversion and the joyful experience of reconciliation. From a deeper understanding of penance as a virtue and of the need for reconciliation to be an act of the faith community, and not only of its ordained representatives, they have identified a number of areas for development. That which seems to have attracted most attention is the recreation of an order of penitents. The inspiration for this comes from the Rite for the Christian Initiation of Adults (RCIA) and its process approach. As RCIA recognizes that there are many different stages between interest in Christianity and baptism and admission to communion, stages that require appropriate preparation and celebration, so the advocates of a process approach to penance see stages between the evangelization that makes a person aware of sin and the reconciliation that makes them healthy members of Christ's Body.[55] Favazza compares the two processes on page 87.

A Comparison of the Process of Christian Initiation, Modelled in the RCIA, with a Suggested Process of Sacramental Reconciliation Modelled in a 'Restored' Order of Penitents

	RCIA	EXPERIENTIAL PROCESS	ORDER OF PENITENTS	
1st Period	Precatechumenate/Inquiry	Crisis Event/Situation of Change		
Stage 1	Rite of Becoming a Catechumen	Personal Story Questions of Meaning	Evangelization Welcoming Confession of Sin	1st Period
2nd Period	Catechumenate	————————	Rite of Becoming a Penitent	Stage I
Stage II	Rite of Election	Linking Personal Story with Christian Story	Lenten Conversion and Penance	2nd Period
3rd Period	Enlightenment/ Illuminaton	Deepening in Faith ————————	Rite of Reconciliation	Stage II
Stage III	Baptism/Confirmation/ Eucharist	New Level of Conversion and Personal Integration	Postreconciliatory Reflection	3rd Period
4th Period	Mystagogia	Growth in the Sacramental Life Entry into Active Ministry		

Whether such an approach could be recovered remains to be seen. Certainly some of the communal celebrations of penance allowed in the new Rite have met an obvious need. The more solemn and liturgical celebration, with its stages, would not oust individual reconciliation, but its implementation would be an acknowledgement that the post-Tridentine form is not appropriate to every individual or situation. In particular, it has little to say to the truly alienated if they seek reconciliation and, with its heavy emphasis on absolution, it lacks a clear ecclesial dimension which affirms the damage that sin does to the Church. It is probably the case that the liturgical approach to penance is suffering from the sort of self-conscious archaeologizing that accompanied eucharistic reform. New official rites will emerge only when that approach gives way to an approach based on the experience of using experimental rites. It may be true that confession is in crisis, but penance and reconciliation are enjoying a period of unexpected attention and fruitfulness.

Notes

1. H. Focillon, *The Art of the West: I Romanesque* (Oxford, 3rd edn 1980), p.3.
2. A. Veilleux OCSO, 'The Origins of Egyptian Monasticism', in W. Skudlarek OSB, ed. *The Continuing Quest for God: Monastic Spirituality in Tradition and Transition* (Collegeville 1982), p.44.
3. D. Knowles, *Christian Monasticism* (London 1969), pp.25–6.
4. J. Leclerq, 'Monastic Spirituality Critically Discussed', in *Aspects of Monasticism*, Cistercian Studies Series 7 (Kalamazoo MI 1978), p.330.
5. Leclerq, ibid.
6. P. F. Palmer, *Sources of Christian Theology: Sacraments and Forgiveness* (London 1960), p.150, n6.
7. Palmer, pp.153–4.
8. B. Poschmann, *Penance and the Anointing of the Sick* (London 1964), p.139.
9. Palmer, p.155.
10. Poschmann, p.141.
11. Gregory the Great, *Homiliarum in Evangelia lib. ii.*, xxxiv. 15.
12. B. Mondin, *St Thomas Aquinas' Philosophy in the Commentary to the Sentences* (The Hague 1975), p.2.
13. *A Scholastic Miscellany* (London 1956), p.226.
14. Tentler, *Sin and Confession on the Eve of the Reformation* (Princeton 1977), pp.20–1.
15. Poschmann p.168.
16. Tentler, p.24

17. Poschmann, p.169.
18. F. Oakley, *The Western Church in the Later Middle Ages* (Ithaca NJ 1979), p.126.
19. Oakley, p.127.
20. Tentler, p.53.
21. Tr. in G. G. Coulton, *Life in the Middle Ages* (Cambridge 1967), pp.105f.
22. G. G. Coulton, *From St Francis to Dante: A Translation of all that is of primary interest in the Chronicle of the Franciscan Salimbene (1221–1288)* (London 1906) pp.273f.
23. Cited by S. Ozment, *The Age of Reform 1250–1550* (New Haven CT 1980), pp.217–18.
24. *Calvin: Theological Treatises*, tr. J. K. S. Reid, The Library of Christian Classics, vol. xxii (London 1954), pp.184–216.
25. pp.213–14, 215–16.
26. Full text in Palmer, pp.240–54; J. Neuner and J. Dupuis, *The Christian Faith in the Doctrinal Documents of the Catholic Church* (hereafter ND) (London 1983), s.1615–34 decree, s.1641–55 canons; DS 1668–93, 1701–15.
27. Poschmann, p.202.
28. *The Catechism of the Council of Trent*, tr. T. A. Buckley (London 1852), ch. V; references, given in round brackets, are to questions. The importance of the Catechism is illustrated by an observation of N. Alexandre. *Theologia dogmatica et moralis* (1693), t. I, praef, quoted by Y. Congar, *A History of Theology* (New York 1968), p.178: '(we understand as) dogmatic and moral theology, in which, having set aside all Scholastic questions and questions of positive theology . . . only those things are treated which are defined or handed out as dogmas in the Council of Trent, or explained in the Catechism of this same Council.'
29. On the priest as judge, see also Question XLI.
30. Confession seems to have carried its own set of problems. John Bossy suggests that the obligation of annual confession was frequently unfulfilled. Apart from concubinage and other sexual sins, 'where shame seems to have been the governing instinct and it was often difficult or embarrassing for them to say anything', it seems that the main cause of failure was a state of hostility with a neighbour in which the 'penitent' intended to remain! When they came to confession it was by all accounts 'in an aggressive and self-righteous mood, determined not to concede their own faults without emphasizing the superior iniquity of others' (J. Bossy, *Christianity in the West 1400–1700* [Oxford 1985], p.47). We can also see how experience tempers practice. Detailed explanation of the circumstances of sins, no matter how prudent and modest, has its dangers. Cardinal de Richelieu, when Bishop of Luçon, contributed to a small book published under the name of his grand vicar and former Sorbonne instructor, Jacques de Flavigny, *Brief and Easy Instruction for Confessors*. Here the danger involved in shaming is frequently stressed. If absolution is withheld, Richelieu warns, it must be so 'discreetly, so that

no one is aware of it'. The priest must be 'cautious and restrained' in questioning those under his direction about lechery, especially women, who are timid about confessing sins of the flesh. One can be tactful: it is not necessary to ask for details or explicit avowals. The priest is forbidden to exact public penitence for private sins and he is instructed to take care that feelings of shame are not so intense that they deter the penitent from making future confessions. (E. W. Marvick, *The Young Richelieu* [Chicago 1983], pp.115–16.)

31. On Tridentine practice, see D. Borobio, 'The Tridentine Model of Confession', *Concilium* 190 (1987), pp.21–37.
32. *Introduction to the Devout Life*, chapter 19 (London Everyman Library, 1961), p.79.
33. de Sales, p.81.
34. J. N. Grou, *Manual for Interior Souls*, quoted in J. M. Neufelder and M. C. Coelho, ed. *Writings on Spiritual Direction* (Minneapolis MN 1982), p.82.
35. Robert Taft SJ, 'Penance in Contemporary Scholarship', *Studia Liturgica*, vol. 18, no.1 (1988), p.7.
36. *see* 'A Guide to Further Reading', p.206.
37. J. A. Jungmann, *Die lateinischen Bußriten in ihrer geschichtlichen Entwicklung*. Innsbruck 1932.
38. *Theological Investigations* (London 1967), vol. iii. p.177.
39. *Theological Investigations*, vol. iii, p.193.
40. *Theological Investigations*, vol. iii, p.197.
41. *Theological Investigations*, vol. iii, p.200.
42. *Spiritual Exercises* (London 1967), pp. 86–8.
43. *Foundations of Christian Faith* (London 1978), p.421.
44. *Osservatore Romano*, 27 February 1975.
45. J. A. Jungmann in H. Vorgrimler, ed. *Commentary on the Documents of the Second Vatican Council* (London 1967), vol. 1, p.52.
46. G. Diekmann, 'The New Rite of Penance: A Theological Evaluation', in Nathan Mitchell OSB, ed. *The Rite of Penance: Commentaries*, The Liturgical Conference, Washington DC 1978, vol. 3, p.82.
47. The ICEL text published in *The Rites* (New York 1976), vol. 1, is a direct translation of the Latin Rite in the Roman Ritual.
48. *The Rites*, p.349; my emphasis.
49. p.358, s.37.
50. p.355, s.31.
51. J. Dallen, *The Reconciling Community*, New York 1986.
52. L. Hamelin, *Reconciliation in the Church*, Collegeville 1980; J. D. Crichton, *The Ministry of Reconciliation*, London 1974.
53. p.122.
54. p.122; emphasis in original.
55. For recent developments in research and practice, see P. E. Fink SJ, ed. *Alternative Futures to Worship – Vol. 4 – Reconciliation*, Collegeville MN 1987; J. Lopresti SJ, *Penance: A Reform Proposal for the Rite*, Washington DC 1987; J. A. Favazza, *The Order of Penitents: Historical Roots and Pastoral Future*, Collegeville MN 1988.

5 The Anglican Tradition: from the Reformation to the Oxford Movement

Geoffrey Rowell

One of the proximate causes of the Reformation was the perceived abuse of the penitential system of the medieval church. It is not therefore surprising that Reformation theology, both in England and on the Continent has much in the way of protest against the abuses, real or imagined, of auricular confession. There were protests against the breaking of the seal of the confessional, attacks on the power that the auricular confession gave to the priesthood, and a questioning of its grounding in both Scripture and tradition. None the less Reformation theology was clear that the ordained ministry of the Church possessed 'the power of the keys'. The Westminster Assembly in 1646 resolved that 'those that are rulers of the Church have the keys of the kingdom of heaven committed to them, to shut it against the impenitent, and open it to the penitent sinner . . . both by Ministry of the Word and by censure and absolution respectively as occasion requires to retain or remit sins.' The preaching of the Word was the primary ministry by which both God's judgement and forgiveness were brought home and to ministers, as authorized preachers of the word, the power of the keys was given, for the discipline of the Church, whether in excommunication or in absolution.[1] There is much in the order and practice of the Protestant Churches concerned with the enforcement of moral discipline and the penalties of excommunication.

If there was excommunication there was also restoration of the penitent to communion. This involved the exercise of ministerial authority in the lifting of ecclesiastical penalties, but it was acknowledged that John 20.22–3 gave authority to absolve penitent sinners. The medieval Catholic discipline of an annual confession to a priest, established by the Lateran Council of 1215, was generally repudiated. Such compulsion, it was held, had no warrant in Scripture or in the faith and practice of the primitive Church. None the less the Reformation churches did not completely turn their back on either the pastoral benefits of confession in private to an ordained minister, nor for the most part deny that the absolution of the penitent in such a context was either inappropriate or erroneous.

In the Lutheran Churches the practice was continued and encouraged. Luther himself wrote in the *Babylonish Captivity* (1520) that 'the secret (private) confession . . . though it cannot be proved from Scripture, is in my opinion highly satisfactory and useful or even necessary'. In the *Short Catechism* there is an instruction on confession for simple folk: 'I, a poor sinner, confess myself guilty of all sins before God . . .'. The confessor is instructed to absolve the penitent with the words, 'Dost thou believe that my forgiveness is God's forgiveness?' *Answer*: 'Yes, reverend sir.' Then let him say: 'As thou believest, so be it unto thee. And by command of our Lord Jesus Christ, I forgive thee thy sins, in the name of the Father, the Son and the Holy Ghost. Amen. Go in peace.'[2] Zwingli, on the other hand, maintained that confession was for consultation not for remission of sins. Calvin, beginning from the exhortation to mutual confession in James 5.16, urged that pastors are best qualified to receive such confessions:

> Let every believer, therefore, remember that if in private he is so agonized and afflicted by a sense of his sins that he cannot obtain relief without the help of others, it is his duty not to neglect the remedy which God provides for him, namely, to have relief for a private confession to his own pastor, and for consolation privately implore the assistance of him whose business it is, both in public and private to solace the people of God with Gospel doctrine.'[3]

Furthermore Calvin approves of such recourse being had immediately before a partaking of the Lord's Supper and of an absolution by the pastor being part of such a preparation.

> Nor is private absolution of less benefit or efficacy when asked by those who stand in need of a special remedy for their infirmity. It not seldom happens that he who hears general promises which are intended for the whole congregation of the faithful, nevertheless remains somewhat in doubt and is still disquieted in mind, as if his own remission were not yet obtained. Should this individual lay open the secret wound of his soul to his pastor, and hear these words of the Gospel specially addressed to him 'Son, be of good cheer; thy sins be forgiven thee' (Matt. 9.2), his mind will feel secure, and escape from the trepidation with which it was previously agitated.[4]

General confessions and absolutions became part of most reformed orders of service. Private confession was none the less seen as part of Christian ministry and pastoral care, even though the Reformed Churches did not count it as sacramental and the context of its use was for the quieting of conscience and the assurance of God's forgiveness.

In the writings of the English Reformers we find both attacks on the abuses of the Roman confessional and also a recognition of its value and place when freed from such abuses. William Tyndale could maintain that 'shrift in the ear is verily a work of Satan. . . It began among the Greeks, and was not as it is now, to reckon all a man's sins in the priest's ear; but to ask counsel of such doubts as a man had.'[5] Preaching was the way to forgiveness and absolution. Yet Tyndale could also acknowledge that confession to a priest 'if restored to right use' was not damnable.[6] Thomas Becon in his *A Potation for Lent*, can maintain that he sees no reason for the abolition of confession, rather what is needed is its reform. There is great need of wise confessors and physicians of the soul, who will lead the penitent to a deeper spirituality and away from confession by rote.

> For many care not to what priest they go unto, be he learned or unlearned, wise or foolish, modest or light, of good conversation or of naughty living, so that to satisfy the custom they come to one and receive their absolution and go away never better instructed, nor with the more penitent hearts.[7]

Becon cites six reasons why confession is to be valued:

1. It 'engraffeth in us a certain humility, submission and lowliness of mind, and depresseth all arrogancy and pride, while we humbly are contented to confess to our ghostly fathers such offences as wherewith we have offended God.'
2. It is a means for leading us to shame for sin and love for virtue.
3. 'It bringeth us to knowledge of ourselves, while we hear those things of the priest that are necessary to be known of every Christian man.'
4. We learn both abhorrence of sin and ways to avoid it.
5. It is a means of Christian assurance.
6. 'In confession the ignorant is brought unto knowledge, the blind unto sight, the desperate unto salvation, the presumptuous unto humility, the troubled unto quietness, the sorrowful unto joy, the sick unto health, the dead to life. . . Confession bringeth high tranquillity to the troubled conscience of a Christian man, while the most comfortable words of absolution are rehearsed unto him by the priest.'

The absolution, 'a preaching of the free deliverance from all our sins through Christ's blood', is 'the most sweet and comfortable salve of God's word'. The words of absolution are to be received with 'earnest faith', 'being undoubtedly persuaded that your sins at that time be assuredly forgiven you, as though God himself had spoken them, and according to the saying of Christ. "He that heareth you heareth me", and again, "Whose sins ye forgive are forgiven them". '[8] Coverdale, likewise, stresses the pastoral and healing character of such confession. Priests are the 'true physicians to give due medicine for every sickness, which ordinance, if it were right kept. . . I suppose no man could reprove it.'[9] For Coverdale the abuses of the confessional were prurient questioning of penitents, breaches of confidentiality, and compulsion, which made it the only channel of God's forgiveness.[10] Bishop Ridley maintained that confession to a minister who was able to 'instruct, correct, comfort and inform the weak, wounded and ignorant conscience' was something which might do much good in Christ's congregation.[11] Hugh Latimer argues that those who are content with the general absolution have no need of private confession. Those whose consciences are troubled may resort to private confession and counsel. Latimer adds: 'as for satisfaction, or absolution for our sins, there is none but in Christ. . .'[12] Edmund Grindal maintains that 'confession, if it be discreetly used is a laudable custom, and to the unlearned man and feeble conscience so good as a sermon'.[13] James Pilkington, Bishop of Durham, expressed a similar view.

> Confession is left free to all that feel themselves burdened in conscience and want either counsel or comfort, and the weak and ignorant are moved to resort to a learned minister to receive the comfortable promises of absolution and forgiveness of sin by the lively word of God, applied to so troubled a mind as a sovereign salve for all such griefs.[14]

Liturgical provision was made for private confession in the 1549 Prayer Book, where the form of absolution in the order for the Visitation of the Sick is also to be used 'in all pryuate confessions'. The form of absolution to be given after such special confession was derived from the Sarum Manual and ran as follows:

> Our Lord Jesus Christ, who hath left power to his Churche to absolue all sinners, which truely repent and beleue in hym: of his great mercy forgeue thee thyne offences: and by his autoritie committed to me, I absolue thee fro all thy synnes, in the name of the father, and of the sonne, and of the holy gost.

The same form of absolution was retained in the Prayer Book of 1552, hough with the omission of the instruction that this form was to be used in all private confessions, and with the substitution of the words after thys sorte' for 'after this forme' in the introductory rubric. Queen Elizabeth's 1559 Prayer Book and the Latin Prayer Book of 560 retain the same formula, the Latin Prayer Book having the ubric, '*et finita confessione, Minister utetur hac forma absolutionis*'.

In the 1549 Book the exhortation in the Communion service (which ormed part of Cranmer's 1548 Order of Communion) concluded with n encouragement to private confession:

> And yf there bee any of you, whose conscience is troubled and greued in any thing, lackyng comforte or counsaill, let him come to me, or to some other dyscrete and learned priest, taught in the law of God, and confesse and open his synne and griefe secretly, that he may receiue such ghostly counsaill, aduyse, and comfort, that his conscience maye be releued, and that of us (as of the ministers of GOD and of the churche) he may recuie comfort and absolucion, to the satisfaccion of his mynde, and auodying of all scruple and doubtfulness: requiryng suche as shal be satisfied with a generall confession, not to be offended with them that doe use, to their further satisfiying, the auricular and secret confession to the Priest: nor those also whiche thinke nedefull or conuenient, for the quitnes of their awne cosciences, particuliarly to open their sinnes to the Priest: to bee offended with them that are satisfied, with their humble confession to GOD, and the generall confession to the churche. But in all thinges to folowe and kepe the rule of charitie, and euery man to be satisfied with his owne conscience, not iudgyng other mennes myndes or consciences; where as he hath no warrant of Goddes word to the same.

The 1552 Book, followed by the Book of 1559, amended this xhortation by removing the explicit reference to 'the auricular and ecret confession to the Priest' and by excising the passage exhorting hose who did not find any personal need of such confession to refrain om judging those who sought such ministry. Anyone who cannot uieten his conscience is to resort to some 'discreet and learned inister of God's word' and receive 'gostlye counsail, aduise and oumfort' for the relief of his conscience, 'that by the ministery of od's word he may recieue coumfort and the benefite of absolucion, to e quietting of his conscience, and auoiding of al Scruple and oubtfulnes'. None the less the personal and authoritative form of osolution was retained in the Visitation of the Sick. This differed

from, though was influenced by, the forms in the *Consultation* o
Archbishop Hermann of Cologne (English translation 1547) and fron
that in the 1548 Order of Communion. It differed also from the longe
and more communal form in Martin Bucer's Order for the Visitatio
of the Sick, which, having expounded the reasons for the assurance o
forgiveness, proceeds: 'With this confidence, in the name of th
Church of God and the authority granted to it, we absolve this ou
brother (*or* sister) from his sins in response to his petition and on hi
giving sufficient indication of repentance and also of desire for an
faith in the redemption of Christ.' It should also be noted that Cano
113 of the Canons promulgated in 1603–4 binds the minister t
absolute secrecy as to the confession of secret and hidden sins that h
has received.

In the Sixth Book of *The Laws of Ecclesiastical Polity* Richar
Hooker treated of the 'Power of the Keys', the nature of spiritu
jurisdiction in the church, and, in that context, of confession an
absolution. He refers to Ignatius of Antioch – 'a bishop doth bear th
image of God and of Christ; of God in ruling, of Christ i
administering holy things'.[15] 'We are', writes Hooker, 'to make n
doubt or question, but that from him which is the Head hat
descended to us that are the body now invested therewith' spiritu
power of authority. This power and authority is for the cure of soul
to lead us to repentance. The inner reality of repentance is the 'secre
repentance of the heart' before God, and this belongs to daily praye
and devotion. Outward forms of penitential discipline are als
appropriate and established by authority of the Church.

> Repentance being therefore either in the sight of God alone, or els
> with the notice of men: without the one, sometimes through
> performed, but always practised more or less, in our dail
> devotions and prayers, we have no remedy for any fault; where
> the other is only required in sins of a certain degree and quality: th
> one necessary for ever, the other so far forth as the laws and orde
> of God's Church shall make it requisite: the nature, parts, an
> effects of the one always the same; the other limited, extende
> varied by infinite occasions.[16]

Having discussed the nature of spiritual authority and the character
repentance, Hooker affirms on the basis of Matthew 16 that Chri
gave to his apostles the power of discipline. This power was exercise
in the early Church by public confession and penitence until it w
found to offer occasions of scandal, when it became the practice f
such confession and penance to be private. Hooker considers suc

'private and secret confession' to be 'a profitable ordinance'. In common with earlier Reformation divines his objection is to the decree of the Lateran Council of 1215 which laid down the necessity of confession at least once a year.[17] Hooker is sharply critical of scholastic attempts to characterize the sacramental nature of private confession. Some, he says, argue that it consists in contrition, confession and satisfaction, leaving out absolution, others, followed by the council of Trent, making 'absolution, if not the whole essence, yet the very form whereunto they ascribe the whole force and operation of their sacrament'.[18] The healing grace of God is already operative, Hooker seems to suggest, in the acknowledgement and confession of sin, and he does not doubt the reality of spiritual benefit in self-examination and the articulation of particular sins. He cites with approval the words of St John Chrysostom:

> To call ourselves sinners availeth nothing, except we lay our faults in the balance and take the weight of them one by one. Confess thy crimes to God, disclose thy transgressions before the Judge, by way of humble supplication and suit, if not with the tongue, at the least with the heart, and in this sort seek mercy. A general persuasion that thou art a sinner will neither so humble nor bridle thy soul, as if the catalogue of thy sins examined severally be continually kept in mind.[19]

Such confession may be 'in the heart', but Hooker does not despise confession to a priest, of whose authority to absolve in the name of Christ he has no doubt, though such confession is to be practised 'as a virtuous act' not as something 'commanded as a sacrament'.[20]

Hooker's central concern is Christian repentance, holiness and growth in grace and he is well aware of the twin pitfalls of complacency and scrupulosity.

> Because the knowledge how to handle our own sores is no vulgar and common art, but we either carry towards ourselves for the most part an over-soft and gentle hand, fearful of touching too near the quick; or else, endeavouring not to be partial, we fall into timorous scrupulosities, and sometimes into those extreme discomforts of mind, from which we hardly do ever lift up our heads again; men thought it the safest way to disclose their secret faults, and to crave imposition of penance from them whom our Lord Jesus Christ hath left in his Church to be spiritual and ghostly physicians, the guides and pastors of redeemed souls, whose office doth not only consist in general persuasions unto amendment of life, but also in the private particular cure of diseased minds.[21]

He notes that St Gregory of Nyssa had urged penitents to have particular recourse to the ordained ministry: 'Make the priest, as a father, partaker of thy affliction and grief; be bold to impart unto him the things that are most secret, he will have care both of thy safety and of thy credit.'[22] After further detailed examination of the patristic evidence Hooker concludes:

> We everywhere find the use of confession, especially public allowed of and commended by the Fathers; but that extreme and rigorous necessity of auricular and private confession, which is at this day so mightily upheld by Rome, we find not. It was not then the faith and doctrine of God's church, as of the papacy at this present, 1. That the only remedy for sin after baptism is sacramental penitency. 2. That confession in secret is an essential part thereof. 3. That God himself cannot now forgive sins without the priest. 4. That because forgiveness at the hands of the priest must arise from confession in the offender, therefore to confess unto him is a matter of such necessity, as being not either in deed, or at the least in desire performed, excludeth utterly from all pardon, and must consequently in Scripture be commanded, wheresoever any promise of forgiveness is made.[23]

Turning to the Reformation Churches Hooker notes first that confession is acknowledged as a principal duty, 'yea, in some cases confession to man, not to God only'. 'It is not in the reformed churches denied by the learneder sort of divines, but that even this confession, cleared from all errors, is both lawful and behoveful for God's people.'[24] The Lutheran churches, Hooker continues

> agree all, that all men should at certain times confess their offences to God in the hearing of God's ministers, thereby to shew how their sins displease them; to receive instruction for the warier carriage of themselves hereafter; to be soundly resolved, if any scruple or snare of conscience do entangle their minds; and, which is most material to the end that men may at God's hands seek every one his own particular pardon, through the power of those keys, which the minister of God using according to our blessed Saviour's institution in that case, it is their part to accept the benefit thereof as God's most merciful ordinance for their good, and, without any distrust or doubt, to embrace joyfully his grace so given them, according to the word of our Lord, which hath said, 'Whose sins ye remit they are remitted.' So that grounding upon this assured belief, they are to rest with minds encouraged and persuaded concerning the forgiveness of all their sins, as out of Christ's own word and power by the ministry of the keys.[25]

As far as the Church of England is concerned, Hooker commends the general confessions in the Offices and the Eucharist. In regard to private confession and absolution Hooker first acknowledges the clear recognition of the minister's power to absolve, 'the Church [is] not denied to have authority either of abridging or enlarging the use and exercise of that power, upon the people no such necessity [is] imposed of opening their transgressions unto men, as if remission of sins otherwise were impossible; neither [is] any such opinion had of the thing itself, as though it were either unlawful or unprofitable . . .' Carelessness in approaching the general confession is recognized to be all too liable to 'extinguish all remorse of men's particular enormous crimes'; hence the exhortations in the Communion service, and the clear injunction that notorious evil livers are not to be admitted to 'the sacred mystical food'.[26] All are to be pointed to confession, which is necessary for all Christians. Rightly used the general confession and absolution may bring the assurance of God's forgiveness and grace for amendment of life, but there will always be those who need the ministry of private confession and absolution.

> Contrariwise, if peace from God do not follow the pains we have taken in seeking after it, if we continue disquieted, and not delivered from anguish, mistrusting whether we do be sufficient; it argueth that our sore doth exceed the power of our own skill, and that the wisdom of the pastor must bind up those parts, which being bruised are not able to be recured of themselves.[27]

In chapter five of the Sixth Book Hooker considers the question of satisfaction for sin, arguing on the basis of an Anselmian interpretation of the atonement that Christ has already made 'a full perfect and sufficient satisfaction'. No further satisfaction is therefore required by God as a condition of his pardon, but in respect of the effects of sin on others satisfaction may need to be made. Moreover prayer, fasting and almsgiving are 'works of satisfaction' whose effect is to give expression to that grace of true repentance which is

> a spiritual nativity, a rising from the dead, a day-spring from out the depth of obscurity, a redemption from more than the Egyptian thraldom, a grinding of the old Adam even into dust and powder, a deliverance out of the prisons of hell, a full restoration of the seat of grace and throne of glory, a triumph over sin, and a saving victory.[28]

The final question Hooker considers is that of absolution. From Scripture, he argues, it is clear that God acts instrumentally through his ministers, and Christ authorized 'more generally his Apostles and the ministers of his word in his name to absolve sinners'.[29] The force of absolution can never be derived from the act itself but from the concurrent grace of God, 'God really performing the same which man is authorized to act as in his name'.[30] It is 'for the strengthening of weak, timorous, and fearful minds' that God has endued his church with power to forgive sinners. As far as sin is concerned ministerial absolution declares us free from guilt and our restoration into God's favour. In regard to ecclesiastical censures the absolution has an effect of itself.[31] The act of sin God alone remits, washing away the stain of sin by the sanctifying grace of the Spirit, and delivering from the punishment of hell. The ministerial sentence of private absolution 'is no more than a declaration what God hath done'. And Hooker is able to cite Peter Lombard as a witness to the doctrine that 'God alone doth remit and retain sins, although he have given the Church power to do both: but he one way, and the Church another'.[32] Finally Hooker acknowledges that there are those who are overwhelmed with a sense of their sin, are cold and dry in their prayer, and agonized over their condition. To meet their need God has ordained 'for their spiritual and ghostly comfort consecrated persons, which by sentence of power and authority from above, may as it were out of his very mouth ascertain timorous and doubtful minds in their own particular, ease them of all their scrupulosities, leave them settled in peace and satisfied touching the mercy of God towards them.' 'To use the benefit of this help for our better satisfaction in such cases is so natural, that it can be forbidden to no man; but yet not so necessary, that all men should be in case to need it.'[33]

Of seventeenth-century Anglican writers Jeremy Taylor in his *Holy Dying* (1651) expounds the value of confession in the context of the Visitation of the Sick. Jas. 5.16 is the basis for such confession – 'Christian to Christian, Brother to Brother, the People to their Minister'. God has made the minister 'the publisher and dispenser' of pardon for sins; the ministers of the Gospel are ministers of reconciliation.[34] 'The Ministers of Religion,' Taylor writes, 'must take care that the sick man's confession be as minute and particular as it can, and that as few sins as may be, be intrusted to the general Prayer of Pardon for all Sins.' 'For by being particular and enumerative of the variety of Evils which have disordered his Life, his Repentance is disposed to be pungent and afflictive, and therefore more salutary and medicinal. . .'[35]

Like Hooker, Taylor is clear that when a man repents, 'he is absolved upon his contrition and dereliction only; and if he were not, the Church could not absolve him'. It is not necessary to have priestly absolution in private for obtaining pardon,

> yet as to confess sins to any Christian in private may have many good ends, and to confess them to a Clergy-man may have many more; so to hear God's sentence at the mouth of the Minister, *pardon* pronounced by God's Ambassadour, is of huge comfort to them that cannot otherwise be comforted, and whose infirmity needs it.[36]

It is Taylor's view that disputes about the forms of Absolution were vain disputes, and he points out that giving of communion was 'the formality of Absolution, and all the instrument and the whole matter of reconciliation'. 'When that is done, the man hath obtained the peace of the Church; and to do that is all the Absolution the Church can give.'[37]

In *The Alliance of Divine Offices* (1659) Hamon L'Estrange in his comments on the Visitation of the Sick, remarks that the Church approves, though does not command, auricular confession. Again, it is the healing, comfort and assurance of the absolution that is stressed. The sinner's pardon 'is sealed in Heaven . . . at the very first minute of his repentance'. The absolution is the making evident of that pardon and the means whereby 'unspeakable comforts . . . flow [into] a disconsolate soul'. L'Estrange comments that the three forms of absolution found in the Prayer Book (in Morning and Evening Prayer, in the Holy Communion, and in the Visitation of the Sick) reflect to a degree three understandings of absolution – optative or precatory, declaratory and authoritative. After the particular confession encouraged by the Visitation of the Sick, 'authoritative absolution is proper',

> because where the Priest absolves in his own person, his Absolution is not fitly applicable to any, but such as have given him evident tokens of hearty sorrow for their sins . . . extendible it is not to whole Congregations . . . where the confession is too general to be conceived in all real: and a confession at large can at most pretend to be an Absolution at large, effectual only to such as truly and sincerely repent.[38]

L'Estrange is a witness, along with other Anglican writers, that once the focus is shifted from arguments about compulsory private confession and the apparently mechanical effect of priestly absolution in separation from the inner reality of repentance and contrition, private confession is to be valued as medicine for the soul and a way of deepening Christian life.

If we turn to other Restoration divines, John Cosin, Bishop of Durham and John Bramhall, Archbishop of Armagh, we find both continuing controversy with Roman Catholics and a high evaluation of confession. In a controversial work in defence of Anglican orders Bramhall affirms that 'he who is ordained, is enabled by his office many ways to put away sins'.

> 1. By Baptism, – 'I believe one Baptism for the remission of sins'; so saith the Creed. 2. By the Sacrament of the Lord's Supper; – 'This is My blood, which is shed for you and for many, for remission of sins:' so said our Saviour. 3. By prayer; – 'Call for the presbyters of the Church; the prayer of faith shall save the sick; and if he have committed sins, they shall be forgiven him.' 4. By preaching the word of reconciliation; – 'God was in Christ, reconciling the world unto Himself, not imputing their trespasses unto them; and hath committed unto us the word of reconciliation.' 5. By special absolution; – 'Whose sins ye remit, they are remitted.' To forgive sins is no more proper to God, than to work wonders above the course of nature. The one is communicable as the other. The Priest absolves; or, to say more properly, God absolves by the Priest. Therefore he saith, 'I absolve thee in the Name of the Father, and of the Son, and of the Holy Ghost.' God remits sovereignly, imperially, primitively, absolutely; the Priest's power is derivative, delegate, dependent, ministerial, conditional.[39]

Bramhall acknowledges that there is dispute about whether the absolution of the Priest is declarative or optative, but he holds this not to be an essential distinction, noting that there were similar controversies in the Church of Rome. He is emphatic that Protestants have not ' "pared away" all manner of shrift, or confession and absolution.' Private confession is not condemned, so long as it is not made compulsory. For many it is a vital spiritual medicine. As he rather quaintly puts it:

> No better physic for a full stomach than a vomit. Bodily sores do sometimes compel a man to put off natural shamefacedness, and to offer his less comely parts to the view of the chirurgeon. By a little shame, which we suffer before our fellow servant, we prevent that great confusion of face, which otherwise must fall upon impenitent sinners at the Day of Judgment.[40]

Rome has erred in making it a sacrament and necessary to salvation, and by demanding 'a particular and plenary enumeration of all sins'. 'Christ said not, "*what* sins ye remit", but "*whose* sins", giving this caution to the Presbyters, to attend more to the contrition and capacity of their confitents, than to the number and nature of their sins.'[41] Private confession is above all a *personal* ministry.

John Cosin, in his *Notes on the Book of Common Prayer*, is likewise clear that for the Church of England confession is neither sacramental nor compulsory. Yet he describe private confession and absolution as a 'sacred action' and points out that the absolution is the same as that of the ancient Church and of the Church of Rome. Venial sins do not need confession, but mortal sins do. 'If he hath committed any mortal sin then, we require confession of it to a priest, who may give him, upon his true contrition and repentance, the benefit of absolution; which takes effect according to his disposition that is absolved.' In the priest's absolution 'there is true power and virtue of forgiveness, which will most certainly take effect' where there is true contrition and repentance as in baptism. It is Christ's leaving power to his Church to forgive sins which is so vigorously denied by 'the puritans of our days, and their fathers the Novatians, the old puritans of the primitive Church'.[42] But this is not the doctrine of the Church of England. Elsewhere Cosin sets out various forms of 'devout and penitent confessions' to be used especially before receiving the Blessed Sacrament. These are prefaced by the encouragement to private confession in the Exhortation in the Communion Service and the citation of I John 1.9. The Collect for Purity and the Collect for Ash Wednesday are suggested as preparatory prayers. Four prayers of personal confession are provided, two being adaptations of the Prayer Book confessions from the Offices and the Communion service, the other two being Cosin's own compositions, one of which is known from its inclusion in later anthologies of prayer.

> Forgive me my sins, O Lord, forgive me the sins of my youth and the sins of my age, the sins of my soul, and the sins of my body, my secret and my whispering sins, my presumptuous and my crying sins, the sins that I have done to please myself, and the sins that I have done to please others. Forgive me my wanton and idle sins. Forgive me my serious and deliberated sins. Forgive me those sins which I know, and those sins which I know not; the sins which I have striven so long to hide from others, that now I have even hid them from my own memory. Forgive them, O Lord, forgive them all, and of Thy great goodness let me be absolved from mine offences.[43]

Herbert Thorndike (1598–1672) describes the priest as both judge and physician, who first, by the grace of spiritual discernment, makes known the sin, binding the awareness of sin upon the individual's conscience, and then acts as a physician in prescribing the medicine of repentance. Such repentance includes satisfaction not to God, but to the Church showing that the sinner recognizes and embraces the terms of that baptismal covenant by which it is constituted. Thorndike further recognizes that the congregation, along with the ministry, has a responsibility of prayer and intercession for the repentance and conversion of the sinner. Taking as an analogy the raising of Lazarus, he comments that 'Lazarus was first dead before he was bound up in his grave-clothes; and when he was restored to life, he remained bound, till he was loosed by the apostles'. The Lord raises to life from the death of sin; the apostles release from the binding of the grave-clothes. Like Bramhall, Thorndike links ministerial absolution with the work of reconciliation implicit in the whole activity of ministry – in baptism, in preaching and teaching, and as presiding over the eucharistic assembly.[44]

It is noteworthy that in 1661 at the Savoy Conference the Presbyterian request that the Form of Absolution in the Visitation the Sick be made 'declarative and conditional, as "I pronounce thee absolved" ', instead of being authoritative was rejected. The bishops appealed to John 20, where it is not 'Whose sins you *pronounce* remitted' but 'whose sins you remit'.[45] In Ireland, where Bishop Bramhall and Archbishop Ussher drew up the canons in an amended version of the English canons in 1634, canon 19 ordered the tolling of the church bell the day before the administration of the sacrament 'that if any have any scruple of conscience or desire the special ministry of reconciliation, he may afford it to those who need it'. Ministers are to receive those who come, giving them advice and counsel, 'as the benefit of Absolution likewise, for the quieting of their consciences, by the power of the keys which Christ hath committed to his Ministers for that purpose'.[46] Rather later Archbishop Wake, in the *Exposition of the Doctrine of the Church of England*, wrote that the Church refused no sort of confession, either public or private. All are encouraged to confess their sins before receiving Holy Communion.

> We propose to them the benefits, not only of ghostly advice how to manage their repentance, but the great comfort of absolution too, as soon as they shall have completed it. . . . When we visit our sick, we never fail to exhort them to make a *special confession* of their sins to him that ministers to them, and when they have done it, the absolution is so full, that the Church of Rome itself could not desire to add anything to it.[47]

Wickham Legg, in his study, *English Church Life from the Restoration to the Tractarian Movement* (1914), gathers a number of examples of the practice of confession linked with spiritual direction, particularly in the Restoration Church. John Evelyn used Jeremy Taylor. Dean Granville of Durham made a general confession to Bishop Gunning of Ely, 'receiving after the same a solemne absolution on my knees.' Books of devotion often commended private confession and absolution, notably *A Daily Office for the Sick* by Zacchaeus Isham, chaplain to Dr Henry Compton, Bishop of London. Isham comments: ''Tis fit also . . . to observe; that though our Church presseth *particular Confession* to a Priest, only when the Conscience is disquieted with sins of deeper malignity, yet it doth not discountenance the more frequent use of it; and this too is so comprehensive a Case, as to take in great numbers that neglect it.'[48] One curious piece of evidence suggests that private confessions might be made silently to God *sotto voce* and then the absolution given. This occurs in John Warton's *Death-bed Scenes and Pastoral Conversations* (1827). The minister in one of the stories recounted in this book urges the dying Mrs Barton to make her confession according to the pattern of the order for the Visitation of the Sick, then, he says, he will do what he has never done before – pronounce the absolution over her.

> Upon hearing this, the poor woman, who was lying at her length in the bed, reached out her hands: and, clasping them above her, with a wonderful expression of fervour and devotion; her eyes too, which were black, yet keen and piercing, being fixed with a stedfast undeviating gaze upwards; with convulsed and quivering lips she seemed to be laying open her inmost soul to God. She was speaking rapidly, but uttered no sounds.
>
> The spectacle was striking in an uncommon degree. I stood in silent awe. After a few minutes exhausted by this powerful feeling she dropped her hands, and said with difficulty, 'I am ready, Sir: I desire it from my heart.'
>
> Immediately I pronounced aloud the solemn form in the most solemn tone of which I was capable.[49]

When the minister goes on to explain the different forms of absolution to his penitent, he describes the form in the office as a simple declaration of those whom God will pardon, the form in the Eucharist as the expression of a devout desire that God may pardon those who are at his altar, the third in a Visitation service as the only proper Absolution. He continues,

> But it must be understood . . . not as necessary to your salvation; nor as if *I* were the person who forgave you your sins; but acting in the name of *him*, who alone is able to forgive sin; and acting as his minister and instrument whom he has authorized and employs to declare his great mercy to sinners; for the express comfort and satisfaction of your conscience troubled with the remembrance of many iniquities and longing earnestly for an authoritative assurance that God accepts your faith and penitence; I have pronounced this particular form of absolution, being assured by the glad tidings of the Gospel that a person under the circumstances in which I suppose you to be, is indeed forgiven in heaven.[50]

The practice of private confession and ministerial absolution remained constant in the Church of England from the Reformation onwards, most especially in relation to confession of sin in sickness, but not confined to such times. On the verge of the Oxford Movement the Irish layman, Alexander Knox, could write:

> Whatever evil may be charged upon (auricular confession), one undeniable good has resulted from it; namely a more exact and experimental acquaintance with the movements of the human mind, in religious matters, than we see attained by any who have wholly abandoned this species of discipline. I say, wholly abandoned, because various Protestant sects have resorted (some statedly, as the Wesleyan Methodists in their class meetings, others occasionally, as the Independents and Anabaptists in their admission of members) to practices not wholly of a different nature.[51]

Knox goes on the commend the discipline and spirituality of many Roman Catholic writers as leading to an interior piety, 'learnedly examined and judiciously guarded.' There is a great need, he suggests, for a truly inward religion combined with discipline and order, an interior piety that does not become fanaticism.

That discipline the Tractarians sought to revive and renew. In so doing they were both building on a long tradition and at the same time bringing into prominence a discipline that by the beginning of the nineteenth century was neglected as never before in the Church of England.[52] Nonetheless in their understanding of confession they were not alone, as we can see from the comments on absolution by one who was a high churchman but not a Tractarian, Christopher Wordsworth, later to be Bishop of Lincoln. He wrote in his *Theophilus Anglicanus*:

> No one can be admitted through the door of Pardon, who has not

passed through the door of Penitence. Christ alone 'openeth, and no man shutteth; and shutteth, and no man openeth'; and He turns the key in the hands of His ministers *only* when it is moved *aright*. . .

God, in this as in other cases, is pleased to work by *means*, and to use the agency of His creatures, especially of men, as *instruments* in conferring His benefits upon other men; and though *His power* is not tied to means, yet, when *He* has *appointed* certain means for dispensing His grace, *our salvation is* restricted to the due and reverent *use* of them. He remits the punishment of *original* sin by means of the Sacrament of Baptism; and in the case of *actual* sin, He confers the grace of His own pardon by the *instrumentality* of priestly Absolution, ordinarily and where it may be had, and whenever justly pronounced and duly received; and thus He makes *repentance available* to the true penitent, through the declaration and pronunciation of pardon by the Minister of Christ, acting by His authority, at His command, and by His power. Absolution does not *give* repentance, but *makes* it *effectual*; as the *loosing* of Lazarus did not give him *life*, but the full and free *use* of it.[53]

Both Evangelicals and Tractarians had a high doctrine of the Christian life, a strong sense of the gravity of sin, and equally a lively sense of the grace supplied by God to enable growth in holiness. In their sacramental teaching the Tractarians laid great weight on the doctrine of baptismal regeneration. As Pusey put it, baptism is 'a changing of the whole man, making him another self; before, out of Christ, now in Christ, new born, new created, a member of Christ, a son of God, new-formed "after the Image of Him who created him." '[54] The Christian, so re-born by the Spirit in baptism, had as his destiny no less than a sharing in the Divine nature. Yet that way of holiness was not something automatic, nor was the righteousness of Christians no more than the imputed righteousness of Christ, but a righteousness that was imparted. Sin after baptism was all too real, and for those called to Christian holiness penitence for sin was a necessary part of the Christian life. As Pusey again put it: 'In Baptism, sins are suddenly and painlessly blotted out through grace; deep sins after Baptism are forgiven, but upon deep contrition which God giveth; and deep contrition is, for the most part, slowly and deeply worked into the soul, deepening with deepening grace.'[55] In his sense of the genuine *grace* of penitence and sorrow for sin, Pusey stands in the tradition of the Fathers, who recognized the grace of compunction and the gift of tears as an important part of the Christian's transfiguration into the likeness of Christ.[56] It is not surprising that the revival of sacramental devotion and the recovery of Catholic insights that the Oxford Movement brought about led before long to a revival in the practice of sacramental confession.

Keble and Pusey characterized the prevailing understanding at the time when the Oxford Movement began as 'every man his own absolver'.

> Since we are mostly on easy terms with ourselves, the terms of self-absolution were commonly very easy. It was a quiet easy-going time, and so repentance partook of the general easiness. There was apparently little memory of past deadly sin, except an occasional thankfulness, that anyone was no longer guilty of it. . . No wonder then that an unqualified teaching of the gravity of post-Baptismal sin fell on people's hearts like a thunder-clap.[57]

Pusey claimed that the revival of confession began with men rather than with women.[58] In Newman's *Autobiographical Writings* there is an account of the first confession Newman heard, when he was Vicar of St Mary's in Oxford.

> Oriel College. March 18, 1838.
> (This is the first instance of my hearing a confession)
>
> March 18. – On Wednesday Evening March 15, as I was sitting in my rooms, a young (person) man came in, and (in the course of conversation) by degrees said he wished to confess to me previously to receiving the Sacrament of the Holy Eucharist on Sunday next (today) and asked if I should object to receive his Confession. I said I should feel it painful, both from the responsibility and the distressing trial of hearing it; and that I would think of it. He said he should go elsewhere, if I would not – yet he wished me rather, and yet should be sorry to pain me. I saw him again the next day, when he said his reason was to gain peace of mind & that he had thought of it for two years & more, & latterly from reading Bishop Taylor. – and when I reminded him that if he began he must tell me *all*, he (assented as being) said he was aware of it. Then I told him that I felt that Confession could not be separated from Absolution, referring to the Exhortation to the Communion – and while I thought it would be well for many of us at least in certain seasons of our lives, if we were in the practice of *Confession*, that I was thus far decided as to the use of *Absolution*, that it was a removal of the disabilities & bar which sin put in the way for our profiting by the Ordinances of the Church – that I did not see it was more than this, though I had

not a clear view on the subject, that if it was more I trusted I should be guided to see it – but that any how the act was *God's*, & He could as really use me as His instrument, though ignorant, as He could the inanimate element in Baptism. This was the *substance* of what I said, and I added I should be ready to receive him at seven o'clock on Saturday morning in the Chancel of St Mary's.

So yesterday the 17th at the time appointed I was there, and sat down against the rails at the Altar at the North end to get out of view from chance intrusion – I sat in my Surplice – and he came and knelt before me. Then I stood up and said over him the Collect, 'O Lord we beseech Thee mercifully hear our prayers and spare all those who confess &c.' On sitting down again I said 'What you are to say, is said not to me but to God' & he began his Confession – when it was ended, I asked, if he had told me all. Then I tried to make some remarks for his direction & comfort. Then I repeated the last answer in the Catechism 'To examine themselves &c' and asked him if he could sincerely concur in what was there set down; he said he could. Then I stood up, and holding my hands over his head, pronounced the Absolution from the Visitation Service. Then when he had done praying, I took hold of his hands, raised him up and dismissed him.[59]

The Tractarians were in no doubt that the Prayer Book taught confession, that it had been practised and encouraged by many Anglicans, even if it had greatly diminished in the century or so preceding the Oxford Movement. They emphasized that the Ordinal specifically gave authority to absolve in the ordination of a priest with the words from John 20, 'Receive the Holy Ghost for the office and work of a priest, whosoever sins you forgive they are forgiven, whosoever sins you retain they are retained.' They suspected that those who objected to the revival of sacramental confession did so on a number of grounds. First there was a general suspicion of a practice that might be labelled 'un-English' and 'popish'. Second, there was an objection to the role and authority of the priest in pronouncing absolution. Third, there was concern about priestly interference in family life, sacerdotal manipulation, and supposedly prurient questions about breaches of the seventh commandment put to 'delicately nurtured females'. In 1858 two curates were prosecuted for asking improper questions in the confessional. They were acquitted.[60] Anti-Catholic literature, such as W. Hogan's *Auricular Confession and Popish Nunneries* (1847), made much play with sacerdotal seduction as well as improper innuendo. The confessional like the convent could all too easily be portrayed as part of a conspiratorial undermining of the virtues of Victorian Christian manliness. Much of the opposition to the revival of sacramental confession in the context of the ritualist controversies of the 1860s and '70s belongs to the realm of propaganda and sensationalism rather than to sacramental theology.

The fullest Tractarian response was provided by Pusey in his Oxford University Sermons of 1846, *Entire Absolution of the Penitent*, and in the extended preface to his translation of the Abbé Gaume's *Manual for Confessors* (1878), and by Thomas Thellusson Carter in his book, *The Doctrine of Confession in the Church of England* (1864), a careful study which remains one of the most balanced and perceptive expositions of the history and theology of confession in the Church of England. Mention should also be made of the substantive Declaration on Confession and Absolution issued in 1873, following controversy over the manual, *The Priest in Absolution*, published privately by the Society of the Holy Cross (SSC) and condemned by Lord Redesdale in the House of Lords.[61] The Declaration affirms, with reference to the form of absolution in the Order for the Visitation of the Sick, 'that in these words forgiveness of sins is ascribed to our LORD JESUS CHRIST; yet that the Priest, acting by a delegated authority, and as an instrument, does through these words convey the absolving grace'. It concludes by stating that, although the formularies of the Church of England 'do not authorize any Priest to teach that private Confession is a condition indispensable to the forgiveness of sin after Baptism, and that the Church of England does not justify any parish Priest in requiring private Confession as a condition of receiving Holy Communion' none the less 'all who . . . claim the privilege of private Confession are entitled to it, and . . . the Clergy are directed under certain circumstances to 'move' persons to such confession.'[62]

Pusey argued against those who objected to any idea of a specific authority to absolve being located in the priesthood, that the same objectors would not take exception to a doctor applying 'to the cure of diseases the medicines which God has given him the knowledge and skill to use'. 'Why', he asked, 'is it undue "power" to bind up the broken-hearted, to pour into their wounds the wine and oil of penitence, to lift them up when desponding, to loose them, in Christ's Name, from the chains of their sins, and encourage them anew to the conflict?'[63] To acknowledge an authority to absolve in the ordained ministry of the Church is not to substitute that ministry for Christ, but to recognize that the ministers of the Church were instruments of Christ. As Chrysostom put it: 'Whatsoever the priest hath entrusted to him is of God Alone to give – And why say I priests? Neither Angel nor Archangel can effect any thing as to the things given by God, but the Father, Son, and Holy Spirit dispenseth all; yet the priest lendeth his tongue and affordeth his hand.'[64] He pointed out that Wheatley, the eighteenth-century commentator on the Prayer Book, had noted that the 'Priest pronounced *THE* Absolution', not a *Declaration* of Absolution, and that the word 'pronouce' was used deliberately, 'signifying, as *Pronuntiare*, "to give sentence".'[65] Recognizing that the words of John 20.22–3 may indeed be understood with reference to Baptism, Pusey argues that it is 'even more natural to understand them primarily of some distinct gift of remission'. 'To perform a Divine office, He clotheth them with a Divine power; and to fit them for the ministry of their office, He imparteth the Holy Ghost, Whose is the right and the power to forgive sins.'[66]

The sermons on the *Entire Absolution of the Penitent* were preached in 1846. That same year Pusey made his own first confession to John Keble, though he had himself heard confessions since 1838. He was already meditating publishing a translation of Gaume's *Manual for Confessors*, and wrote to his friend Copeland: 'I feel more and more that we need a system of confession, and that there is no remedy to our great practical evils, or any adequate guidance without it.'[67] When his translation of Gaume finally appeared almost thirty years later the practice of sacramental confession had become much more common in the Church of England (though still controversial). Pusey prefaced Gaume's work with a substantial essay covering both earlier Anglican testimony to the practice and importance of sacramental confession and endeavouring to meet objections and demonstrate the importance of the discipline of sacramental confession as a means of sanctifying grace. He referred to a letter he had published in *The Times* in 1866 replying to objectors.

> The Prayer-book, not we, taught confession. As a fact, the practice of confession was revived, while (scarce) a word was said about Absolution. The teaching followed the practice; and as it began, so has it continued. The use of confession among us all, priests and people, is very large. It pervades every rank, from the peer to the artisan or the peasant. In the course of a quarter of a century . . . I have been applied to, to receive the confessions from persons in every rank, of every age, old as well as young, in every profession, even those which you would think least accessible to it – army, navy, medicine, law. But in almost every case . . . the desire came from the persons themselves.[68]

Pusey rebutted the accusations of improper questions being put in the confessional. 'They who have acted the zealot for the purity of our English families,' he wrote, 'have themselves libelled them, as though they would have allowed their ears to be profaned by what was unbefitting for a pure-minded woman to hear.' And he continued by urging the value of confession as a remedy against the sexual sins and temptations of Victorian public schools.[69] Turning to post-Reformation support of sacramental confession, Pusey noted that the response of the Church of Rome to the Augsburg Confession only required two additions to be made to what the Confession said about private confession and absolution: that confession should be required every year, and that preachers should exhort to diligent examination of conscience and confession of the sins such examination brought to mind.[70] He noted the significant number of Church of England bishops who in the seventeenth century had included questions about confession in their visitation returns.[71] Among the many advocates of confession Pusey cited, were Bishop Duppa, the author of *The Guide for the penitent*, and Bishop Thomas Wilson, the saintly eighteenth-century bishop of Sodor and Man. Duppa had urged use of 'holy confession before receiving the Sacrament, or in times of sickness or when a particular sin lay heavy on the conscience'. 'Disburden yourself of it into the bosom of your confessor, who not only stands between God and you, to pray for you, but hath the power of the keys committed to him, upon your true repentance to absolve you in Christ's Name from those sins which you have confessed to him.'[72] Wilson's qualifications for a good confessor are noted with approval: 'a blameless life. Of an inviolable secrecy, a sweet behaviour to allure and to comfort sinners. Courage to reprove and prudence to apply fit remedies to troubled consciences, and to let them know that God respects sincerity of heart above all things.'[73] Keble, he recalled, had commented that 'we go on working in the dark . . . until the rule of systematic confession is received in our Church.'[74] Pusey himself came to value regular confession, and believed that it was a means of grace whereby the conscience grew 'more delicate, more truthful, more alive to the truth; more real, more simple, more earnest, more exact'. Yet there could no more be a single, enforced rule, than there could be with receiving communion.

> The Centurion was devout, who said, 'Lord, I am not worthy that Thou shouldest come under my roof'; and Zacchaeus, 'who received Him joyfully'. The streams of Divine grace are not pent up like the water in a canal, at one dull, even, unvarying level. We cannot make one unvarying law for souls which God has made so varied, and forms so variously.[75]

In his study of the doctrine of confession T. T. Carter examines the evidence of both Scripture and the early Church, concluding that

> according to ancient belief and practice, the remission of sins after baptism, at least those of the gravest kind, was ordinarily to be obtained only through Penance, preferably through public Penance, and consequently with the use of Confession, as part of Penance, true repentance being held to be always necessary as a condition of its profitable use. Holy Baptism was not supposed of itself by any prospective or implied gifts to remedy its own losses in the case of the excommunicate. Nor was the Blessed Sacrament of the Eucharist, though applying the full benefits of the Atonement, to be approached by those who had thus fallen, without a previous cleansing. Penance was held to be a distinct ordinance, having its own proper place and efficacy, renewing the pure baptismal position, and removing the hindrance which deadly sin causes to the vivifying and profitable reception of our LORD's Blessed Body and Blood.[76]

That being acknowledged Carter was clear that the Fathers recognized that sins might be forgiven outside of the Church's penitential discipline.

> The availing power of true contrition alone, through the merits of CHRIST, was ever believed to be such that, even in the case of sins for which the law of the Church properly required Penance, grace was supposed to overflow its ordinary channels in response to its appeal, through direct and secret intercourse of the soul with GOD, though the safer course, and that which reverent and careful minds would ever follow, was universally held to be only through the ministry of the Priest.[77]

The 'profound consciousness of the living energy and love of the HOLY SPIRIT, and the closeness of communion between the elect soul and the Divine indwelling Presence' enabled the Fathers to affirm the 'grace of sacerdotal absolution' and yet not scruple 'to ascribe an absolute value, irrespective of all outward means of grace, to the living force of true contrition, at the same time not supposing that the acceptableness of contrition superseded the use or value of a subsequent absolution. They affirmed both principles, and left them to be held equally and in common.'[78]

At the Reformation the Church of England, Carter noted, might have been expected, in accordance with its stand on the teaching and practice of the primitive Church, to have provided only 'precatory or optative' forms of the absolution. That the English Reformers retained the indicative form, despite its comparatively recent origin in the West, was, Carter believed significant, and an indication that they regarded it as a true expression of the primitive faith. The alterations made, however, in the medieval form were, he believed, significant.

'By the authority of the Blessed Apostles, Peter and Paul', is replaced by 'Who hath left power to His Church'; thus bringing out the idea of the Church, the Body of CHRIST, as the organ of the HOLY GHOST, instead of seeming to confine the transmission of His grace to individual Apostles. 'All thy sins', is substituted for 'all the sins which thou hast confessed to me, and from all thy other sins, which, if thou hadst remembered, thou wouldst have fully confessed'; thus apparently excluding the positive obligation of 'numbering' sins. 'All sinners who truly repent and believe in Him', is inserted instead of, 'with a contrite heart and with thy mouth'; the later expression being removed, perhaps as seeming to imply that oral confession is itself an essential condition, and necessary title to forgiveness. Lastly, 'I restore thee to the Sacraments of the Church' is omitted, because properly applicable only where Church censures had been imposed.[79]

Likewise Carter notes that the Reformers were careful to retain the specific authority to absolve in the formula of Ordination even though this, like the indicative form of absolution, was of comparatively recent origin in the Ordinal. The 'ultra-Reformers', Carter comments, 'sought to magnify preaching to the detriment of the inner ministry of Confession. The leading directors of the English Reformation rather aimed at restoring the balance between the two, seeking earnestly to develop and intelligent use of the Word of GOD, as the truest means of giving life to sacramental ordinances.'[80] He went on to argue that since the Reformation

> two principles have striven for mastery in the West – one preserving the priestly office entire, with its Apostolic exercise of the power of the keys; the other, a reaction, as extreme, from the extreme Roman view of Penance, limiting pastoral intercourse to mere confidential conversation on the side of the penitent, counsel and exhortation on that of the Priest. A constant effort has been made to introduce into our Offices this latter mode of dealing with penitents, as the sufficient and more desirable exercise of the ministerial office. The Church has as uniformly and as steadily resisted it.[81]

Carter devotes a chapter of his book to absolution, paying particular intention to the indicative form of absolution. He notes that th

Catholic Church has never defined absolution, any more than in the early centuries baptism and the Eucharist were defined. Absolution was recognized as an extension of the baptismal ministry.

> Absolution, as a subsequent and distinct act (to baptism), is the restoration of this baptismal grace, when lost; its renewal, when decayed. . . If Absolution may be viewed on the one side as the extension of Baptism, it may be also regarded on the other as the anticipation of the holy Eucharist. The ordinance looks both ways, sin necessitating it in both cases; in the one to restore grace lost or deteriorated, in the other to ensure greater grace yet to come.[82]

He goes on to adduce comments from Jeremy Taylor (paralleling absolution and the cleansing of lepers by the Jewish priesthood), from St Augustine (comparing absolution and the loosing of Lazarus), and from St Ambrose ('Men pray, but it is God who forgives: it is man's obsequiousness, but the bountiful gift is from God . . . He who is invoked by the Priest, is imparted by God; in which transaction there is God's gift, the Priest's ministry'). Carter comments: 'The type of the Levitical priest cleansing the leper, represents the declaratory view of absolution; that of loosing Lazarus implies an effectual act in the renewal of life, while St Ambrose's words explain the living grace to be a direct gift of the Holy Ghost renewing the soul, though conveyed through an earthly ministry.'[83] These are different sides of the truth, and the definition of absolution varies according to the view taken of the remission of sins.

'If remission of sins be regarded simply as a judicial act, a pardon of the offence, then absolution is but declaratory. Pardon, under this view is but an external fact, which the Priest attests, his sentence coinciding with the sentence of God. If, however, remission of sins be viewed internally, as more than mere pardon, as a communication of fresh life, then Absolution becomes a channel of quickening grace.'[84] Carter continues,

> To attribute the Absolution more than a mere declaration of forgiveness,' May seem to derogate from the supremacy of God. But the ministry of the means of grace is not the same with the gift of grace: the channel of the current is not identical with the stream. To assert for the Church's ministry a delegated instrumental power, through which God vouchsafes to act by covenanted promise, is not to claim any Divine power.[85]

In Christ the power of God operated through human means – that is a necessary corollary of incarnation. The ministry of forgiveness is Christ's ministry, 'His own inalienable prerogative, but exercised mediately through others, through a line of subordinate agency, His own commissioned ministers, deriving from Himself in an unbroken continuity of living grace'. 'His words,' says Carter, 'were so understood by the bystanders; for "they marvelled and glorified God, Who had given such power unto men".'[86]

The Anglican tradition witnesses to the view that 'remission of sins is not a mere judicial process . . . but an actual internal change from evil to good.'[87] Absolution, unlike baptism, 'presupposes a gift of grace'.

> There must be a regenerate nature before any effect can result from the ministration of Absolution. It is remedial, not initiatory, and thus implies a previous grace, a pre-existing fitness for its reception. On this account Absolution is never administered to the unbaptized. They may confess, but they cannot be absolved. . . Baptism is in itself a gift of life, involving the new, the heavenly nature, and uniting the soul to God in Christ. There is thus a spiritual principle on which the grace of Absolution can act, an already existing power, and, however dormant it may have become through neglect, such as may be renewed and increased.[88]

Having painstakingly examined the theology of absolution Carter concludes with further comment on the indicative form of absolution. He is clear that the form of absolution used for the first 1200 years of the Church's history was precatory and not indicative, and that is the continuing tradition of the Christian East. The *absolvo te* came to be added to the prayer for forgiveness (which was essentially that which appeared following the absolution in the Prayer Book Order for the Visitation of the Sick). The prayer implored the desired grace, the declaration sealed its assured possession. A similar variance between precatory and indicative forms was to be noted both in the gospel records of the Lord's words in healing or forgiveness, and in baptismal liturgies.

> The form of administering Baptism was originally precatory, and this usage still obtains in the East, while the Western use has become indicative. There is no greater claim implied in the 'Ego absolvo te', than in the 'Ego baptizo te'. In both cases alike the idea involved is not the power of bestowing grace, but only the exercise of the instrumental agency through which it is imparted by God according to the terms of the Covenant.[89]

The indicative form of the Prayer Book in fact combines prayer for forgiveness with *ego absolvo te*, for first the Priest prays, 'of His great mercy forgive thee thine offences', and only then adds 'I absolve thee.'[90]

Pusey and Carter, as perhaps the most notable defenders of the place of sacramental confession as both freeing from the guilt and power of sin and enabling holiness of life, reminded their nineteenth-century opponents of a long line of post-Reformation Anglican witnesses to the value of this sacramental means of grace. As Pusey wrote in the preface to his first 1846 sermon: 'What we need is, that men's hearts should be restored, the longings after a more inward, or more watchful, more devoted life, fostered, the desire of greater strictness with self, and conformity to the Will of God strengthened, the indistinct feeling after a higher standard of duty confirmed and more defined.' He urged that those who found it strange should not 'declaim against remedies which they have not tried, nor seek to deter the wounded of Christ's flock from being bound up'.[91]

Notes

1. J. L. Ainslie, *The Doctrines of Ministerial Order in the Reformed Churches of the 16th and 17th centuries* (Edinburgh 1940), pp.66–70.
2. Quoted ibid., p.79.
3. *Institutes*, iii.iv.12, q. ibid., p.80.
4. *Institutes*, iii.iv.14, q. ibid., pp.80–1.
5. *Obedience of a Christian Man* (1528), Tyndale, *Doctrinal Treatises*, PS (Parker Society) 36, p.363.
6. *Exposition of First Epistle of St John*, PS44, p.150.
7. Becon, *Works*, PS11, p.100.
8. ibid., pp.101–2.
9. Coverdale, *Remarks*, PS26, p.481.
10. ibid., pp.482–3.
11. Ridley, *Letters* (1554), PS1, p.338.
12. Latimer, Sermon 1552, *Sermons*, PS18, p.13.
13. Grindal, *Works*, PS9, p.57.
14. Pilkington, *Works*, PS3, p.524.
15. *Ad Smyrn.*, c.9; *Laws of Ecclesiastical Polity*, VI.ii.2.
16. VI.iii.1.
17. VI.iv.3.
18. ibid.
19. Chrysostom, *Hom. in Hebr.* 30; q. VI.iv.4.
20. VI.iv.5.
21. VI.iv.7.
22. ibid.
23. VI.iv.13.

24. VI.iv.14.
25. ibid.
26. VI.iv.15.
27. ibid.
28. VI.v.5.
29. VI.vi.1.
30. VI.vi.4.
31. VI.iv.5.
32. VI.vi.8.
33. VI.vi.18.
34. *Holy Dying* (1700 edn), p.192.
35. ibid., p.202.
36. ibid., p.209.
37. ibid., p.210.
38. L'Estrange, *Alliance of Divine Offices* (London 1659), pp.298–9.
39. J. Bramhall, *Works*, LACT (Library of Anglo-Catholic Theology, Oxford), V, pp.213–14.
40. ibid., p.222.
41. ibid., pp.222–3.
42. J. Cosin, *Works*, LACT, V, pp.163–4.
43. ibid., II, p.283.
44. H. Thorndike, *Works*, LACT, I.i, pp.56–60; IV.i., p.202.
45. W. Cooke, *The Power of the priesthood in Absolution* (London 1858), pp.82–3.
46. ibid., pp.107–8.
47. q. ibid., pp.112–13.
48. Wickham Legg, *English Church Life from the Restoration to the Tractarian Movement* (London 1914), pp.263ff.
49. J. Warton, *Death-bed Scenes* (London 1827[2]), I, pp.366–7.
50. ibid., pp.370–1.
51. A. Knox, *Remains* (London 1836[2]), I, pp.63–4.
52. K. Denison 'Pusey as confessor and spiritual director', in P. Butler, ed., *Pusey Rediscovered* (London 1983), p.212.
53. C. Wordsworth. *Theophilus Anglicanus or Instructions concerning the Church and the Anglican branch of it* (London 1854[7]), pp.130–1.
54. E. B. Pusey, *Entire Absolution of the Penitent* (Oxford 1846), p.25.
55. ibid., pp.25–6.
56. cf. I. Hausherr, *Penthos, the doctrine of Compunction in the Christian East*. Kalamazoo MI 1982.
57. E. B. Pusey, *Advice for those who exercise the Ministry of Reconciliation through Confession and Absolution, being the Abbé Gaume's Manual for Confessors . . . abridged, condensed, and adapted to the use of the English Church* (Oxford 1878) (hereafter *Gaume*), p.vi.
58. ibid.
59. J. H. Newman, *Autobiographical Writings*, ed. H. Tristram (London 1956), pp.214–15.

60. E. Jay: *The Religion of the Heart: Anglican Evangelicalism and the Nineteenth Century Novel* (Oxford 1979), p.113.
61. Text of the Declaration in T. T. Carter, *Doctrine of Confession* (London 1885[3]), pp.207–302; and in Pusey, *Gaume*, pp.clxxi–clxxiv.
62. Carter, pp.293, 301.
63. Pusey, *Entire Absolution*, p.xvii.
64. ibid., p.5,9; Chrysostom: *In Johan.Hom.*, 86 fin.
65. ibid., p.10n.
66. ibid., pp.33–5.
67. Denison, 'Pusey as confessor', pp.215 and 210–27 *passim*.
68. *Gaume*, p.viii.
69. ibid., pp.xix, xxi–xxv.
70. ibid., p.xxviii.
71. ibid., pp.xlii–xliii.
72. ibid., p.cxxi.
73. ibid., p.cxxxiii.
74. ibid., p.cxliv.
75. ibid., pp.clv–clvi.
76. Carter, pp.34–5.
77. ibid., p.31.
78. ibid., pp.36–7.
79. ibid., p.130.
80. ibid., pp.146,150.
81. ibid., p.182.
82. ibid., pp.255–6.
83. ibid., pp.260–1.
84. ibid., p.261.
85. ibid., pp.261–2.
86. ibid., p.263.
87. ibid., p.265.
88. ibid., p.267.
89. ibid., p.281.
90. ibid., p.282.
91. Pusey, *Entire Absolution*, pp.xv–xvi, xviii–xix.

6 A View from the Foothills: Some Observations on Orthodox Practice of the Sacrament of Confession

Christine Hall

> And there is no limit to the process of perfection, because the perfection of the perfect is indeed endless. Therefore repentance is not restricted either in seasons or in actions, even till death.[1]

Evidence and experience indicate that doubt about the intrinsic value of the sacrament of reconciliation lies behind the breakdown of penitential practice in the Western Church. Unhelpful experiences of spiritual direction or of making confession have led many to conclude that for them the process is neither helpful nor meaningful.

Although, for a Westerner, the task of comparing the western position with that of the East is as difficult as conducting the survey of a high mountain peak whilst remaining confined to the foothills, nevertheless the view from the foothills is very interesting and informative. The view indicates that Orthodox theology of the sacrament of confession shows a strong inner cohesion in its understanding of the meaning and purpose of the sacrament, whilst at the same time showing a wide variety of practice. Evidence suggests that its inner cohesion is maintained by its vision of the human person, destined for union with God and moving towards that union in company with other persons, within the communion of the Body of Christ, the Church.

In Orthodox terminology, the title 'sacrament of confession' is preferred by many priests and in many manuals, as well as in the popular speech, because there is strong emphasis on the fact that confession is as much a confession of faith as it is a confession of sin. From the priest's point of view, the pastoral and teaching opportunities provided by the sacrament are very important. It is not unusual to begin a confession by taking the penitent through the Creed. The principle underlying this practice is that belief determines action and understanding of sin, and penitents cannot be expected to be or behave in any way except in accordance with what they believe. Confession is also an occasion for building up confidence before Christ in penitents who, as Khomiakov put it, 'can condemn themselves but have no right to absolve themselves'.[2]

Orthodox manuals of dogmatic theology (Andrutsos, Chitsescu and others) stress the dominical institution of the sacrament of confession, quoting John 20.23, 'For those whose sins you forgive, they are forgiven; for those whose sins you retain, they are retained'. The subsequent linking of the exercise of this authority to a visible act of confession results from recognition of the Church as a visible institution which links grace to visible signs and offers it through sensible means.

The visible elements of the sacrament, as celebrated in Orthodoxy, are repentance with the necessary accompanying desire not to sin again; confession and absolution. Although a wide variety of authoritative canonical material exists to help confessors to establish suitable penances, the giving and performing of a penance is not regarded as essential to the sacrament and is very often omitted.[3]

REPENTANCE

Repentance is of those sins committed after baptism, hence the title 'second baptism', which is often given to the sacrament of confession. As St John Climacus (*c.* 570–649) wrote, 'If God in his mercy had not granted to men this second baptism, few indeed would be saved.'[4]

The healing aspect of repentance and the idea of reconciliation with the Christian community, emphasized comparatively recently in Western practice, is fundamental to Orthodoxy. Some Orthodox theologians have accordingly stated their preference for the use of the Greek word *metanoia* which expresses this spiritual therapeutic process better than the Latin *paenitentia*.[5] The presence of the priest encourages dialogue, and this breaks the solitude of the separated. The penitent's sorrow for sin is accompanied by the hope of forgiveness and the deep yearning for lost innocence. Against this background, sin is told aloud and thus externalized, becoming, as it were, objective. It is then possible for it to be faced from outside and overcome. 'Only sacramental absolution destroys it for good and gives complete healing.'[6]

Whilst recognizing the distinction between venial and mortal sin (1 John 5.16), Orthodoxy has produced no catalogue of which sins fall into which category. Repentance is an 'act of the heart' acknowledging its offence against the mercy of God, without analysis or classification. The concept of a 'state of grace' would have little meaning in this context, where 'no limit is set to the process of perfection, because the perfection of the perfect is indeed endless'.

Furthermore, the idea of 'quieting the individual conscience' would be seen as a distortion, because the individual is inseparable from the community and the confession of particular sin is firmly placed within the dynamic movement of the whole community towards participation in the life of God himself. As the Greek theologian Christos Yannaras warns, if repentance is thus distorted and sin regarded as no more than individual guilt, acts of repentance become a series of 'cases' requiring predetermined 'penalties'. The whole process becomes a legal transaction; 'remission of sins' – a phrase which refers directly to the existential transfiguration of man accomplished through repentance – is identified with legal 'justification' and release from the pangs of guilt.[7]

CONFESSION

The apostolic authority to adjudicate on the spiritual condition of penitents cannot be exercised unless that condition is known, hence the need for an act of confession. The account in Acts 19 of the confession of the exorcists of Ephesus is taken by some Orthodox theologians as indication of the introduction of the practice of confession from apostolic times, and 1 John 1.9 ('. . . if we acknowledge our sins, then God who is faithful and just will forgive us our sins') is seen as the Church's early recognition that confession is necessary before forgiveness can be obtained.[8]

'If anyone loves me, he will keep my word, and my Father will love him and we shall come to him and make our home with him' (John 14.23). In certain circumstances, Orthodoxy would accept that penitents who have what the West has called perfect contrition but who cannot, for reasons beyond their control, confess to a priest, may indeed receive God's forgiveness and be indwelt by him. This does not however indicate acceptance of widespread use of individual and private confession without a human witness, for only God knows the existence and outcome of such a confession; and such a practice implies that the absolution given by the priest has no real effect, but is only a simple declaration or an announcement that the penitent's sins have already been forgiven. By contrast, in conferring apostolic authority to bind and loose, Christ implicitly made forgiveness conditional on confession and absolution.[9]

ABSOLUTION

The corporate dimension of the sacrament of confession is focused in the bishop, who, as successor to the Apostles, is the one who exercises the 'economy' of the sacrament. At an early stage in the Church's history, bishops began to delegate this authority to priests. The *Apostolic Canons*[10] mention a '*presbyteros epi tēs metanoias*' at Constantinople as early as the fourth century. In the canonical literature of the Orthodox Church it is indicated that the authority to absolve cannot be taken for granted by any priest but must be specifically delegated to him by the bishop by laying on of hands, a custom which is still practised. This helps to emphasize the corporate dimension of the celebration of the sacrament of confession. It would perhaps be desirable in the Anglican context to institute such a practice, accompanying it with the expectation that those who assume the spiritual direction of others are themselves under close direction.

In the Orthodox Churches, formulae of absolution vary, and the development and use of different confessional rites has been discussed at length in many learned sources. Generally speaking, in the Romanian and Russian Churches, the confessor uses the indicative form, 'I forgive'; in the Greek Church the deprecative form, 'May God forgive'. The indicative form, adopted in the Romanian and Slav Churches in the eighteenth century, is attributed to the latinizing influences of Petru Movila, Moldavian (Romanian) Metropolitan of Kiev. The use of the deprecative form should not be taken to imply that the Orthodox priest does not absolve as his Roman Catholic counterpart does. The deprecative form may accentuate the role of God, but in essence the meaning is the same; the penitent receives God's forgiveness through the priest.[11] The dominical authority to forgive has been given, and when the authority is exercised, the forgiveness is efficacious. The absolution must be given orally, to the penitent alone; other forms of communication are inadmissible, as they would normally be in the West.

PENANCE

The juridical notion of 'satisfaction' is absent from Orthodox theology. The *epitimia* (penance) is not a chastisement but a therapeutic remedy, the purpose of which is to place the penitent in a position in which he or she will not be further tempted. Repentance is itself a 'gift', and 'purification is therefore achieved in consolation and joy'.[12] There is an organic link between the state of the sick person and the therapeutic means, not (as the Western doctrine of satisfaction would seem to imply) between the gravity of the offence and the nature of the punishment or retribution. Apart from its therapeutic objective, penance also aims to protect other Christians from the effects of the penitent's sin.[13] 'Educative penances are always intended to guide us to physical participation in the realization of our freedom.' They are not to be 'interpreted as a price for the redemption of our sins'.[14] When compared with this evident attempt to keep in view what the person is in the process of becoming, the idea of satisfaction seems to tie penitents to the past, from which they can be extricated only with difficulty.

Despite the insistence by some Western theologians that sacramental satisfaction cannot be adequately explained in terms of juridical law but must also be concerned with the healing and saving character of penance,[15] even Orthodox theologians writing within the last five years, continue to imply that the juridical view of redemption colours penitential practice in the West. Is this because they are badly informed; because Western positions on the matter are unclear to outsiders, or because, despite changes in the rite used, modern penitential practice continues in reality to be underpinned by legalism?

The juridical view of redemption, developed by Anselm of Canterbury, and further developed by Thomas Aquinas, reached its inevitable canonical formulation at the Council of Trent: 'Dominus noster Iesus Christus, qui . . . sua sanctissima passione in ligno crucis nobis iustificationem meruit et pro nobis Deo Patri satisfecit'. Commenting on Anselm's view,[16] the Russian theologian Vladimir Lossky drew attention to St Gregory Nazianzen's insistence that it is impossible to use juridical notions to prove rationally that the work of redemption was necessary. St Gregory posed two questions: 'The most precious and glorious blood of God . . . why was it shed and to whom was it offered?' We were, he argued, in bondage to the devil and sold to sin. A ransom is paid to someone who holds people in his power. To whom was it paid in our case and why? If it were paid to the devil, this would be outrageous; the robber receiving a ransom, and not just a ransom from God but God himself. On the other hand, the ransom could not possibly be paid to the Father, for it was not the Father who held us in captivity. St Gregory concluded:

> Is it not evident that the Father accepts the sacrifice not because he demanded it or had any need for it but by his dispensation? It was necessary that man should be sanctified by the humanity of God; it was necessary that he himself should free us . . . and that he should recall us to himself by his Son . . . Let the rest of the mystery be venerated silently.[17]

Orthodox theology never excludes the wider vision of man as capable of reaching union with God, of participating in the divine life. In consequence, Lossky could only describe juridical ideas of redemption as 'constricted horizons'. Salvation from sin 'will be in its ultimate realization in the age to come our union with God, the deification of the created beings whom Christ ransomed'.[18] It is evident that a non-juridical view of redemption and an emphasis on ultimate union with God could not possibly co-exist with a doctrine of satisfaction and hence with its extension, the notion that, by the performance of penances whose extent corresponds to the gravity of the sins committed, the repentant sinner shares in the 'payment' made by the Saviour.

CONFESSION AND THE HOLY EUCHARIST

The Lateran Council of 1215 laid down that 'every faithful of either sex who has reached the age of discretion should at least once a year faithfully confess all their sins in secret to their own priest'.[19] By contrast, Orthodox theologians are wont to point out that no canon of an Ecumenical Council recognized in Orthodoxy binds all the faithful to the use of auricular confession. There are however canons of ancient Councils prescribing public penance for idolatry, murder and adultery; these are, at least theoretically, still in force.[20]

In practice, there is no suggestion that the sacrament of confession may be dispensed with any more than any of the other sacraments may be, although there are those who see it as a necessary preparation for every (or almost every) act of Communion, and those who see it as independent from Communion but indispensable to growth in the spiritual life.[21] Orthodox Christians receive Holy Communion from their baptism and chrismation onwards, whatever their age. If they are children, they are expected to make use of the sacrament of confession as soon as they know the difference between right and wrong. Opinion varies about what age this is likely to be; the general consensus is about seven or eight. Interestingly, the Pravila of Targoviste says that the years of discretion will probably be fourteen for boys and twelve for girls.

In some Orthodox communities, confession is not practised frequently. Some writers explain that there are historical reasons for this, but do not give details. Despite the difficult political situation in which the Romanian and Slav Orthodox find themselves, and despite the fear of many of them that the confidentiality of the sacrament of confession is open to political pressure, evidence suggests that, in general, the faithful of these traditions make much greater use of the sacrament than the Greeks do, and that they are normally expected to do so before each act of communion. In some places, practice is inevitably determined by the numbers involved. Before a major festival, particularly one at which those who communicate rarely usually come for communion, queues for confession may run into hundreds. This only gives the confessor time to say the preparatory prayers with the assembled crowd and then to take each person separately for a very short time. In places where it is still customary to receive communion no more than three or four times a year, the close relationship between confession and communion still seems to hold. In places where the custom of frequent communion exists or has been restored, confessors may, at their discretion, give penitents permission to receive communion more than once before returning again to confession.

PENITENTIAL CANONS

From about the fourth century onwards, after the period of persecution had passed, a large number of penitential canons (penances) was formulated by ecumenical and local councils to regulate the life of the Church. Those ascribed to St Basil the Great, fourth century Bishop of Caesarea, are among the most severe. They prescribe the number of years a penitent should be deprived of Holy Communion for certain sins; for example, fifteen years for homosexual activity; six years for false witness; three years plus 200 prostrations daily and some dietary restrictions, for allowing a child to die unbaptized.[22] The later canons of John the Faster, Patriarch of Constantinople from 582 to 595, show a moderating tendency, prescribing no period of deprivation longer than three years. The tendency continues in the canons of the Quinisext Council of 692 (also called the Council in Trullo), which codified and categorized penitential canons from many sources, including those canons of local councils which had proved their universal validity. Some scholars have seen this as an indication that

> unlike the truths of faith, which do not change but remain in substance the same, even if they are expressed in new ways, the canons of the Church are an instrument which the Church must use as is most appropriate to every age. In its canons, the Church must demonstrate a permanent capacity for adaptation and renewal, in order that its saving mission may be best served.[23]

A number of penitential canons are included in the Molitfelnic (Euchologion) for the use of confessors. They are accompanied by the instruction that confessors should hold strictly to the canons, not considering themselves wiser or more forgiving than the holy Fathers who formulated them, except in cases where penitents show the greatest repentance and humility and have truly forsaken the sins they have confessed. Such dispensation is in accord with patristic opinion that 'the return of the sinner depends on the rending of the heart and can be achieved even in a single day'.[24]

In its second canon, the Quinisext Council described the purpose of penitential canons as being 'for the care of souls and the cure of diseases'. In his study of the canons as 'limits set to life', Yannaras emphasizes that they are to be healing and therapeutic in character, not legal and juridical.[25] The penances imposed by such canons 'do not represent penalties to buy remission'. They represent rather the 'length of the journey which human freedom has to traverse in order to accord with the Trinitarian mode of existence within the Church body'. The canons have however 'always been relative and subject to economy . . . this does not mean necessarily that canonical penalties are reduced, but it does mean that they are adapted as closely as possible to the distinctiveness of each personal failure'.[26] As usual, it is the bishop who has the authority to exercise the canons and the authority to set them aside, by virtue of his apostolic grace to bind and loose. The purpose of the canon is, according to Yannaras, to 'mark the limits of life'. They 'distinguish sin only to mark the starting point for repentance'. They do not set out to be a legal code which is systematic and definitive. It should perhaps be noted here that the canons are administered with great attention to each personal case. For example, a person suffering from a terminal illness will not normally be deprived of communion for twenty-five years. During the period of deprivation, the penitent is still expected to attend the Liturgy, perhaps allowed to receive the *antidoron*, given holy water to drink, and required to say certain prayers or to follow some other instruction given by the confessor, who will review the situation regularly with the penitent and modify his instructions accordingly. 'The canons are subordinated to the life of the Church which is love, in order to manifest her healing character.'[27]

The Church is a eucharistic community, whose penitential canons regulate 'not only external relationships having to do with her administrative structure and the good order of her human organization, but also the conditions for each member's participation in her body or personal severance from it'.[28] This explains the canons' preoccupation with admission to or exclusion from the Holy Communion. To put it bluntly, those who are not in communion with Christ are not allowed to go on behaving as if they are, but are led from recognition of their distance away from God through repentance and purification to a more loving relationship with him.

INDIVIDUALITY AND PERSONHOOD

The modern western mind seems to have immense difficulty when asked to consider and to understand the limits of individuality and the value of personhood-in-community. This, admittedly ungainly, expression is used advisedly, to avoid the term 'corporate personality', which might come more readily to mind. 'Corporate personality', whilst it may speak to us of mutual support also seems to convey to many people the idea of loss of identity, despite the very clear analogy of the Body of Christ put before us by St Paul, in which no member is confused with any other or loses its specific value, and in which the whole is infinitely more than a sum of its separate parts.

It has been claimed that 'Orthodox asceticism cannot be understood unless the Orthodox conception of "integral" human nature, created after the pattern of Christ's nature, is fully grasped'.[29] For Orthodoxy, the true state of nature is its state at creation, and sin is a condition alien to nature. In this sense, what we commonly call 'human nature' is not human nature as created by God at all. Similarly,
as Lossky identified, what we 'habitually call a human person is not truly a person but an individual'.[30] Our nature, as it was at creation, has been recapitulated in Christ, but, as fallen creatures, we do not know true unity of nature. In our individual autonomy, we are still merely distinguishable parts of our shared human nature, experiencing all the inadequacies and limitations on freedom which this implies. Yannaras speaks of the 'tragic divide between person and nature'[31] and Lossky emphasizes that 'persons as such are not just parts of nature. Although linked with individual parts of the common nature in created actuality, they potentially contain in themselves, each in his fashion, the whole of nature.'[32]

The tension has to be held between the idea of the person as joining with other persons to form the whole Body of Christ (unity in communion) and that of the person as embodying that whole. In this context, the purpose of the sacrament of confession is the same as that of all the sacraments, to restore life to fulness of freedom and love. The penitent has in effect taken a decision to escape from autonomy and separateness, and seek instead to be incorporated into the loving communion of the Church and the life of God the Holy Trinity. This communion does not destroy distinctiveness but is paradoxically the 'ontological precondition for distinctiveness and freedom'.[33]

Repentance is important above all for the transfiguration of man from individual autonomy to the freedom of communion and personhood.

> I call the Church to be a partaker in my inadequacy: I ask and receive the love of the Church, the love of God, which is not a 'feeling' of pity or a legal absolution, but life. It is grace, the gift of transforming my alienated person into an image of the Son of God, the Son of the Father's love.[34]

It is evident from this that the sacrament of confession goes far beyond the level of man's individual psychological requirements, the psychological experience of relieving guilt feelings and the 'quieting of the individual conscience'.

SPIRITUAL FATHERHOOD

> Parallel to the 'apostolic succession' of the clergy, which maintains the unity of the Church in her organic historical continuity, the succession of spiritual fatherhood preserves the unity of the Church's spiritual experience, the orthodoxy of the Church's mind and life.[35]

The ministry of spiritual fatherhood is the ministry of spiritual direction within the framework of confession. The *pneumatikos patēr* is above all one who is born of the Spirit; who knows the heart and has the gift of discernment (*diakrisis*) of spirits and thoughts. This discernment is the result of a particular gift from God, not just of a long experience in understanding people. Absolution is reserved to priests but the spiritual father, or indeed spiritual mother, need not necessarily be a priest. He or she may be a simple monastic, and it is not uncommon in Orthodoxy for those whose regular confessor and spiritual director is their parish priest to have a monastic spiritual father to whom they will go once or twice a year. The mysteries of the spiritual life are passed on from generation to generation through the relationship of spiritual father/spiritual disciple.

Much could be said about the use and role of the spiritual father both in the monastic life and outside it. Suffice it to say, for the purposes of this comparison that the paternity of the spiritual father is a figure of the fatherhood of God and has no connection whatever with any moral or psychological paternalism which militates against maturity. It is the task of the spiritual father to initiate the discipline gradually and appropriately into the mysteries of the spiritual life and, by so doing, to facilitate the disciple's reconciliation with God. But, it is grace which accomplishes everything; the love, trust and obedience which the disciple shows to the spiritual father are not directed to him as man but to Christ whom he represents.

It is appropriate that the transition from individuality to personhood, of which Yannaras and other Orthodox theologians write, should take place within a living relationship; that the life of the Church should become accessible through a living and personal event.

> Ultimately [the relationship with a spiritual father] is a relationship and a bond which 'hypostasises' the person in the unity of the Church's life – it is a birth into life, not mere instruction; 'for though you have ten thousand instructors in Christ, yet you have not many spiritual fathers: for in Christ Jesus I have begotten you through the Gospel. (1 cor. 4.15)[36]

LIFE IN GOD

The purpose of the sacrament of confession is to restore human beings to life, the life which exists within God and the ecclesial community. Restoration is accomplished through knowledge of the truth which leads to freedom. It is in fact truth, not virtue, which is the purpose of repentance.

> Virtue exists for truth; truth does not exist for virtue. Thus he who practises virtue for the sake of truth is not wounded by the darts of vainglory. But he who concerns himself with truth for the sake of virtue has the conceit of vainglory as his associate.[37]

Yannaras sees this statement as summing up the whole of Christian ethics and summarizing the end and purpose of the sacrament of confession. Sin is then identified as the rejection of a relationship of loving communion. 'Against thee alone have we sinned; thee alone do we worship.'[38] By contrast, the juridical understanding of sin as a violation of codes of behaviour, and of salvation as individual justification, requires objective 'reform'. This confines the penitent to individual effort and individual morality, whereas in reality: healing can only come through gradual understanding and dynamic experience of the truth of the mystery, through bringing one's sin to the Church again and again until one gains real humility and this humility encounters the love of the Church – until *life* does its work and the deadened nature is raised up.[39]

It is in this way that the healing of the sacrament of confession is closely bound up with the transition from individuality to personhood, and that 'maturity of repentance is inevitably revealed as transfiguration; an involuntary change coming from without, and a spontaneous testimony to the fact that God saves the person who approaches him'.[40]

Notes

1. Isaac the Syrian, d. *c*. 700, *Mystic Treatises*, 55.
2. A. S. Khomiakov, *L'Église latine et le protestantisme au point de vue de l'Église d'Orient* (Lausanne 1872), pp.271–2.
3. T. Ware, *The Orthodox Church* (Harmondsworth 1980), p.297.
4. Monk of the Eastern Church, *Orthodox Spirituality* (London 1980), p.47.
5. For example, P. Evdokimov, *L'Orthodoxie* (Neuchatel 1959), p.289.
6. ibid., p.290.
7. C. Yannaras, *The Freedom of Morality* (Crestwood NY 1984), p.151.
8. N. Chitsescu, *Teologia Dogmatica si Simbolica* (Bucharest 1958), p.899.
9. ibid., p.901.
10. Canon 51, PG (Patrologia Graeca) 67; 613–16.
11. Chitsescu, p.902.
12. Evdokimov, p.291.
13. H. Andrutsos, *Dogmatica Bisericii Ortodoxe Rasaritene* (Sibiu 1930, tr. from Greek), p.410.
14. Yannaras, p.151.
15. For example, B. Haring, *The Law of Christ* (Cork 1963) pp.468–72.
16. V. Lossky, *In the Image and Likeness of God* (Crestwood NY 1974), pp.101–2.
17. *Oration* 45,22. PG36; 653.
18. V. Lossky, op. cit., p.103.
19. J. Neuner and J. Dupuis, *The Christian Faith in the Doctrinal Documents of the Catholic Church* (London 1983), p.453, para. 1608.
20. Monk of the Eastern Church, op. cit., p.45.
21. See Hieromonk Silouan, 'Confession before Holy Communion' (*Sourozh*, February 1984;) and A. Kniazeff, 'On the Sacrament of Repentance' (*Sourozh*, May 1985).
22. Molitfelnic of the Romanian Orthodox Church (Bucharest 1937).
23. Liviu Stan, *Codificarea Canoanelor* (Bucharest 1959), pp.637–8.
24. See M. Colotelo, 'Nomocanonul slav', *Studii teologice*, No. 5–6. Bucharest 1960.
25. Yannaras, p.180.
26. ibid., pp.181–2.
27. ibid., p.191.
28. ibid., pp.173–4.
29. Monk of the Eastern Church, p.50.
30. Lossky, p.107.
31. Yannaras, p.145.
32. Lossky, p.107.
33. Yannaras, p.144.
34. ibid., p.146.
35. ibid., p.157.
36. ibid., p.156.
37. St Maximus the Confessor, *Ambigua*, PG90; 369A.

38. Orthodox Vespers of the Sunday of Pentecost.
39. Yannaras, p.150.
40. Archimandrite Vasileios, *Hymn of Entry* (Crestwood NY 1984), p.24.

PART TWO

The Contemporary Church: Pastoral and Theological Perspectives

7 What has been Lost? Penance and Reconciliation Reconsidered

Brian Horne

I

In 1972 Hans Urs Von Balthasar felt obliged to come to the defence of the practice of personal, individual confession. This he did in an article the title of which indicated the apologetic nature of the exercise: 'Personliche Beichte überholt?'[1] That the sacrament of penance (as it used to be called) should have needed to have been defended in this way would have astonished earlier generations of his fellow churchmen for whom regular visits to the confessional were as normal and indispensable a part of the Christian life as regular participation in the Eucharist. The same attitude, if not precisely the same practice, could have been observed in earlier generations of Catholic Anglicans. By the time of Balthasar's article, however, it was impossible to ignore the fact that, not only had the practice of private confession declined rapidly, there was also confusion about both the theology and the liturgical celebration of this sacrament.[2] By 1970 the traditional penitential system seemed to have broken down both in the Roman Catholic Church and also, though less obviously and dramatically, in the Churches of the Anglican Communion. In an effort to restore the sacrament to the faithful the new liturgy of reconciliation, *Ordo Penitentiae* was presented in 1974. The *Alternative Service Book* of the Church of England of 1980 made no mention of the sacrament of reconciliation of course; but six years later the bishops of the Church of England commended a new set of services for Lent, Holy Week and Easter which contained in addition to rites for corporate acts of penitence a form of absolution for cases of individual confession. In doing this they were following the example of sister Churches of the Anglican Communion which had already provided such rites in their own revised liturgies. It remains to be seen whether any of these attempts at re-vitalizing the penitential liturgy will be able to capture the imagination of Catholic Christians and restore to them a sacrament which they seem to have lost – or rejected.

II

We have only begun to investigate the reasons for the decline of the celebration of the sacrament in the latter part of the twentieth century.

Some are sociological and are connected to the changed cultural and political circumstances of twentieth century Christians: circumstances which somehow encourage them to regard the traditional practices as irrelevant to their spiritual and psychological needs. Others are theological and arise out of the way in which the penitential discipline was formed and how it has developed down the centuries: it is a real question whether a rite celebrated appropriately in certain historical conditions is equally appropriate in very different conditions. It is just as important to ask whether beneath the changing forms of the rite certain elements should remain constant and unchanging. All would agree that without contrition, confession and absolution there can be no reconciliation. What about the element of *penance*? The new rites and the contemporary theologians are ambivalent.

From the end of the fourth century to the beginning of the sixth (a crucial period for the history of the celebration of the sacrament in Western Christendom) the Latin Church, growing rapidly and changing in numerous ways to accommodate its altered position in society, began to shape both the theology and the practice of the sacrament in ways that were to determine its future for the next fourteen centuries. It is not unreasonable to suppose that, just as certain aspects of civil law were beginning to influence theological interpretations of the atonement, so these same influences came to be felt liturgically in the practice of the penitential discipline. One might cite as an instance of this Pope Gregory I's argument, at the end of the sixth century, that, while the death of Christ could be said to free the baptized from the consequences of original sin, when it came to sins committed *after* baptism it availed to convert the eternal punishment into temporal penalties which could be discharged in this life only by an adequate amount of suffering – either self-imposed or imposed by the Church. Penitence thus became the prelude to a forgiveness that could only be obtained or realized (perhaps one should use the term *earned*) in, what came to be called *satisfaction* (Moralia XVI). While it is true that Gregory's teachings were never incorporated into official pronouncements by the Church, his influence was pervasive, and notions of satisfaction became a constant theme and in some later periods even a dominant theme in both soteriology and liturgy. In particular, satisfaction was linked to that part of the penitential rite to which the name penance was given.[3] (Nine centuries later it was this interpretation of salvation in terms of satisfaction that Martin Luther rejected when he tried to fit the penitential discipline into the framework of a doctrine of justification by faith.)

Gregory's main concerns were pastoral and practical: the theological issue of how and whether confession could be said to be a *sacrament* was not a matter which he addressed directly. But by the twelfth and thirteenth centuries the theological issue was very much to the fore. This was a world in which the details of sacramental theology and practice had become an important part of scholastic debate. By 1215 the practice of repeated private confession to a priest had been commended and officially recognized as the Sacrament of Penance. Scholastic theologians now disputed about its precise nature, its resemblance to other sacraments, its correct 'matter' and 'form'. What words should be used when pronouncing absolution? Did the priest possess the power to forgive sins? Was it the interior disposition of the penitent or the formula uttered by the confessor that caused the removal of guilt? Were the forgiveness of God and reconciliation with the Church separate actions or part of a single rite? On all of these questions opinions differed, but in this controversy, as in so many others, the genius of Thomas Aquinas prevailed and the substance of his views, somewhat modified, passed into the teaching of the Council of Trent[4] which in turn lasted until the present century. Thomas identified the acts of penance – imposed by the priest and accepted by the penitent – as the *matter* of the sacrament and the words of absolution pronounced by the confessor as the *form*.[5] Only the combination of both elements could properly constitute and validate the penitential rite as *sacramental*. Contemporary theology has moved away from the scholastic terminology of *matter* and *form*; but before we dismiss Thomas's distinctions as medieval quibbling, it is worth noting Karl Rahner's comment on the Thomistic 'synthesis': '. . . this teaching of St Thomas was inspired by his deep theological insight which urges him to let the personal and sacramental moments in the process of justification permeate one another as intimately as possible.'[6] We shall return to Thomas Aquinas later for it may be that his 'deep theological insight' can help us, in our present doubt and confusion, to see more clearly what the sacrament is.

The 'process of justification' was, of course, one of Martin Luther's deepest concerns, and he initially advocated private confession, recognizing a spiritual value, even a psychological necessity, in the practice. But he became unable to accept that the priesthood had special powers of absolution and, more significantly, he saw that the idea of *penance* was inextricably linked to that of *satisfaction*. 'This is an important point for we cannot evade the question of whether this is so, and whether the idea must necessarily be interpreted in a way that seems to contradict what is taught about forgiveness in the New

Testament. If penance can only be seen in terms of a false medieval conception of *satisfaction* i.e. as the individual sinner trying to 'make up' for his transgression or 'pay back' what is owed to God, then Luther's rejection must be correct. But, of course, the central teaching of the medieval Church recognized this as a perversion; no human being could accomplish his own atonement, that was achieved by the work of Christ and the grace of God. However, if that was so, what was the point of penance? Was not confession and absolution enough? I do not think this dilemma was ever properly resolved. Penance was retained, but its purpose was variously understood, and in practice – sometimes in theology – absolution came to be regarded as the more significant element. Consequently, in both the Roman Church (despite the specific teaching of the Council of Trent)[8] and the Anglican tradition penances have usually been perfunctory affairs with all the emphasis falling on the 'binding and loosing' powers of the minister. The focus has become the words of absolution.

III

The new *Ordo Penitentiae* shows a movement away from the sacramental theology of the Council of Trent and, perhaps deliberately, offers the possibility of different ways of interpreting the sacrament. It is clear from all the new forms that an effort has been made to rid the celebration of both its juridical connotations and the excessively individualistic notions of sin and forgiveness which have been a feature of its practice since the later Middle Ages. Reconciliation is now the keynote of all the rites: as the Body of Christ in the world the Church identifies her own mission with that of her Head. This sacrament (for individuals) is to be seen as but one part of the whole movement of Christ's reconciling work; one of the means by which the reconciliation is expressed and achieved. The Church (and its individual members) is seen as a penitent people. To display this new understanding the rites have been extended with Scripture readings and prayers, the latter enabling the minister to be seen not only as the one who, in the name of Christ, absolves the sinner, but also as the one who, in the name of the Church and by the power of the Holy Spirit, intercedes for the sinner.

The idea of confession as an opportunity for spiritual growth is indicated in both the individual and communal celebrations of the sacrament. In the former, the anonymity of the old style is abandoned; instead a face-to-face encounter between the priest and the penitent is envisaged so that in addition to the usual ingredients of a more ritual kind there can be discussion of moral problems and the laying on of hands. More significant of the move away from Thomas' theology is the emphasis, especially in the communal rite, on absolution. This has now become the essential 'sign' of the sacrament. It is assumed that when an individual, private confession is made, acts of contrition and penance will be enjoined and performed, but in the new communal rite penance is not mentioned even though the absolution given by the presiding minister is specifically referred to as 'sacramental'. Is penance then merely a pious adjunct to the rite of 'binding and loosing' and not an essential element of the sign of reconciliation?

The question can be posed more sharply. Every celebration of the Eucharist is prefaced by, or contains within its structure, a penitential rite. What, if any, is the difference between such a confession and absolution and the confession and absolution in a communal service of repentance such as is provided in the *Ordo Penitentiae*? Is the celebrant of the Eucharist also celebrating the sacrament of reconciliation in every penitential rite at every Eucharist? Monika Hellwig in her extensive examination of the new attitudes to reconciliation in the Roman Catholic Church, seems to suggest that this is not the case. 'These special rites of repentance within the Eucharistic celebration are not an addition to the meaning and content of the Eucharist but serve to emphasize and draw out the meaning that is intrinsic to it.'[9] Is there a separate and distinct sacrament of reconciliation, and how should it be celebrated?

Nothing at all is said about the *sacramental* nature of confession in any of the new Anglican service books which contain rites of reconciliation. In the recently-published *Lent, Holy Week, Easter: Services and Prayers* provided by the Bishops of the Church of England we are given two rites that are intended for communal use (A) and (B) and what appears to be a rite for individual use (C) which comes with the rubric which repeats the formula to be found in the Book of Common Prayer: A form of absolution '. . . which may be used for the quieting of the individual conscience'. Why it should be thought that the announcement of forgiveness which then follows would 'quiet the individual conscience' more effectively than the declaration of forgiveness heard after a general confession made during a church service is left unexplained. And what exactly is meant by the 'quieting' of a conscience? Is it meant to suggest reconciliation or psychological relief? I suspect the latter, for if the former were intended surely some mention would be made of the restoration of the sinner to the body of the faithful. I am not wanting to drive a wedge between psychological and spiritual healing; there is a connection, but they are also distinct.[10] I can believe that wise advice from an experienced and sensitive counsellor would have the desired psychological effect, but that is a matter of the personal gifts and training of the minister. The sacraments, on the other hand, have never been made to depend upon the individual talents of the minister for their efficacy in the lives of those who receive them. There is, moreover, no mention of *penance* in any of the Anglican rites.[11] Max Thurian argues strongly that the confessional is not the proper place, ordinarily, for spiritual direction, or, presumably, long discussions about moral problems.[12] In this I am inclined to agree with him and am wary of the claim of Balthasar when he writes: 'The less personal confession is practised in the Church, the greater will be the pressure on the office hours of the psychologists where the need for doing away with personal guilt feelings and situations of guilt is met in a different way.'[13] Of course Balthasar recognizes that psychiatrists and confessors work differently and he is concerned to stress the essentially sacramental character of confession: 'Someone who in thoughts, words, or deeds has offended seriously against the spirit of the holy Church of Christ must personally come forward and responsibly confess . . . reconciliation with this communion requires a genuine, personal incarnational act which is provided for by Jesus as a normal ecclesiastical act in the authorization of the disciples.'[14]

IV

In view of the wide variety of interpretation of the meaning of confession in the history of the church, and the present confusion about its character and practice, is there not a case for proposing that it cease to be regarded as a separate and distinct sacrament? We need not feel ourselves bound to defend the medieval classification of seven sacraments of which penance is one. What necessity is there for describing it and wanting to define it as *a* sacrament? It would seem that, for those who recognize their sinfulness, the only requirement for God's forgiveness and restoration to the relationship of love is genuine acknowledgement of sin and the repentance which follows such acknowledgement. Self-accusation, confession and the willingness to accept judgement is both to receive forgiveness of the One who judges and to surrender oneself to the power of the Holy Spirit for the healing of wounds and the growth in holiness. Repentance then is a constant attitude of mind and heart of the believer; and if this is thought too individualistic, there is always participation in the celebration of the Eucharist which may be seen not only as the centre of all sacramental life but also as a sacrament of reconciliation. It is in the offering of the sacrifice of Christ for the sins of the whole world that forgiveness is received. Even Thomas Aquinas argued that the sacraments were ordered to the Eucharist as their end and goal. In this celebration the Body of Christ is healed and restored.

There is no doubt that part of the problem of the old rite as it was practised in the West was not only that its discipline was exercised juridically, so that it was perceived purely as a discipline, but that it was excessively individualistic, as though confession was nothing more than 'the expression of a sensitive soul which is concerned with its private individual blamelessness' instead of 'a confession of guilt through which the Church herself must join in suffering and expiating'.[15] However, even when all that has been said and the errors of our history have been acknowledged; even when we have recognized the possibility of 'social' sin, the gospel forces us to personal decision and repentance. Whatever evils there may be in society, and however we may be caught up in them, it is sentimental to pretend that it is not the individual who sins; so it is the individual who must acknowledge the evil in his own heart, the individual who must seek true personhood, the individual who must find himself sacramentally in the Body and must enter the new humanity offered by God in the baptismal community. There may be time for corporate repentance, there must also be time for individual confession. What I have identified as 'sentimentality' Hans Urs Von Balthasar calls 'infantilism'. He accuses some charismatic groups of this as he sees a 'flight into community' which fails to nourish the inner person in a sacramental way. 'One sign that this accusation is not far-fetched lies in today's tacit agreement that penitential services in common can completely, or almost completely, replace personal confession. At this point, precisely the most personal and the most unrelinquishable act of the entire sacramental life is suppressed.'[16]

If we are to retain this sacrament, how shall it be celebrated? As I have said, many Catholic theologians now writing are concerned to emphasize the power of the Church to 'bind and loose', though not in any harsh, juridical way. Michael Schmaus is typical: 'Within the total life of the Church this sacrament is a special concrete form of that spirit (of penitence). Its particular sacramentality lies in the fact that a visible sign performed by the Church is the guarantee of God's receiving again into his kingdom someone who has fallen away'.[17] The essential sign of the rite is thus the pronouncement of forgiveness, and the Thomistic 'synthesis' – penance and absolution – is set aside: there is now no obligation on the part of the penitent to *do* anything apart from receiving the gift of forgiveness in thankfulness and humility.

This approach has certain clear advantages. There can be no question of anyone earning forgiveness, no danger of believing that satisfaction must be made to God before he is prepared to welcome the sinner back from his estrangement. The penitent cannot cause the grace of reconciliation any more than he can cause the grace of baptism or the Eucharist. But the apparently tidier and simpler interpretation still does not answer the question raised earlier: is there a distinction between our everyday confessions and the more solemn rites of 'sacramental' reconciliation?

V

It is time to introduce the concepts of justice and mercy and to return to Thomas Aquinas who, when talking about sacraments directs us always to consider what sacraments are for. They are to sanctify us, make us holy. And how, in the context of sin and repentance are we actually made holy? What is the process? It will involve the operation of justice and mercy. With his 'deep theological insight' he presents us with his synthesis of penance and absolution: the signs of justice and mercy. The conditions under which the sacrament can be celebrated are repentance and confession; the sacrament itself is a combination of forgiveness pronounced and penance performed, the visible symbols of mercy and justice respectively which achieve a special kind of reconciliation that draws the sinner more intimately into the life of the One from whom he has been estranged. The release from the prison of guilt is accomplished at all levels, natural as well as supernatural, by that operation of justice and mercy which we call the act of pardon. In this act, whether it is human or divine, there will always be a *mutuality*, a kind of exchange between the forgiver and the forgiven, and forgiveness, if it is to begin the process of healing and restoration, will require in its declaration a kind of acceptance which is more than a mere mental act and disposition of the will. It is perhaps this dimension of reconciliation that is in the mind of Monika Hellwig when she writes of the genuine problems people have with the rite of confession.

> The outer signs are expected to signify and mediate reconciliation with the unseen God without any inner experience of integration, focus, conversion (which would already be part of the reality that is signified and would therefore powerfully point further to the reality that cannot be experienced directly). It seems as though the ritual itself is supposed to be the sign and pledge enough, without any personal transformation. But the people are not satisfied with this hollow sign.[18]

If the rite is to be more than a hollow sign and become the experience of true reconciliation it should be recognized, in the first place, that, unlike the sacraments of baptism and Eucharist, the *ministers* of the sacrament are both the one who is representing Christ and his Church and also the one who is confessing the sin; and, in the second place, that the elements of justice and mercy must interpenetrate one another. We demand justice and we need mercy and the complex mystery of God's redeeming love can only be realized sacramentally when the two are really signified. We have here the two parts of Thomas Aquinas's synthesis: penance and absolution. The mutual exchange of love which occurs in any genuine act of pardon involves the sinner in a deliberate movement into the new relationship which is offered by the pardoner. I can agree with J. D. Crichton when he says that the sacrament actualizes 'not only the forgiveness of Christ but also the repentance of the sinner', but I cannot agree with him when he goes on to say that the 'actualisation has happened when the absolution is given. All the rest is discipline.'[19] I do not see penance as 'discipline', I see it as the effective sign of God's justice, just as absolution is the effective sign of God's mercy. It is therefore not a matter of making an effort to pay back what one owes (satisfaction) nor of trying to make amends (putting things right), it is the visible expression of the acceptance of judgement and the desire to be reunited to the one from whom one has become separated. Here in the penance the sign (the sacrament) of reconciliation reaches completion and spiritual healing begins. If self-examination and confession are the means by which we come to recognize past sinfulness, penance is the means by which we lay hold on this knowledge.[20] So in accepting both the justice and the mercy of God as mediated by His Church we can progress towards holiness.

Perhaps the most searching examination of this mystery of 'pardon in operation' is found, not in any work of theology, but in William Shakespeare's play *Measure for Measure*. As the play draws to its end Shakespeare's humanist imagination reaches out beyond the bounds within which it usually works to touch and portray Christian truth. (Perhaps, in the end we shall discover it to be, simply, human truth too, however paradoxical it may seem.) In the extraordinary last act, when every past action and every motive is revealed, the wicked are brought before the Duke. Those who will find redemption do not excuse their sins or ask their evil to be set aside by the Duke's gracious behaviour, they acknowledge their viciousness and demand, albeit with sorrow and fear, the penalty they know as just: measure for measure. The Duke refuses to impose the requested and apparently appropriate penalties: there is a different kind of measure to be reckoned. If there is only the penalty of justice there can be no possibility of reconciliation. On the other hand, the wickedness of the past cannot simply be forgotten; if there is only the forgiveness of mercy there will be complicity in a lie: it is an illusion to pretend that innocence can be recovered. Christian forgiveness (for this is what we are dealing with in this play) must be of a special kind: one that redeems the past by the double exercise of justice and mercy. So the Duke imposes penalties, but they are not those which have been demanded and which strict justice requires; they are acts which will bring about the reconciliation of those who perform them with those whom they have wronged. It is something like this that Adrienne Von Speyer has in mind when she talks about penance as

> both an end and a beginning. It is imposed as punishment for what has been but it is spoken from within the new attitude. . . The Lord has had us confess so that we may be redeemed, but being redeemed is meaningful only if we seek the path to God anew and assume a new attitude of prayer toward him. Penance should bring this about in us. It is not only a deed performed externally but is also something that should shape us and bring us closer to God, the seed of a new fruit.[21]

The penance therefore should be appropriate to the needs of the penitent, and the frequency with which the sacrament is celebrated would, similarly, depend upon the needs, character and situation of each individual. It should never be a harsh imposition 'from above' nor a sullen shouldering of a burden 'from below'. My interpretation leads me to suppose that the celebration has a solemn character and need not necessarily be a frequent occurrence, but might be seen rather as the occasional focus of the entire life of repentance and reconciliation which is the Christian way. I am not pretending that a renewed understanding of the significance of the element of penance within the sacrament will do anything to revive the celebration of the sacrament – the sociological as well as the theological reasons for its decline have not yet been seriously addressed – but I am suggesting that what I have said will help to give its celebration greater coherence. However, the deep and complex mystery of pardon and reconciliation so poignantly intimated in human relations still awaits adequate articulation in the liturgy of the Church.

Notes

1. *The Von Balthasar Reader*, eds M. Kehl and W. Losev (Edinburgh 1982), pp.278–82.
2. See Karl Rahner's prescient essay, 'Forgotten Truths Concerning the Sacrament of Penance', written more than ten years before Balthasar's article, in *Theological Investigations* vol. ii (London 1963).
3. See B. Poschmann, *Penance and the Anointing of the Sick* (London 1964), ch. 2, pp.122–54.
4. See J. Neuner and J. Dupuis, *The Christian Faith in the Doctrinal Documents of the Catholic Church* (London 1983), 1615–1634.
5. *Summa Theologica*, III, iv, QQ 84–90.
6. Rahner, p.156.
7. See *The Pagan Servitude of the Church*, 1520.
8. See Neuner and Dupuis, 1630–33.
9. M. K. Hellwig, *Sign of Reconciliation and Conversion. The Sacrament of Penance for our times* (Wilmington DE 1986), p.30.
10. Some perceptive remarks on the distinction between spiritual healing and psychotherapy are made by Jeremy Young in his article 'Guilt or Neurosis? The Sacrament of Penance and Psychotherapy'. He points to a frequent confusion between neurotic (or existential) guilt and theological (or actual) guilt. Neurotic guilt, a psychological state in which the patient, though *not* guilty, obsessively imagines himself to be, is that state of imprisonment which psychotherapy 'can remove if the patient has sufficient motivation to change; theological guilt is that which sacramental confession removes if the patient is contrite'. He quotes Victor White: 'In short, the primary and direct concern of the sacrament is wilful misdeeds: the primary and direct concern of analysis is with a certain kind of involuntary misfortune.' *Kairos 3*, Easter 1981, pp. 16–19.
11. The rite of the Episcopal Church of the USA: 'Before giving absolution the priest may assign to the penitent a psalm, prayer, or hymn to be said, or something to be done, as a sign of penitence and an act of thanksgiving.'

    The rite of the Church of Canada: 'The priest may suggest appropriate devotions or actions to be performed by the penitent after the conclusion of the rite.' Here we have the explicit exclusion of penance from the rite.
12. M. Thurian, *Confession* (London, 1985), pp.121–2.
13. von Balthasar, p.280.
14. ibid.
15. Rahner, p.151.
16. 'Flight Into Community' in *New Elucidation* (San Francisco 1986), pp.108–9.
17. M. Schmaus, *Dogma* vol. v: *The Church as Sacrament* (London 1975), p.206).
18. Hellwig, p.109.

19. J. P. Crichton, *Christian Celebration: The Sacraments* (London 1974), p.223.
20. If there is some truth in the suggestion that the Church seems to have intellectualized this sacrament by expecting penitents to be far more articulate about the state of their spiritual life than they are capable of being, a renewed awareness of the importance of this element of penance might help to reduce the intellectual content. This does not mean that the intellectually capable should become slovenly nor that others should return to the trivial recitation of little lists provided in manuals of devotion.
21. A. von Speyer, *Confession* (San Francisco 1985), p.190.

8 Not as Judge but as Pastor

John Gaskell

I came out of the Army in April 1949. With a school friend similarly released I went on pilgrimage to Our Lady of Walsingham. We went by the newly nationalized boring LNER with its black engines and yellow rolling stock to Huntingdon, whence we walked. At Ely we stayed in a room over a fried fish shop, but I had the ecstatic experience of seeing the bishop celebrate the 'early service' in the cathedral. He was wearing a chasuble. To my untutored eye it was both antique and Spanish, but in any case 'extreme'. I had no idea that bishops ever celebrated 'early service' in chasubles or otherwise, and it seemed a good omen for a Catholic adventure, and I was anxious to be Catholic. Arrived at Walsingham via Norwich – church upon church! – and Wymondham – Comper of course! – I got up early to go to confession at some preposterous hour like 7.30 a.m., ready for the early Mass. I went to the confessional, made my anxious confession, and was given a penance, absolved and dismissed. I could not believe my ears! I had spent careful thought and prayer on my confession and had tried to make it a 'good' one – *had* I neglected to receive instruction in the Catholic faith? Yes, I had, but the Army in the Far East hardly seemed the setting for it. *Had* I been impure in thought, word or deed, by myself or with others? Alas yes by myself and alas no with others! *Had* I left God out of my life? Was that possible I wondered? Yet all my careful Catholic reflection was dashed by the priest's seeming lack of interest. Of course I was absolved, I thought, but he might have said *something*. Ill humour was dissolved later, however, when an earnest fellow pilgrim told me over coffee that the Holy Father was encouraging us to 'pray the Mass'. Wryly I reflected that the rector at home had told me that Cranmer had thought up that one exactly four hundred years before, and the rector did *not* hear confessions.

Going to confession and giving counsel in reconciliation is a very personal thing. I write only from my own experience of it. These are some impressions of how things have seemed to move in these last decades. I am aware that they owe little to knowledge of change among Roman Catholics: they are the excogitations of an Anglican Catholic. As an Anglican Catholic I underwent a severe shock in that box at Walsingham because as a penitent – and years later as a confessor – my approach to confession was moulded by the guidelines of the Prayer Book. I *expected* counsel.

In the Book of Common Prayer, since 1662, the first Exhortation has placed the sacrament of penance in a quite particular setting, preparation for receiving Holy Communion. The priest and his people with him look forward to the celebration of the Eucharist. He invites the congregation to self-examination, private prayer of penitence and to public acts of reconciliation. But he goes on:

> And because it is requisite, that no man should come to the Holy Communion, but with a full trust in God's mercy, and with a quiet conscience; therefore if there be any of you, who by this means cannot quiet his own conscience herein, but requireth further comfort or counsel, let him come to me, or to some other discreet and learned Minister of God's Word, and open his grief; that by the ministry of God's holy Word he may receive the benefit of absolution, together with ghostly counsel and advice, to the quieting of his conscience, and avoiding of all scruple and doubtfulness.

The impulse for the priest is pastoral – he is to absolve, to counsel and advise with a view to the spiritual peace of his flock. He is not to be judge primarily or to administer a code but to minister to grief, the burden and tangle of sin in which men and women find themselves. During the Anglican centuries this Exhortation may have been little heard and less acted upon, but it has set the style for the administration of this Catholic sacrament among us, as a sign of love and peace and of the Good Shepherd knowing his sheep through the sacramental ministry of his lesser shepherds.

So the priest in the confessional is to sit not as judge but as pastor. It is true that he will be called upon to exercise the gift of judgement again and again, but he does not deal with his fellow sinner as a man or woman or child on trial, but as one who guilty comes to a sacramental encounter with God in his mercy and with Our Lord who is the Way. The shock of my Walsingham confession was that it dealt with the past but had no word of God for the future. It gave me no help on the way. If I ask myself now what role I am to fulfill as I speak in counsel at confession I think of myself as a coach and an encourager. I am beside the penitent, joining together with him or her in seeking the way. When I went to Walsingham the confessions I had made in the previous four years had all been met with priestly words of encouragement, kindness and support. While clearly the pronouncement of absolution was a sacrament of forgiveness that made me 'just as if I were newly baptised', as an Army chaplain once told me, the words of the pastor contained a word of God that often enough dismissed despondency and encouraged well-doing.

Over the last twenty-five years the main impression I have is of growth in expectation of the sacramental counsel element in the transaction of the sacrament of penance. When in 1961 I started hearing confessions the penitent told his sins to God: the priest listened in to them: then he gave his comments, his advice or his instruction. Often enough the confession was made in formalized terms derived from devotional handbooks, which left the confessor clear about the penitent's sins but quite at a loss as to what the penitent was like. The portrait was all shade and no light. Today, however, the penitent has usually had little or no recourse to a questionnaire of sins, explains more about what is involved, and rarely is concerned with failures in the impedimenta of devotion. In the mid 1960s one would hear a good deal about failures to keep the rules of sodalities, omissions of grace or the Angelus, or the problem of the mind wandering during High Mass. These were sensible anxieties about prayer and belief, but they were seen as sin. Because confession was a church thing that some Anglicans did it was very much bound up with the style and witness-bearing of differing strands of the C. of E. so that missing a Lenten Compline which loyalty to the dear vicar might suggest as a grave omission could sound as bad as telling a lie to the boss at work. I think that it is a grace that that sort of 'churchy' confession is increasingly rare. I myself have to be careful not to think ill of it, however, because it often enough expresses recognition of our need for order and discipline for growth as men and women in Christ.

What is the counsellor in the sacrament of reconciliation to say? Briefly the answer is that he must say whatever is good news from God for the penitent man, woman or child. What the words actually are must be left to the inspiration of the moment from the Spirit of Christ in priest and penitent. The clue lies in listening to the person rather than to the list of sins, great or little. Many will remember Percy Thrower, who had a long career in broadcasting and journalism as a popular communicator of wisdom about gardening. In broadcasting he tended to work without a script. 'If you know your subject,' he explained, 'the plant tells you what it wants you to say.' Percy Thrower looked at the plant: the confessor listens to the penitent. So the confessor sits there wondering how best he can help the penitent. That means attending to the person, with unsaid hopes, fears and successes, as well as to the specific things that are said.

When I first heard confessions I was paralysed with anxiety as to what I was to say. After all, that is what is expected of priests. We know; we have opinions, positions, views. But one of the things I have learned is that over and over again the penitent tells you what to say. The essential text is St John 7.38. 'If anyone is thirsty let him come to me: whoever believes in me let him drink. As Scripture says, "streams of living water shall flow out from within him".' Here the evangelist sees Jesus as refreshment for men and women. He meets our need: thirst is met by drink and with faith comes the great discovery that life, renewal, personal refreshment, unexpected resources of spirit, imagination and new purpose can be released from within. Christ the Word is an inner source to be evoked by Christ the Word supernatural and transcendent, the crucified and risen Lord of the Gospels and of present glory. Again and again this inner Christ speaks, and the confessor's role is to hear his Word and for him to express it to the believer. 'Water shall flow from within.'

Transferred to the confessional situation the evangelist teaches that the life of Christ is there in the penitent waiting to develop, grow and take over. The confessor's absolution does not give life: it liberates the life of Christ already suffering and wounded in the penitent to a new if temporary Easter in the penitent. The ear of the confessor must listen to the words of the penitent for the clues – the jealous who are not thankful, the quarrelsome who are in reality outspoken, the angry who are vain. Thus so often the way forward is pointed by the very language in which people couch their sins – one of the reasons that the slump in sin lists is such a blessing – so that one can hear them say 'I hoped; I tried; I wondered if'.

The possibility of cautious attention to the tone of voice and the demeanour of the penitent is one of the good results of the decline in the use of the purpose-built confessional. In a face-to-face situation in counselling room or study the priest has the proper conditions for casting about to discover what the penitent wants to hear. The confessional box or screen besides exaggerating the horror of sinfulness unfortunately distances from each other the two Christians who are engaged in a rite of God's utter love and wish for reconciliation. Questions or reciprocation are difficult. True through a grille the sinner may be desperate enough for help to insist on a question or the confessor assured enough to venture on a joke, but the encounter outside the box gives a freedom in Christ which itself makes men and women ready for growth. Admittedly the penitent kneeling looking in one direction and the confessor sitting and looking in another is a useful sign of man's penitence before God's holiness, of the seal of the confessional, and of the Church's authority to minister forgiveness among its members. But it is irksome and frightening, if not awesome, for many, and it is in practice inferior for pastoral aptness to the decent study or specific room. The advantage of the confessional or confession kneeler in the church is that it largely ensures privacy and secrecy, although I have twice had to ask 'winos' to retire to a decent distance rather than press an ear to the panelling of the confessional! If, however, you are going to hear confessions at home in a non-specialized room you have got to be strong minded – no answering the phone, no running to the front door, no quick queries as to whether it shall be sprouts or cabbage. When a fellow Christian is taking the opportunity through you to open his or her conscience to God he or she must be assured of your attention. Therefore it must be impossible for others to intrude. In my own study I am clearly visible to anyone who takes particular trouble to look in from the street and more than once until I learned my lesson have had the celebration of the sacrament of personal peace and quiet celebrated against persistent ringing and knocking at the front door by people who could see I was 'only having a chat'. So do think about privacy for your penitent, often hard to get when a clergyman's home or office is rightly regarded as open to all and we find it hard to refuse to respond to a bell. But God has given you the penitent; others can wait.

Doing without a confessional cannot mean doing without an order. The priest traditionally has blessed – 'Bless me Father, for I have sinned' – but perhaps better now he can petition our heavenly Father *ad libitum* at the opening of the confession for grace, guidance, and the realization of the presence of the crucified and risen Lord, in priest, in penitent, in their words, and in the formula of absolution. Traditional forms of *Confiteor* can be uttered happily by penitents face to face or side by side or they can be encouraged to make up their own formulae of confession. If they do that they may well be helped to go on to do what in any case they want to do: say their own sins in their own words.

Should we press people to use the sacrament of reconciliation of penitents? I have gone to confession since I was seventeen and my first confession was my conversion experience. No Evangelical can embarrass me with the question 'Are you saved and when?' I still find it easy to include confession in my musts as a Catholic Christian for myself and for others. It is a means of grace and it must be used. So the answer is clear for me, although I recognize that fellow Anglican Catholics or Catholic Anglicans don't all see it that way. For one thing we are not as guilty as we were – I write of my experience of the 'C. of E.' – partly because of the way we are raised and partly because the preachers don't make us feel bad. Nor does the Liturgy. I recall once being asked by a patient in a breakdown to ensure that *all* the Communion devotions words from the 1662 Mass were used in giving a sick communion – '*not* that abbreviated nonsense!' As I laboured through the Collect for Purity, Invitation, Confession, Comfortable Words, Prayer of Humble Access and gazed down at the patient, I saw there the sad and unhappy product of one side of BCP spirituality. The very wording of the sacrament of grace for body and soul expressed a point of view that burdened both. But a good deal of that has gone. A liturgy of Christians being brothers and sisters together does not encourage guilt, and with the permanent backdrop of Hitler and Amin and political lies it is hard to understand why I should be kind to my wife's mother. Confession too frequently can also be boring, particularly in devout people for whom grace actually has had some victories. Someone once said to me 'I'm so tired of going to confession'. I told her to stop and await some chances of temptation and some craving for grace, for if someone recognizes that quite clearly the sacrament of penance is one of God's gifts available in the Body of Christ he or she can afford to await the need of it.

This need of it and the use of it has to be evoked by the priest *outside* the confessional. When I was being encouraged by Church Literature Association pamphlets to go to confession or to keep going to confession forty years ago I was always reading that 'the priest will understand', 'he won't be shocked', 'he's a sinner like you are'. It was hard to believe. Clergymen are now and were then a group who often do understand yet greatly disapprove, who constantly go on record as being shocked or upset at how ordinary human beings live, and who as constantly give the impression of difference or superiority. Any reader of this book knows that such superiority is a delusion. This false impression is, however, often to be found among churchpeople, and it is in no wise corrected by the secret goodness and kindness of priests in the confessional. So we need to take care about the way in which sins and shortcomings are denounced in the pulpit or the parish magazine. If the preacher tells his congregation that he simply cannot imagine any decent man or woman thinking a particular thing or pursuing a specific line of conduct what are his hearers to do if they think that thing or engage in that conduct? High moral tone in the pulpit should not be contrasted in the parish or in hearing confessions with individual loving pastoral concern for individual failures: the mercy needs to be proclaimed as part of the open message. So the priest offers to his fellow Christians a sacrament of freedom and encouragement as an integral part of God's good way with us. Clearly the gift of forgiveness will be offered to deal with some of the crises of life, when perhaps a Christian will find himself or herself in quite unexpected territory of sin or temptation, simply 'needing God'. But the sacrament comes into its own as a grace from God in disaster because it is ordinarily used as a recognizably essential part of Christian living. We are in some measure always penitents and we need to sacramentalize that fact.

So, again, what can we say to God's people in the sacrament of reconciliation? The priest's counsel *must* always in some form include the proclamation of God's goodness and welcome to sinners and his presence in our sufferings. This element seems to me literally 'crucial'. Over and over again I have been most greatly struck by the power released in telling people of Christ's compassion with us as sinners. The tempted and those rendered unhappy by their sins and problems very often feel themselves cut off from God. Often they have been given imagery of sin separating us from God and they have learned to regard failure – fear, insufficiency, lack of prayer or prayerfulness – as signs or examples of such separation. Yet the message of Gethsemane, Calvary, the Garden, or the Lakeside is of God incarnate suffering our life's passion and resurrection. It is there that we may find him. His presence does not alleviate pain or make joy feel religious: yet 'through his Spirit he is with us now' and suffers our suffering and enjoys our joy. It is his presence there that brings men and women and children to confession and to find his presence there again. People say 'I have neglected God, I have lived in my own strength' and of course they are telling a truth. But God has not neglected them, and their own strengths are themselves his gift. In the household of faith we are exposed to God's renewing grace by Christ all the time, so that confession and absolution do not occur as a sudden interruption in the pattern of our daily life. Even if the confessor sees the penitent infrequently he sees him or her as part of the providential continuity of that life. The old pattern of accumulation, confession, absolution, start again is psychologically intolerable. For that reason the confessor never says 'all will be well now', but he can say that God will be loving through temptation and sin. The risen humanity of Jesus is the guarantee and that we can with confidence say. It is the message of the cross. That is what the confessor as counsellor is to proclaim.

Sometimes people wonder what 'ordinary' confessions are like so I venture now to give two imaginary ones, with some comments. I am no Iris Murdoch so this penitent may not convince! His words are, however, intended to demonstrate two possible ways in which a man's confession might be expressed. In the first example the penitent is to be imagined simply kneeling at a confession place beside his confessor in church; in the second think of the penitent seated in the vicarage study, occasionally prompted and questioned by the priest.

'I confess to Almighty God and to you my Father that I have sinned in thought, word and deed through my own most grievous fault; especially I confess that since my last confession which was at Easter I remember the following sins: I have failed to attend Mass on four Sundays and Ascension Day. I've allowed my mind to wander often at Mass and at times of prayer and I have often omitted my morning and evening prayers. I have talked critically about the clergy. I have taken God's name in vain twenty times or so. I have sometimes been unkind in thought and word to my wife and children and I'm often angry with one of them unreasonably. I know I'm not thankful enough. Life's so difficult! I have been disloyal to my wife. I've been several times impure in thought and word. I have given way to angry thoughts quite frequently. I committed gluttony occasionally. I really can't think of anything else: I'm afraid that its always the same. For these and all my other sins which I cannot now remember I am heartily sorry, humbly ask pardon of God, and of you, my Father, penance, advice and absolution, and I ask Blessed Mary, all the angels and saints and you father to pray to God for me. Amen.'

Now this is how much the same confession might be made more informally:

'Since I came to confession at Easter there are three areas in which I am conscious of sin. First of all there's the Church. It all hardly seems worth while really, the way the bishops and the Synod behave. It's all so depressing. When I go to Mass I feel angry and critical and I talk unkindly about the vicar. I'm very judgmental and I don't really want to go to church at all. I feel that I'm failing God and I find it very hard to concentrate at Mass or when I say my prayers. I use God's name as a swear word occasionally. I think I'm difficult at home. I've a wonderful wife and we are very happy but I know I don't trust God enough. If I had faith I wouldn't worry about the future. I keep wondering what's going to happen and I'm far too critical of my wife and children. I'm often very sharp with one of the children. I'm not thankful enough for all my blessings and I'm not loving enough. Occasionally I've been angry and sworn at home. I've occasionally flirted with one of the girls at the office. In myself I'm aware that I'm angry a lot of the time. I'm not the sort of loving person I pretend to be. If I were a better Christian I suppose that everything would go better but it seems to me I never change. Occasionally I give way to all sorts of sexual thoughts and a lot of the time I wonder if I shall ever get any better. I used to like church but there's no vision now somehow. God my Father these are all the sins and I am very sorry for them and I ask you to forgive me for Jesus Christ's sake. Amen. I think that's about all, father. Oh I think I eat too much and should look after myself better.'

These two fictions give a rough idea of ways in which one man's condition might be expressed. The conscience has been opened to God, and there is a fairly clear picture of what has been going on, and while the confessor cannot guess at what is missing or what may be mistaken he can hear that the penitent is a bit discouraged, not terribly wicked, but sensitive about his family life and sufficiently a churchman to be affected by the Church's supposed state. He has made a 'good' confession.

In response the confessor's temptation might be to engage in a discussion of what is wrong with the Church. The Church can be making the penitent angry because there are or because there are not going to be women priests, or because it is left or right or liberal or reactionary. Take your pick! These issues are irrelevant to particular counsel. The confessor as pastor has to encourage the penitent's church membership and help develop such trust in God and Our Lord that the penitent has, and arguing about the Church's dilemmas will not help. On the other hand, the penitent's distress should not be coldly ignored, and it would be appropriate in a confessional to suggest a meeting later with a discussion in view. Because of the seal of course the initiative for such a meeting would have to come from the penitent once the confession time was over. In the more discursive situation of an open confession it would be foolish not to allude to church problems, but folly to expect to settle them! Any consideration of them should only be with a view to establishing the perspectives relating to the penitent's call to holiness, which is heard in a Church always in need of reform. So the confessor should not engage in a discussion of the many things that are wrong with the Church. He might find that the penitent and he agreed, but the penitent is not in need of confirmation of opinions. He wants encouragement to persevere, and his confessor can best help him by reminding him of the grace of God available in the Eucharist, that he need not be disheartened if his prayers are poor, and that the clergy are not beyond criticism. Finding that we are having a bad time is to discover an invitation from God himself not to lose heart. If the confessor himself has doubts and queries about the Church, the sacrament of penance is not the time to share them. He invites the penitent to do his best in his Mass-going and praying because God always is the loving Father and receives worship and prayer through Our Lord.

The slight note of desperation to be heard must be met by a practical application of the doctrine of justification by faith. 'You are a man of faith and God loves you, don't ask if your faith is enough: God's love is.' The confessor will be aware that Christians often think that all is up with them but nevertheless they survive as believers. 'Do your best and you will be OK in the long term' is not dismissive if the confessor encourages the penitent to use the means of grace.

The penitent sounds like a happily married man experiencing the usual tensions of family life. Again the confessor will need to remind the penitent that Christian living in family relationships as in the Church are very much a matter of maintaining our highest hopes whatever the shortcomings. Mutual acceptance and forgiveness in the family after conflict actually tell us more about each other and deepen our love, and the penitent's reference to thankfulness suggests good things about his family life: it's not all rows. It also suggests to the confessor an opportunity for encouraging a particular line of prayer – thanksgiving – that does in fact greatly open people up to the goodness of God and encourages them in reflecting that goodness in their own humanity. It is through conflict that understanding can come and love grow. The pastor should not say that he thinks that all would be well and life would be easier if the penitent had more faith or fulfilled his Christian duties better. That can too easily sound like a reproach. The end of conflict will come only with the final vision of God.

It is obvious from these unsubtle comments that responding to a confession does not mean the quick composition of a sermonette! Very occasionally as a penitent I have heard in response to my heart's burdens a nice little chat on 'this lovely season of Ascensiontide' or a brief run-down on the cardinal virtues. Such remarks are full no doubt of truth, but the truth needs to be precisely focused on the particular man, woman or child the priest is with. Our celebration of reconciliation is a pause on the particular providential path that the penitent is pursuing. So we need to particularize. This will often of course mean drawing out the personal significance of biblical material.

Over and over again the patterns of salvation history and the varying points of view of the New Testament writers are what speak clearest to the sinner. The question of what is 'more probable' or 'right or wrong' most often needs to be met not with a brief discourse in moral theology but by placing the penitent, who is already 'in Christ', mentally in the framework God provides. Men and women who do not know where to turn or how to free themselves from circumstances find themselves united with the Crucified. So fear of life or of death or just of tomorrow – retirement? – directs the mind straight to Gethsemane; the un-pious or non-churchy are in fact fellow citizens of Nazareth – Jesus in his ministry knew anger and tears; the prayerless hear Paul's words of encouragement in Romans; the people who are fed up with God or life find themselves in the Psalms. The priest hears confessions in the context of revelation and the means of grace attendant upon it and it is from that context that priest and penitent learn.

In the days when confessions were more devout I used to say to myself quite often as I listened to the list 'that's not a sin'. It still happens, but with a major difference, that they are problems which are brought, not venialities. The penitent needs to be told that his problems may not be sins, but it is important not to discount or to give the impression one discounts what is said. For the penitent the problem is something that comes between him and God, or it may be matter with which 'he travails and is heavy laden'. If I am unhappy about something in my life I don't want to be told by God's representative that it doesn't matter or should be dealt with by another department! By God's help and the care of the priest the penitent may come to that view later and the start may be with a word or two about the difference between problems and sins. This is probably best done in the study because in the closed privacy of a confessional it may not be easy to deal with problems because they really need a ministry of the word that entails exchange. So one can offer a private ear on another occasion, but remembering that the seal requires the penitent to raise the matter not the priest.

Never guess. I once decided 'never to go to confession again' after a confessor *guessed* what my confession meant. As a first year priest I was in charge during an interregnum, overstretched and novice at the same time. When I went to confession my usual confessor was away. After giving me his kindly advice, proposing a penance, absolving and blessing me the visiting priest who had never seen me before and who I at once determined should never see me again rose to his feet, loomed above the confessional screen and proclaimed, 'Of course Father the trouble with you is you don't work hard enough! Do some work, man!' He sat down, and I left, penance unsaid! The confessor had made a guess about the circumstances of my sins and he had got it wrong – or at any rate I thought so! Now it seems to me folly to suppose that the confessor only deals with what he hears, for implications and possibilities cannot be lost upon him unless he is very unimaginative or not interested in life. But you must use your guesses to prompt your questions, not telling what you guess but putting points so that you elicit what you need to know. Never be nosy or try to get something clear in your mind unless there is reasonable chance that the information given will help the advice. On occasion it may be difficult to understand what exactly a penitent is talking about, for the vocabulary he or she uses may be wrong or the details too complicated. At such moments the confessor remembers that the confessional is a sacrament of God's mercy and man's guilt and penitence and that the priest is there to speak for the God who knows already. The information is not the priest's but God's and if the priest does not quite understand it there is no harm. He remains puzzled under the seal and leaves his fellow-Christian to God.

If he should not 'guess' should he 'remember'? As a student at Theological College in my early thirties I was amazed at the apparent insouciance with which contemporaries went to confession. It was absolution that mattered, so the confession seemed to cause no anxiety. The furniture of the *box* implied a wonderful *now* with God of the sort I so unhappily endured at Walsingham. But the habit of people returning to confession carries with it for me an implication of memory, of a common experience of the sacrament upon which penitent and confessor can build. The confessor does not idiotically cry out 'But you've never done that before!', but he can say to himself that 'This is – I *think* – the chap who hates Matins!' The stated hours for confession, the queues and the confessional box or place are blessings which I would be sad to end. On the other hand with those who will it is far better to engage a time, to form a relationship, and to develop a pattern. If you are running seriously you need a coach. In such a partnership memory will play a part. It is therefore inevitable and right for the confessor to remember at least the sort of picture he has of the penitent. His picture will be partial, but he would be foolish if he did not submit his memories to the guidance of the Holy Spirit as he and penitent talk together. You don't want to give the impression that sin is so great that it can't be forgotten, but the pilgrimage to holiness will include wisdom learned from the ills of the past.

These are personal impressions of counselling in the sacrament of reconciliation. I have learned from my own confessors and from my penitents much for my own ministry as a pastor in reconciliation. In many ways talk about this particular work is difficult because of the absolute secrecy of the confessional's seal and I cannot tell you what I aid to my last penitent because his confession was not for my hearing ut for God's. I know that priests can be jokey about confessions but hey are very imprudent to be so, for their approximating witticism an give the impression that the seal is not secure. It must be secure, owever, in order to free for utterance people sometimes frightened or mbarrassed or sad. So while we may be unsure what to say in our ounsel we can be sure that of it we can speak not at all. There at least I an venture on an instruction uncompromising and clear. I am also ure that if the priest comes to this sacrament in a non-directive and vocative frame of mind, refusing to be the penitent's conscience or lecision maker, he must also come expecting to encourage life in the ong tradition of the Church's rule of faith. God by his Spirit helps nen and women and children to be human by their going to Mass, by ngaging in prayer, by participation in varying degrees in the life of he Mystical Body, by stewardship of time, money and talents. All hese are the aids by which through the grace of Our Lord Jesus Christ Christians discover how to be themselves. Through penitence and ope they discover in themselves the ultimate love who is God.

9 Social Joys: Renewal in Preparing for Confession

Andrew Greany

'Lights twinkled from the many windows, flowers scented the night air, voices grew in volume welcoming friends, neighbours and family members flown the nest'.[1] So Christy Nolan sets the scene for the twice yearly 'Station', survival of the days of the Irish Penal Laws, when Mass had to be celebrated in households and isolated farms. Now, an ancient custom still lingering on in the childhood home of the writer's mother, the Station expresses community celebration, the cementing of neighbourliness, the continuity of family contact; and before Nolan goes on to a moving description of the Mass, Christ among his people, of his own 'cradling' of his family in his prayers, and of the feasting which followed, he tells of the arrival of the 'accounter of pardon'. 'Conversation took on a low key as one penitent after another sampled forgiveness for confessed sins. "Anyone else for Confession?" was questioned from one room to the next all the way down to the Kitchen, and back went the answer, "Everyone's been".'[2] This passage is remarkable for its setting of confession, together with the Mass, in the context of family feasting and celebration, and for the natural simplicity of the question 'Anyone else for Confession?'; it is instructive to set it alongside memories of thirty years or so ago, when there would be something of a shadow over our household as Christmas approached, or as the days of Holy Week went by. For all would be conscious that the journey to the sacred tribunal would soon have to be made. Deep sighs would be heard from one armchair as father's pencil was held poised; and in the kitchen mother might be making, *sotto voce*, such comments as, 'I really don't know what to say', or, 'I don't think I can go to Father X'. No doubt the various struggles were in part the fruit of different personalities finding their way through a particular forest of thorns – one with an apparently clear view of right and wrong, and capable of a strict and detailed application of it to the thoughts, words, deeds and omissions of the preceding months; another with a much more general sense of 'not being quite the person I would like to be'. Perhaps there were confused ideas about repentance, amendment and the grace of absolution floating in the dark waters of these hours; little might have been heard or remembered about Lombard and contrition, of quinas and the matter and form of the sacrament, of Pusey and the rousing of longings after a more inward, more watchful and more levoted life. There was still a straightforward pressure to do what narked out a 'true Anglo-Catholic'. But the waters were also dark in he sense that the '*metanoia*' of those occasions was a gloomy and nxious business. And why not, it would have been said? The rodigal's decision to return, and many of his thoughts as he travelled, vere no doubt painful.

Lord, breathe once more
On that sad mirror
Let me be lost
In mist for ever
Rather than own
Such bleak reflections.[3]

f the joy of liberation and restoration were acknowledged, it was omewhat grudgingly so in that household, and simply as the nmediate fruit of the words of absolution; even there, I think, in the omewhat limited form of 'well, at least that's over for another few nonths.'

Much has changed; the loss of a cohesive Anglo-Catholic ethos, the pread of psychotherapy and counselling, the questioning of absolute tandards of morality and the authority of the Church and its ministry re all factors which may be adduced as causes for the disappearance f such household scenes as I have recalled. Maybe, indeed, we should ejoice that the days of conscience 'reduced to the function of a kind of piritual cash-register, making up all our sins (according to number nd gravity)'[4] appear to be gone, along with the pressure to conform to party line on so sensitive an area, and that there should be a decline the unwilling use of a means of grace which could so easily either be ivialized, or bring oppression and guilt rather than liberation. Yet e cannot easily set aside the voice of Christian tradition and xperience (and of much contemporary and continuing witness), articularly to the 'gift' of personal absolution, and to the value of wning personal responsibility for what must be vulnerably acknow-dged as sin, and thus to this sacrament as a positive and life-nhancing enrichment of the Christian's life, much more than a mere lotting out of sin.

The traditional Anglican (as opposed to Anglo-Catholic party) pproach, in making penance an *optional* extra for those of notably nquiet conscience has not only made it a *rare* extra, but has also ontributed to the confusion of Anglicans who may have been told or taught about it. Part of the price that has to be paid for the view that 'none must' is the conclusion that those who do must be strange indeed! The contrast with Nolan's Station and 'Everyone's been' is most striking. But if Anglican suspicion of rigorism and compulsion is a barrier to a fruitful use of the sacrament of penance, so too is a 'cash-register' mentality and an unthinking and depersonalized application of absolute standards of morality in the confessional. In particular, it is crucial that the joy of the vision and the life of God should be discerned and appropriated in the *process of repentance* as well as in the gift of personal absolution; that gift, moreover, must be experienced as 'community gift', as a social joy, reinforcing that sense of belonging to God's redeemed community which some of the traditional language of confession ('before the whole company of heaven', 'to you my brothers and sisters') has expressed. For that is the company which has shared the awareness of human frailty, the liberation of acknowledging it, and the joy of God's forgiveness.

In *The Christian Priest Today*, Michael Ramsey pleaded for a 'deep and wide recovery of repentance'. He spoke of the turning and change of mind which are *metanoia*, as God's gift, and went on 'We begin with a glimpse of the vision of God in his power and wonder and beauty and goodness.'[5] The doctrine of the Trinity teaches us that there is a continual movement within the Being of God; Adrienne von Speyer speaks of the mutual revelation and communication within the Trinity. In particular, she argues that in gratitude to the Father for his showing of himself, the Son 'shows himself to the Father in an attitude that is the archetype of Confession',[6] and then the Son 'awaits the return manifestation of the Father, in order to direct himself ever anew according to him. So in confession . . . we aim at opening ourselves fully, acknowledging ourselves as what we are, so as to experience God equally fully, and out of this experience to order our lives anew'.[7] Such grounding of the human experience of confession, forgiveness, recreation and redirection in the very life of the Trinity is one way of redeeming the process of repentance from a mechanical and self-centred exercise. We expect too the activity of the Holy Spirit, who comes to us in our weakness, and aids us in the painful process of making ourselves vulnerable, of revealing ourselves as persons with cracks in our self-image. But the continuing work of the Spirit is concerned with the formation in us of the mind of Christ, and of a sense of participation in the life of the Son, in order that we may cry 'Abba, Father', and know ourselves to be loved, just as the Son knows that he is loved, and himself loves the Father. In itself, such a sharing in the attitude of the Son to the

Father, the 'archetype of Confession', as von Speyer describes it, is indeed 'social joy'.

But this grounding of repentance, confession, and forgiveness in the life of the Trinity must lead to a renewal of the manner of our self-examination. Jesuit writers in particular emphasize the dangers of a moralistic examination of *conscience*; a sense of sin should not be the product of shame and depression at a failure to keep rules, but part of our recognition that God's love is asking for our love in response. Ignatian 'Examen of *Consciousness*', prayerful and positive reflection on the day, or on a longer period of time, might well be a fruitful way of feeding the more particular exercise of preparing for confession, and of discovering a new joy in making that preparation. 'What is happening in our consciousness', as one Jesuit writer puts it, 'is prior to, and more important than our actions which can be delineated as juridically good or evil.'[8] It is instructive that in Ignatius' own scheme for the daily examen, prominence is given to prayer for enlightenment by the Spirit – that is, the exercise of allowing the Spirit to show us what our own natural powers would never be capable of discerning unaided; and to thanksgiving – for the giftedness of our lives, in small and great things. Such prayer and thanksgiving are both concerned with placing us in a God-centred attitude, asking and expecting him to show us what he wills, and acknowledging all as gift. This is a vital, and liberating, contrast to the examination of *conscience* which begins with a man-centred approach to individual successes and failures in the keeping of rules. In the element of the Ignatian examen sometimes described as the 'practical survey of actions', we are closer to the 'traditional' material of preparation for confession. But again, prior questions are to be asked, concerned with the discernment of ways in which God has been at work in us, and of what he has been asking of us. Awareness of interior moods and feelings, joy, pain, turmoil, anger, anxiety, harmony, may reveal to us the nature and the quality of our response to the callings of God. From our inner attitudes, revealed by our moods and feelings, will have sprung our actions and choices. The sorrow which we feel, and must express before God, in so far as we are made aware of failures to respond to his callings, is not so much shame or depression at our weakness, but an experience of faith, part of the deepening of our realization that God desires us to love him, to be indwelt by him, and to co-operate with him. Finally, the examen may be related to the traditional 'intention to amend', for it asks for resolutions for the future, a greater sensitivity to God's activity in our lives, and a readiness for change in a particular area.

This approach has the potential to develop in us a deep joy and thankfulness in the process of repentance, and in the calling to mind of specific sins in preparation for personal confession; and this joy and thankfulness will be the more marked if we understand ourselves as beings-in-community, social beings, with the potential for that mutual love which is the life of the Trinity, as members of the Body of Christ, which, weakened as it is by the individualism and selfishness of us all yet remains a living reality, and finally as part of the whole of humanity which inhabits the 'communal home which has been given to us by the Creator, and which he loves'.[9]

Joy and thankfulness then, proper elements in any prayer understood as life in God, are to be the springs of a self-examination which truly grows out of attention to the Creator and his world by the enabling of the Spirit, and with the mind of the Son. The pain which is felt will be the pain of the love of God which looks at the brokenness of the world, and at the failure of this particular penitent to see its needs, and to respond to them; but it will not be the pain of lonely guilt or anxiety. Our consciousness will be raised, and our sensitivity attuned to the 'voice of the pain of God', both at a global level, and also 'in our neighbourhood, on our street, at work with us'.[10]

Yes, that's how I was. . .
Careless of the claim
Of the world's sick
Or the world's poor. . .[11]

But the voice of God's pain we do not hear alone; 'whether in the Church, or in society, we must listen to it together'.[12] Such heightened awareness and sensitivity are themselves, again, ways of identity with God and with others; but they are no cause for any lack of particularity in what as individuals we are called to confess and amend.

This then is to underline the proper joy of true repentance and careful self-examination, seen as part of life with the Father in Jesus Christ, by the enabling of the Spirit, and as part of our identification of ourselves with him and with humanity. It is to question the wisdom of so emphasizing the (very real) joy of the gift of the 'Ego te absolvo' that what goes before the hearing of those words becomes shrouded in anxiety, guilt and loneliness. It is also to suggest that from the perspective of moral theology we do not forget the connection of goodness and happiness – happiness, that is, understood as the fitting result of the fulfilling of God's purpose.[13] Christians are not called primarily to follow a system of morality, but to find their true end and fulfilment in God. 'He shall be like a tree planted by the waterside that will bring forth its fruit in due season'.[14] Again, life hidden with God in Christ has a 'proper' fruit, in its 'proper' place; and the 'natural law', that which is proper to the fulfilment of humanity, is not so much the reading off of exact prescriptions from biology, or so-called 'laws of nature', as a common (perhaps more common, more widely shared, than our relativistic age is sometimes prepared to acknowledge) way of looking at the world and its inhabitants, and a common search for what makes for their flourishing in relation to one another. Though this way, and this search, may be (and often are) shared between Christians and non-Christians, the Christian faith brings them to a particular sense that God is both their instigator and their end. If his image is marred, it remains his image, and is fit to contain his fulness. Helen Oppenheimer quotes St Augustine in his *Homilies on the First Letter of John*:

> Empty out that vessel that is to be filled with good, pour away the evil. God will fill you, shall we say, with honey; where will you put it if you are full of vinegar? What your vessel held must be poured away, and the vessel cleansed . . . so that it may be fit to hold – did we say honey? Gold? Wine? Speak as we may of that which cannot be spoken, call it what we will, its proper name is – God.'[15]

The process of repentance is concerned with the vessel which, happily, has a 'proper' use; however sour and unpleasant the vinegar, the task of repentance is a happy one, since it is inspired by the vision of God who alone is the proper fulness of the vessel.

'Ego te absolvo' is the effective sign that the penitent is in that moment participating in the joy of restored fellowship with God, with the Church and with humanity; it is a sign of the Kingdom. The joy of the life of God, and the reality of belonging with God the Holy Trinity, are hallmarks, therefore, of the state of the penitent absolved, as well as of engagement with the process of repentance; it is worth reflecting how careful attention to the choice of a penance, discussed in Chapter 7, may serve to enrich these characteristics of joy and belonging. One possibility is for the penance to be practical action, a specific act of generosity, the fulfilling of a commitment to a particular task at a particular time; this may make real, in action, the joy of fulfilling our true nature, which brings happiness not as a reward, but simply because in doing it, we are being the persons we are truly called to be. This connects with the vital notion of the need to make restitution and satisfaction, where that is possible, but goes beyond this in the sense that it is more than a mechanical putting straight of the record. It connects also with the importance of making a penance appropriate to the particular condition and need of a penitent but strengthens it by making it one of deed as well as of word or thought. A further possibility is the co-operation of confessor and penitent in working out the penance; this might have particular advantages in enhancing the sense of the corporate, as we continue the Christian pilgrimage enriched by the particularity of the moments of confession and absolution. For we would be effectively reminded of the shared responsibility for our progress in the life of Christ, if the decision about a penance is in part our own.

These reflections began with memories that were somewhat chilly and grey; a cold coming we had of it. Yet journeying in the cold was itself part of the way in which the potential of the sacrament of penance was valid. It is perhaps too easy to say that the discipline, the sense of obligation, even the fear and trembling were wrong; but is it too naive, risky even, to suggest that the way of repentance, as well as the gift of absolution, should be the place of joy, and that the owning of personal responsibility, as well as the moment of formal restoration to the community should demonstrate our belonging? The Church corporately, as well as many individual Christians, will know the 'cold' as part of the history of the sacrament of penance; that is inevitable, but hopeful too.

R. S. Thomas writes of 'The Belfry':

I have seen it standing up grey,
Gaunt, as though no sunlight
Could ever thaw out the music
Of its great bell; terrible
In its own way, for religion
Is like that. There are times
When a black frost is upon
One's whole being, and the heart
In its bone belfry hangs and is dumb.

But who is to know? Always,
Even in winter in the cold,
Of a stone church, on his knees
Someone is praying, whose prayers fall
Steadily through the hard spell
Of weather that is between God
And himself, perhaps they are warm rain
That brings the sun and afterwards flowers
On the raw graves and throbbing of bells.[16]

This chapter is intended to suggest that the sun and the flowers may be discerned in the whole process of repentance and absolution, despite, and even because of the fact that there has been a gaunt greyness for many in their experience of this sacrament; and it is the setting of that process within the social life of the Holy Trinity, and within a confident search for the happiness of human fulfilment in God, which may revitalize the use of the sacrament.

Notes

1. C. Nolan, *Under the Eye of the Clock* (London 1987), p.126.
2. op.cit., p.126.
3. R. S. Thomas, *Judgment Day: Selected Poems 1946–1968* (Newcastle upon Tyne 1986) p.64.
4. F. Kelly, 'Towards an Adult Conscience': *The Way* (October 1985), vol.25, No.4, p.283.
5. M. Ramsey, *The Christian Priest Today* (London 1972), pp.50–1.
6. A. von Speyer, *Confession* (ET London 1964), p.21.
7. op.cit., p.21.
8. G. A. Aschenbrennery SJ, *Review for Religious* vol.31 (1972), p.15.
9. Kelly, p.288.
10. op.cit., pp.289–90.
11. Thomas, *Judgment Day*.
12. Kelly, p.290.
13. In connection with this paragraph, see especially H. Oppenheimer, *The Hope of Happiness* (London 1983), chs 1–3.
14. Psalm 1.3.
15. Augustine, *Homilies on the First Epistle General of St John*, quoted by Oppenheimer, pp.3–4.
16. Thomas, op.cit., 'The Belfry', p.90.

10 The Role of the Confessional Process in Psychotherapy

Julienne McLean

> The intelligent psychotherapist has known for years that any complicated treatment is an individual, dialectical process, in which the doctor, as a person, participates just as much as the patient . . . the patient can win his own inner security only from the security of his relationship to the doctor as a human being . . . the analyst must go on learning endlessly, and never forget that each new case brings new problems to light and thus gives rise to unconscious assumptions that have never before been constellated. We could say that a good half of every treatment that probes at all deeply consists in the doctor's examining himself, for only what he can put right in himself can he hope to put right in the patient. (Jung, 1951)[1]

I think it understandable that for those unacquainted with psychotherapy – either theoretically, or in practice, many misconceptions can arise. This can be a result of misinformation, difficulties with 'psychological' language, bias, and sometimes simply from fear and prejudice. The theory and practice of modern psychotherapy appears to be a relatively new development in the healing arts, acquiring status and independence only within the last hundred years. In fact, it is the modern successor in a long historical development of healing and therapeutic endeavours. However, within the modern profession of psychotherapy and psychoanalysis, theories, ideas, interpretations and viewpoints about the nature of the psyche have proliferated, diversified and differentiated since its inception in the latter part of the nineteenth century, sometimes almost beyond recognition of common ground. This can be confusing to the layman. In this short chapter, an exhaustive or even adequate consideration of psychotherapy is not possible. These areas are so fundamental, complex, and vast, that I can only attempt a brief glimpse of basic principles and dynamics, with historical antecedents, with the aim of relating the psychological meaning and purpose of 'confessing' in the psychotherapeutic process. I need to stress, however, that the conduct of the therapeutic encounter, and understanding of unconscious processes cannot be learned, or adequately understood from a theoretical or rational position alone – reading a map cannot, in any way, be a substitute for the journey itself.

In essence, psychotherapy is a 'kind of dialectical process, a dialogue or discussion between two persons'. Dialectic was a term which originally described the art of conversation among the ancient philosophers, and later developed to describe the process of creating new syntheses.[2] Psychotherapy is the use of personal relationships to help in the process of healing of the psyche, of relieving suffering and distress, of integrating parts of the individual which are divided or dis-eased, of reconciling the person with disowned and unconscious parts of themselves through being accepted, acknowledged, trusted, understood and supported by another, with the personality, attitudes, empathy, warmth, genuineness, and conscious awareness of the therapist playing a fundamental role.

This process can, of course, occur at many different levels. It can occur in general and informal contexts, or in more formal and specific types of therapeutic relationships. The value of sharing problems and difficulties with friends and family, and receiving comfort and encouragement from others is a common daily experience of great importance. To describe the more formal levels of psychotherapy, I think it would be the most useful to quote from Cawley (1977), who has provided a helpful classification by delineating three types of psychotherapy (see Table I).[3]

TABLE I
LEVELS OF PSYCHOTHERAPY

1	Outer (Support and Counselling)	1. Unburdening of problems to sympathetic listener
		2. Ventilation of feelings within supportive relationship
		3. Discussion of current problems with non-judgemental helper
2	Intermediate	4. Clarification of problems, their nature and origins, within deepening relationship
		5. Confrontation of defences
		6. Interpretation of unconscious motives and transference phenomena
3	Deeper (Exploration and Analysis)	7. Repetition, remembering and reconstruction of the past
		8. Regression to less adult and less rational functioning
		9. Resolution of conflicts by re-experiencing and working them through

The first level is really what any good doctor or professional person in the caring professions should practice in their relationships with their clients or patients – to be able to communicate and empathize with many different people in difficulty effectively and compassionately. This is the basis of less formal psychotherapy, of supportive psychotherapy and counselling. The intermediate level ideally involves recognizing and understanding the nature and origins of the difficulties of the patient, with a more active use of the therapeutic relationship to foster understanding and insight. Many social workers, psychiatrists and general practitioners work at the intermediate level. At the deeper level of exploration and analysis, the practice of dynamic psychotherapy puts greater emphasis on helping patients face the truth and take responsibility for themselves and their relationships, on exploring unconscious parts of the psyche, anxieties and defences. The aim of treatment at the deeper level is reintegration and change in personality functioning towards greater wholeness, maturity and fulfilment.

There are several elements which are of fundamental importance in any therapeutic relationship – there has to be a positive working alliance established between the therapist and patient, where the reliable core is formed by the patient's motivation to overcome his difficulties, his conscious and rational willingness to co-operate, his basic sense of trust in the relationship, where a 'safe space' develops – a space that offers security, trust and hope of benefit and healing. This occurs through the process of transference within the therapeutic relationship. Transference is the experiencing of feelings, drives, attitudes, anxieties and defences towards a person in the present which do not befit that person, but are a repetition of reactions originating in regard to significant persons in their past which are unconsciously displaced on to figures in the present, notably the therapist. Transference reactions offer the therapist an invaluable opportunity to explore the inaccessible past and the unconscious.[4] Every relationship between two persons is a unique event – when two people meet and interact, their 'psychic field patterns' interact – something happens, something clicks one way or another, and their conscious and unconscious patterns 'arrange' themselves relative to each other in a typical fashion. True relatedness between two people depends vitally on the awareness of the quality of the 'field effects' involved.[5] Much of what really happens in relationships we cannot understand logically, or defies causal reasoning or analysis. The task of the psychotherapist is to attempt to identify and understand the underlying processes and patterns within the psyche, to create an 'enabling space' in the search for wholeness and reconciliation.

The central role of the dialectical process with the aim of healing, of relieving distress and suffering, is, of course, a very ancient process, and has been systematized and understood differently by various cultures throughout the centuries. Although the modern systematic investigation of the unconscious mind, and the application of psychodynamic psychotherapy is fairly new, the origins of dynamic psychotherapy can be traced historically through a long line of ancestors and forerunners. Certain medical or philosophical teachings of the past, as well as certain older healing methods, offer a surprisingly high degree of insight into what are usually considered the most recent discoveries in the realm of the human mind.[6] The ancestry of the healing of disease, both psychic and somatic, had its primitive origins in the practice of exorcism, where the cause was commonly thought to be due to the possession of evil spirits. Healing was expected to follow exorcism, and such treatment was usually in the hands of religious leaders, or traditional healers, such as shamans or priests. Alternatively, it was thought that disease might arise from the infringement of taboos – primarily social or sexual in origin, and cure was expected to follow from a type of ritualized expiation – a primitive form of confession. Many primitive populations believe that certain diseases result from the violation of taboos, or from other offences. A comprehensive survey of data relative to the confession of sins was made by Raffaele Pettazzoni, who emphasized that among most primitive populations the 'concept of sin' was identical with the 'breach of taboo'.[7]

As the authority of the Church, and medieval thought in general, was declining in Europe during the Middle Ages, there was corresponding interest in human self-awareness. 'The general conception of unconscious mental process was conceivable (in post-Cartesian Europe) around 1700, topical around 1800 and fashionable around 1870–1880 . . . it cannot be disputed that by 1870–1880 the general conception of the unconscious mind was a European commonplace and that many special applications of this general idea had been vigorously discussed for several decades.'[8]

By 1775, the time of the last executions for witchcraft in Europe, the practice of exorcism as practised by priests gave way to new techniques of healing and therapy, such as hypnosis, stemming from the work of the famous physician, Franz Anton Mesmer. There was also increasing interest by the medical profession and the lay public in the idea of the 'pathogenic secret' that had only formerly been disclosed to priests in confession. The notion of the pathogenic secret gradually became known to a wider public, as evidenced by a series of literary works throughout the nineteenth century on the theme. The first medical reference relating to the systematic investigation of the 'pathogenic secret' and its psychotherapy was the work of the Viennese physican, Moritz Benedikt (1835–1920). In a series of publications that appeared between 1864 and 1885, Benedikt showed that the cause of many cases of hysteria and other neuroses resides in a painful secret, mostly pertaining to sexual life, and that many patients could be cured by the confession of the 'secrets' and working out their related problems.[9] Nietzsche (1844–1900) emphasized the importance of instincts and their sublimation, of self-deception, and of guilt feelings arising from the turning inwards of impulses which could not be discharged outwardly.

Between 1775 and 1900, there was increasing interest in medical circles in all forms of psychic phenomena in psychiatric patients, phenomena formerly thought to be caused by possession, and requiring to be cast out by exorcism, were now attributed to unconscious agencies within the patients, to be reached and revealed through hypnosis. Particular medical attention was devoted to certain phenomena, such as trance states, somnambulism, catalepsy, multiple states of personality, automatic writing, and towards the end of the nineteenth century, interest came to focus more and more on hysteria, with psychotherapeutic methods principally relying on the use of hypnotism and suggestion, with special attention given to the rapport between therapist and patient.

Freud studied at the Medical School at the University of Vienna, graduating in 1881. Hearing of the work of Charcot, the famous medical hypnotist, in Paris, Freud applied for and received a fellowship to study with him; this was to be his first contact with the use of hypnosis as a method of treatment. Back in private practice in Vienna, Freud attempted to use hypnosis in his work with patients, and during this time became impressed with the work of Joseph Breuer, a prominent Viennese physician, who had some years earlier treated a patient suffering from hysterical symptoms, and who had found that if the patient was allowed to talk freely about past events under hypnosis, there was a marked improvement in her symptoms. Freud collaborated with Breuer in 1885, and they worked together for a number of years, jointly publishing *Studies in Hysteria* (1895), with the emphasis on the importance of inner emotional life, and on the significance of the crucial distinction between conscious and unconscious mental activity. In Freud's early career, he used hypnosis in the treatment of selected patients, mainly young women with hysterical disorders, whose symptoms could be traced to dammed up feelings associated with sexuality. Therapy, at first under hypnosis, aimed to uncover repressed memories, and release the feelings held back because they were unacceptable to the patients' view of themselves. Freud was soon to abandon hypnosis, as his translator, James Strachey, describes in the introduction to *Studies in Hysteria:*

> Freud abandoned more and more of the machinery of deliberate suggestion and came to rely more and more on the patients flow of 'free associations'. The way was opened up to the analysis of dreams. Dream analysis enabled him, in the first place, to obtain an insight into the workings of the 'primary process' in the mind and the ways in which it influenced the products of our more accessible thoughts, and he was thus put in possession of a new technical device – that of 'interpretation'.[10]

During the 1890s, the transition from hypnotism to dynamic psychotherapy, and psychoanalysis took place. The history and evolution of Freud's ideas and methods is an immense subject, of which there are several excellent reviews (Jones, 1953, 1955, 1957, Ellenberger, 1970).[11] Freud's achievement, combining the gifts of a great writer and scientist, was to address these ideas to a medical context, in such a way that they have since been given continuing, increasing and quite divergent attention. Freud did not invent psychotherapy and psychoanalysis any more than Darwin invented evolution; he had many ancient forerunners, yet it was the added scientific and medical impetus, and clinical evidence that he collected, which pioneered the way for new understanding, in modern twentieth century terms, pertaining to the realm of psyche and soma.

Before World War I, Carl G. Jung broke away from the then embryonic psychoanalytic movement to found his own school of analytical psychology. Jung did not agree with Freud's predominant biological and developmental emphasis, and moved to a more teleological view of the psyche, which incorporates the retrospective historical, family and racial background, as well as prospective aims, aspirations and expectations for the future, and this insistence on the role of destiny or purpose in human development clearly set Jung apart from Freud. Jung studied mythology, religion, ancient symbols and rituals, the customs and beliefs of ancient peoples, as well as the dreams, visions, the symptoms of neurotics and the hallucinations and delusions of psychotics in his search to understand the relations between conscious and unconscious psychic life, and its meaning for human development. His writings on symbolism in religion and alchemy fill five of the eighteen volumes of his collected works. Jung essentially saw psychotherapy as a process of individuation, of making conscious what is unconscious, the unifying of an individual through discovering the hidden or undeveloped aspects of the psyche.

One of the fundamental principles of psychotherapy is the concept of conflict between different parts of the psyche. The level at which intrapsychic conflict operates, whether it is relatively conscious, or deeply unconscious, is of central importance. The experience of anxiety is often the result of conflict, where parts of the psyche and related experience are sometimes not able to be readily assimilated into the conscious attitude of the individual, because of the anxiety or psychic pain that it may arouse. These aspects which are in conflict may be repressed, and become more or less unconscious within the psyche. As there are different levels of conscious awareness, so there are many different aspects of what is unconscious. We may be unconscious of something merely because we are not aware of it at this particular time e.g. what we had for lunch last Sunday – memories or thoughts that can easily become conscious. Alternatively, ideas, feelings, or memories may be unconscious because they are actively repressed, owing to their unthinkable, inadmissible nature to the conscious mind, to the image or view that we may have of ourselves, of what is acceptable to ourselves and others, and which would cause too much anxiety, guilt or psychic pain if they were to be acknowledged and incorporated consciously. Anxiety, conflict and suffering can develop when an individual experiences a painful discrepancy between their ideal self, that is, what they would like to be, and their actual self, the way I am at this very moment in time. The unconscious has still another side: it includes not only repressed contents, but all psychic material that lies below the threshold of consciousness. Jung called this the collective, or transpersonal, unconscious, which, he said, could be negatively distinguished from the personal unconscious by the fact that it does not, like the latter, owe its existence to personal experience, and is consequently not a personal acquisition. 'It [the Unconscious] holds possibilities which are locked away from the conscious mind, for it has at its disposal all subliminal contents, all those things which have been forgotten or overlooked, as well as the wisdom and experience of uncounted centuries, which are laid down in its archetypal organs.'[12]

The way we deal with aspects of ourselves, either personally or collectively, which, if consciously experienced, might give rise to intolerable anxiety or pain is to develop defence mechanisms. We all develop defence mechanisms, and some use of these measures is quite normal, but, if used excessively, can interfere with development. We can repress what is unacceptable to the conscious mind, we can forget and put it out of conscious reach, we can deny it, or it may be expressed in a disguised form and converted into physical symptoms e.g. unacknowledged anger and hostility can contribute to headaches, and high blood pressure. Alternatively, we can project, or externalize our unacceptable feelings, and attribute to others what is unacceptable to ourselves e.g. a man who cannot admit his own sexual and aggressive feelings will insist that it is others who have such desires. Another form of defence is to adopt attitudes and behaviours that are opposite to what the person really thinks and feels in order to mask negative feelings (e.g. anger, hate) with positive ones (e.g. love, affection), or the masking of positive feelings with negative ones: e.g. an adolescent who is attracted to a young lady, but because of anxiety, is hostile, rude and unapproachable on meeting. Other common forms of defences are rationalization, regression to more childlike and dependant behaviour, phobic avoidance, and in more extreme and serious forms, states of depersonalization and confusion. In any developing psychotherapeutic relationship, patients begin to experience feelings towards the therapist, often relating to significant figures from the past, and unconscious defensive attitudes. What the patient transfers on to the therapist then becomes a tool for investigating the forgotten and repressed past: e.g. the patient may project their anger or disappointment onto the therapist, or, alternatively, may be quite unable to feel any anger, stemming from childhood defences against expressing anger; a patient may experience strong feelings of envy and jealousy towards the therapist, stemming from unconscious sibling rivalry in childhood. Repetition in the transference enables its vividness to be mutually experienced and examined by patient and therapist.

The aim of psychological and emotional defences is to hide thoughts and feelings that arouse anxiety, to deny or falsify the existence of threat or fear, to avoid the frustrations and dangers of new, or threatening situations. These parts of the psyche can then become dissociated from consciousness, and become concealed within the psyche secretly and unconsciously. Jung cogently describes the psychological, emotional and social effects:

> The possession of secrets acts like a psychic poison that alienates their possessor from the community . . . it works like a burden of guilt cutting off the unfortunate possessor from communion with his fellows. If we are conscious of what we are concealing, the harm done is decidedly less than if we do not know what we are repressing . . . the hidden content is no longer consciously kept secret – it then

> splits off from the conscious mind as an independent complex and leads a sort of separate existence in the unconscious psyche, where it can be neither inferfered with, nor corrected by the conscious mind. The complex forms a miniature self-contained psyche which develops a peculiar fantasy life of its own . . . all personal secrets, therefore, have the effect of sin or guilt, whether or not they are, from the standpoint of popular morality, wrongful secrets.[13]

Jung was the first to describe the relation between the process of the confessional, and psychotherapy. Jung considered the process of catharsis, of cleansing, of confession, as the essential preliminary part of the complete psychotherapeutic treatment. He described psychotherapy as consisting, fundamentally, of four stages: confession, elucidation of the transference, education, and transformation, and states that the first beginnings of all analytical treatment could be found in its prototype, the confessional. He describes the psychological effect of confession –

> The aim is to observe the sporadic emergence, whether in the form of images or feelings, of those dim representations which detach themselves in the darkness from the invisible realm of the unconscious and move as shadows before the unturned gaze. In this way, things repressed and forgotten come back again . . . I must have a dark side if I am to be whole . . . and by becoming conscious of my shadow I remember once more that I am a human being like any other. Through confession, I throw myself into the arms of humanity again, freed at last from the burden of moral exile. The goal of the cathartic method is full confession – not merely the intellectual recognition of the facts with the head, but their confirmation by the heart and the actual release of suppressed emotion.[14]

Any real emotional, psychological or spiritual growth can only begin with a sincere and genuine acknowledgement by the individual, to themselves, in their heart, of the stark truth of their situation, and a desire to do something about it. The psychotherapeutic process enables the person gradually to become conscious of what has been denied and repressed, to be able to 'confess' their less desirable and commendable qualities, to be able to 'own' what has been 'disowned' within themselves, to be able to develop the modesty and humility to cut away at their self-delusions to face the true state of their psychic condition, to be able to acknowledge anger, resentment, jealousy, pride, pettiness, cowardice, to be able gradually to withdraw projections – these are the essential beginnings of any true process of development and growth. Jung described the shadow as 'the negative side of the personality, the sum of all those unpleasant qualities we like to hide, together with all the insufficiently developed functions and the contents of the personal unconscious'.[15] Nobody likes to admit their own darkness within themselves, and most people in therapy often put up the greatest resistance to the realization of their shadow. As Ulrich Zwingli wrote in 1525: 'Like an octopus hiding behind its black juice to avoid seizure, a man, so soon as he observes we will be at him, suddenly envelops himself in such a dense hypocritical fog that the sharpest eye cannot perceive him . . . his impudence in lying, his readiness to deny and disown, is so great that, when you think you have laid hold of him, he has already slipped out the back door.'[16]

To acknowledge and become conscious of the 'dark' aspects of our personality cannot occur without considerable moral effort, and generally meets with enormous resistance. But, no growth, development or healing can possibly occur otherwise.

> If you imagine someone who is brave enough to withdraw all these projections, then you get an individual who is conscious of a considerable shadow. Such a man has saddled himself with new problems and conflicts. He has become a serious problem to himself, as he is now unable to say that 'they' do this or that, that 'they' are wrong, and 'they' must be fought against . . . Such a man knows that whatever is wrong in the world is in himself, and if he only learns to deal with his own shadow he has done something real for the world. He has succeeded in shouldering at least an infinitesimal part of the gigantic, unsolved social problems of our day.[17]

Notes

1. C. G. Jung, vol. 16, 'The Practice of Psychotherapy', in *The Collected Works of C. G. Jung* (London 1954), para. 239.
2. ibid., para. 1.
3. D. Brown, and J. Pedder, *Introduction to Psychotherapy* (London 1979), p.95.
4. R. R. Greenson, *The Technique and Practice of Psychoanalysis* (London 1967), p.171.
5. E. Whitmont, *The Symbolic Quest – Basic Concepts of Analytical Psychology* (Princeton NJ 1969), p.299.
6. H. F. Ellenberger, *The Discovery of the Unconscious – The History and Evolution of Dynamic Psychiatry* (New York 1970), p.3.

7. ibid., p.23.
8. L. L. Whyte, *The Unconscious before Freud*. London 1979.
9. Ellenberger, p.46.
10. Brown and Peder, p.106.
11. E. Jones (1953), *Sigmund Freud, Life and Work*. London, Hogarth Press, vol. i, 1953; vol, ii, 1955; vol iii, 1957.
12. Jung, 'Two Essays on Analytical Psychology' in *Collected Works*, vol. 7.
13. Jung, *Collected Works*, vol. 16, paras. 124–9.
14. ibid., para. 134.
15. Jung, 'Two Essays on Analytical Psychology' para 103n.
16. J. Jacobi, *The Way of Individuation* (New York 1965), p.39.
17. Jung, *Collected Works*, vol. 11, Psychology and Religion, West and East, para. 140.

PART THREE

The Liturgies of Penance

11 Rites of Penance and Reconciliation

Martin Dudley and Jill Pinnock

Today's Christians deal with the problem of post-baptismal sin in a variety of ways, and a range of options are available which are determined not only by the theological norms of their tradition, but also by the cultural conditioning of time and place. This volume has set out the history and development of penance in different times, places and traditions. It has amply demonstrated that what we now call the sacrament of reconciliation has signified many different things – reconciliation with God, with the Church, with individual fellow-Christians, with mankind in general and in particular, and with the dark side or damaged aspects of one's own personality. Together with this multiplicity of meaning, and frequently confused with its different facets, has been the element of spiritual direction. The degree of intervention by the minister of the sacrament also varies – he is witness, physician, pastor, judge, counsellor, director – and many modes of restoration have been and are current – deprecatory ('may God forgive you'), declaratory ('I declare you forgiven'), and indicative ('I absolve you'). These options, already discussed, may most clearly be seen in the study of the actual rites of reconciliation, historic and current, Anglican, Catholic, Orthodox and of the churches of the Reformation.

In the study of the texts, certain patterns emerge, and two main groups. The first reflects a fairly businesslike approach to penance as a sacrament efficacious *ex opere operato*. The second finds in penance a rite of passage, a transition and celebration which requires interaction at the human level as well as the divine. For some the former approach has failed and the latter has yet to come into its own. The rites, in their uncompletedness, reflect that striving, in the West at least, for something not yet found. Words are not enough for this. Penance also has its performative nature and is more than words. Proximity to another person, eye contact, gesture, and touch are all part of this. The traditional Catholic confessional stressed anonymity (still and rightly valued by some), by contrast, the 'reconciliation room' affords easy contact and easy transition, perhaps too easy, between confession/absolution and counselling. We should remember that the confessional, placed in an open and conspicuous part of the church and with a grating between priest and penitent, was partly a response to abuse of the sacrament and dates from the sixteenth century, becoming general in the following century. Before that people confessed in the open church, kneeling before the priest or seated at his side. The new Roman rite expects that there will be no physical barrier and that the priest will be able to extend his hands over the penitent in absolution. We find the same recommendation in David Silk's order for Anglican use. The order provided by the United Church of Christ in the USA concludes with the passing of the peace, as can the American Lutheran form, a very tangible indication of reconciliation.

Liturgical forms are still evolving and in that process different aspects of reconciliation are rediscovered or re-emphasized. We have chosen not to subject the existing and authorized texts to detailed criticism; a task which could be usefully performed on the basis of the history and theology already explored in this book, but which would involve too much repetition. We have also not included here those liturgies that might reasonably be called experimental, such as those set out in the volume on reconciliation in the *Alternative Futures for Worship* series (vol. 4, ed. by Peter J. Fink SJ, Collegeville, The Liturgical Press, 1987.) This is not because we do not value them – for ultimately the remaking of liturgies is the most effective criticism of existing forms – but because proper attention must be given to the historical and current forms before we feel tentatively towards the future.

1 THE *CONFITEOR*

At an early stage in the development of the rite of private penance there was no provision of set words. Texts were borrowed mainly from the obsolescent rites of public penance. After the *Confiteor* came to be said before the Mass or after the Office, in the ninth century, it also came to be used in private confessions. The common form, in the Missal of Pius V, came into general use in the thirteenth century. The Third Council of Ravenna, 1314, mentions that a variety of forms were then current and imposes a single use. Religious orders frequently retained their own, shorter form. This is the *Confiteor* from the post-Tridentine Missal:

> Confiteor Deo omnipotenti, beatae Mariae semper Virgini, beato Michaeli Archangelo, beato Joanni Baptistae, sanctis Apostolis Petro et Paulo, omnibus sanctis, et vobis, fratres: quia peccavi nimis cogitatione, verbo, et opere: mea culpa, mea culpa, mea

maxima culpa. Ideo precor beatam Mariam semper Virginem, beatum Michaelem Archangelum, beatum Joannem Baptistam, sanctos Apostolos Petrum et Paulum, omnes sanctos, et vos, fratres, orare pro me ad Dominum Deum nostrum.

English translation from *The Missal in Latin and English* (London, Burns Oates and Washbourne, 1952):

I confess to almighty God, to blessed Mary, ever-virgin, to blessed Michael the archangel, to blessed John the Baptist, to the holy apostles Peter and Paul, to all the saints, and to you, brethren, that I have sinned exceedingly in thought, word, and deed; through my fault, through my own fault, through my own most grievous fault. Therefore I beseech the blessed Mary, ever-virgin, blessed Michael the archangel, blessed John the Baptist, the holy apostles Peter and Paul, all the saints, and you, brethren, to pray to the Lord our God for me.

2 THE ORDER FOR PENANCE IN THE ROMAN RITUAL

Liturgists paid little or no attention to the order for private confession, which was contained in the *Rituale Romanum*, Tit. III, *c.* 1, n. 11. Indeed until the publication of the Roman book in 1614 during the pontificate of Paul V, various dioceses had issued their own rituals. According to the Roman use, the penitent was humbly to approach the confessional and to make the sign of the cross. It was customary to say 'Bless me, father, for I have sinned,' in Latin or the vernacular. In the non-Roman rituals from the end of the sixteenth century the blessing was in a set form:

Dominus sit in corde tuo, et in labiis tuis, ut vere et integre confitearis omnia peccata tua; In nomine Patris, et Filii, et Spiritus sancti. Amen.

The Lord be in thy heart and on thy lips, that thou mayest truly and humbly confess thy sins, in the Name of the Father, and of the Son, and of the Holy Spirit. Amen.

The confessor was instructed to make enquiry into the personal religious state of the penitent, which would have been particularly necessary if the penitent was totally unknown to the confessor. The penitent now made confession, starting with the *Confiteor* in Latin or the vernacular as far as the *mea culpa*. Individual sins were then enumerated and the confession as such concluded with the words

For these and all my other sins which I cannot now remember I am heartily sorry; I purpose amendment for the future, and most humbly ask pardon of God, and of you, father, penance and absolution.

After the priest's admonition comes the absolution. This is the text, with rubrics, from the *Rituale Parisiense*, published in 1839:

Postea Sacerdos, aperto capite, dicit:
Misereatur tui omnipotens Deus, et, dismissis omnibus peccatis tuis, perducat te ad vitam aeternam. Amen.
Et mox, dextera manu ad poenitentem elevata, ei benedicit, his verbis:
Indulgentiam, absolutionem, et remissionem omnium peccatorum tuorum tribuat tibi omnipotens et misericors Dominus. Amen.

After giving a penance, the priest continued:

Dominus noster Jesus Christus te absolvat, et ego auctoritate ipsius te absolvo ab omni vinculo Excommunicationis, Suspensionis et Interdicti, in quantum possum, et tu indiges: deinde, Ego te absolvo a peccatis tuis; in nomine Patris, et Filii, + et Spiritus sancti. Amen.

The reference to suspension was omitted when the penitent was lay. Although it is the latter form, *Dominus noster*, with the *Ego te absolvo*, which became recognized as the form of sacramental absolution, many theologians, including St Bonaventure, held that it was the *Misereatur* that absolved.

The concluding prayer, *Passio*, has been used in this place since the beginning of the sixteenth century and is in the current rite.

Passio Domini nostri Jesu Christi, merita beatae Mariae Virginis et omnium Sanctorum, suffraga sancta matris Ecclesiae, quidquid boni feceris et mali sustinueries, valeant tibi in remissionem peccatorum, augmentum gratiae, et praemium vitae aeternae. Amen.

3 THE FIRST PRAYER BOOK OF EDWARD VI, 1549

The Prayer Book does not include a rite for private confession as such. Instead it provides an Order for the Visitation of the Sick which follows and is derived from that of the medieval Sarum Manual, with the instruction that this is the form also to be used in private confessions.

Here shall the sicke person make a speciall confession, yf he fele his conscience troubled with any weightie matter. After which confession, the priest shall absolue hym after this forme: and the same forme of absolution shall be used in all pryvate confessions.

Our Lord Jesus Christ, who hath lefte power to his Churche to absolve all sinners, which truely repent and beleue in hym: of his great mercy forgeve thee thyne offences: and by his autoritie committed to me, I absolue thee fro all thy synnes, in the name of the father, and of the sonne, and of the holy gost. Amen.

And then the priest shall saye the collette folowyng.

Let us praye.

O most mercifull God, which according to the multitude of thy mercies, doest putte away the synnes of those which truely repent, that thou remembrest them no more: open thy iye of mercy upon this thy seruant, who most earnestly desireth pardon and forgeue-nesse: Renue in hym, most louying father, whosoever hath been decayed by the fraude and malice of the deuil, or by his own carnall wyll, and frailnesse: preserue and continue this sicke membre in the unitie of thy Churche, cosyder his contricion, accepte his tears, aswage his payne, as shall be seen to thee moste expedient for him. And forasmuch as he putteth his full trust in thy mercy: Impute not unto him his former sinnes, but take him unto thy fauour: through the merites of thy most derely beloued sonne Jesus Christe. Amen.

This prayer, 'O most mercifull God . . .' (*Deus misericors, Deus clemens*) comes originally from the Gelasian Sacramentary. It is the solemn form of declaratory absolution used on Maundy Thursday at the reconciliation of those excommunicated at the beginning of Lent.

In the Second Prayer Book of Edward VI, issued in 1552, the form remains the same, but the reference to private confessions is omitted.

4 THE BOOK OF COMMON PRAYER, 1662

The form of indicative absolution remains the same, but is printed here with modern typography and spelling:

Our Lord Jesus Christ, who hath left power to his Church to absolve all sinners who truly repent and believe in him, of his great mercy forgive thee thine offences: And by his authority committed to me, I absolve thee from all thy sins, In the Name of the Father, and of the Son, and of the Holy Ghost. Amen.

Only slight changes are made to the last sentence of the prayer, 'O most mercifull God. . .'

And forasmuch as he putteth his full trust only in thy mercy, impute not unto him his former sins, but strengthen him with thy blessed Spirit; and, when thou art pleased to take him hence, take him unto thy favour, through the merits of thy most dearly beloved Son Jesus Christ our Lord. Amen.

5 THE PROPOSED BOOK OF COMMON PRAYER 1928

The form for confession again appears in the Order for the Visitation of the Sick. For the first time an actual confession appears and follows the earliest type of the *Confiteor*, before the names of the saints were added.

> I confess to God Almighty, the Father, the Son, and the Holy Ghost, that I have sinned in thought, word, and deed, through my own grievous fault; wherefore I pray God to have mercy on me. And especially I have sinned in these ways. . .

The absolution is in the 1549/1662 form and there is a much modified version of 'O most merciful God. . .'

> O most merciful God, who, according to the multitude of thy mercies, dost so put away the sins of those who truly repent, that thou rememberest them no more: Look upon this thy servant, who most earnestly desireth pardon and forgiveness. And forasmuch as he putteth his full trust only in thy mercy, impute not unto him his former sins, but strengthen him with thy blessed Spirit: and whenever thou art pleased to take him hence, take him into thine everlasting favour; through the merits of thy most dearly beloved Son, Jesus Christ our Lord. Amen.

6 ANGLICAN REVISIONS IN THE 1950s and 1960s

The 1954 Prayer Book of the Church of the Province of South Africa contained a separate form for Confession and Absolution. Forms included in the Visitation of the Sick lacked introductory rubrics but these are a major part of the new rite. The traditional form of blessing the penitent is given, a Roman-style confession, and the 1549/1662 absolution. Six years later the Church of India, Pakistan, Burma and Ceylon included an almost identical form in its new Prayer Book (printed below), but added the *Misereatur* and *Indulgentiam*. Both these forms reflect the nineteenth century Anglo-Catholic use based on the Roman rite.

> *The Church does not require of any that, in order to receive forgiveness of sins, he of necessity confess before a Priest, but only that every man be honestly assured in his own conscience of his duty in this matter.*
>
> *And such as shall be satisfied with a private confession to God in prayer ought not to be offended with those that use confession to God before a Priest; nor ought those who think it needful for themselves to confess their sins before a Priest to be offended with those that are*

satsified with their confession to God in private prayer together with a general confession of the Church; but let all alike remember in all things to follow and keep the rule of charity, and not to judge other men's consciences, seeing that there is no warrant in God's Word for so doing.

Every Priest in his exercising of this ministry of reconciliation, committed by Christ to his Church, is solemnly bound to observe secrecy concerning all those matters which are thus confessed before him.

At the time appointed the penitent shall kneel down in some convenient place in the church, and the Priest shall say unto him,

The Lord be in thy heart and on thy lips, that thou mayest truly and humbly confess thy sins.

Then shall the penitent make confession of his sins, using this form or the like.

I confess to God Almighty, the Father, the Son, and the Holy Spirit, before the whole company of heaven, and to you, that I have sinned, in thought, word, and deed, through my own most grievous fault. And especially (since my last confession) I have sinned in these ways. . . For these and all my other sins which I cannot now remember, I am heartily sorry, firmly purpose amendment, and humbly ask pardon of God, and of you counsel and absolution. Wherefore I pray God to have mercy upon me, and you to pray for me to the Lord our God.

After which confession the Priest shall give spiritual counsel and advice, if needed, and prescribe some simple act of devotion, commonly known as a penance; and if he is assured of repentance, he shall absolve the penitent after this sort:

Almighty God have mercy upon you, forgive you your sins, and bring you to everlasting life. Amen.

May the Almighty and merciful Lord grant unto you pardon, absolution, and remission of all your sins. Amen.

[The 1549/1662 absolution, but '. . . and of the Holy Spirit'.]

Then shall the Priest dismiss the penitent with a Blessing.

7 ANGLICAN REVISIONS IN THE 1970s

a. The Anglican Church of Australia, 1978 Prayer Book

The Australian book again includes a form of confession and absolution in the Visitation of the Sick. There are two possible introductions said by the priest and both may be used:

The Lord Jesus welcomes you. He came to call sinners. Have confidence in him.

> The Lord be in your heart and on your lips, and help you to make a true confession of your sins, in the name. . .

There are also two forms of confession, one general and one that allows for specific sins to be confessed. The penitent may, if they wish, use neither of these and make confession in their own words. The first form is simply that of the Holy Common (Second Order) put into the singular. The second is a version of the *Confiteor* form.

> Merciful God, my maker and my judge,
> I have sinned against you in thought, word, and deed:
> I have not loved you with my whole heart;
> I have not loved my neighbour as myself;
> I repent, and am sorry for all my sins,
> Father, forgive me.
> Strengthen me to love and obey you in newness of life;
> through Jesus Christ our Lord. Amen.

> Lord and heavenly Father,
> I confess that I have sinned in thought, word, and deed through my own fault;
> and especially I have sinned in this way . . .
> For these sins I am truly sorry,
> and firmly purpose to amend my life.
> I ask for your forgiveness,
> for Jesus' sake. Amen.

The absolution is the modernized 1549/1662 and there is another version of the prayer, 'O most merciful God . .' based more closely than 1928 on the original.

b. The Episcopal Church of the USA, 1979 Book of Common Prayer

The American book provides two forms of service with a common introduction:

> Concerning the Rite
>
> The ministry of reconciliation, which has been committed by Christ to his Church, is exercised through the care each Christian has for others, through the common prayer of Christians assembled for public worship, and through the priesthood of the Church and its ministers declaring absolution.
>
> The Reconciliation of a Penitent is available for all who desire it. It is not restricted to times of sickness. Confessions may be heard anytime and anywhere.

Two equivalent forms of service are provided here to meet the needs of penitents. The absolution in these services may be pronounced only by a bishop or priest. Another Christian may be asked to hear a confession, but it must be made clear to the penitent that absolution will not be pronounced; instead, a declaration of forgiveness is provided.

When a confession is heard in a church building, the confessor may sit inside the altar rails or in a place set aside to give greater privacy, and the penitent kneels nearby. If preferred, the confessor and penitent may sit face to face for a spiritual conference leading to absolution or a declaration of forgiveness.

When the penitent has confessed all serious sins troubling the conscience and has given evidence of due contrition, the priest gives such counsel and encouragement as are needed and pronounces absolution. Before giving absolution, the priest may assign to the penitent a psalm, prayer, or hymn to be said, or something to be done, as a sign of penitence and act of thanksgiving.

The content of a confession is not normally a matter of subsequent discussion. The secrecy of a confession is morally absolute for the confessor, and must under no circumstances be broken.

The first form again follows the traditional style (blessing, confession, absolution 1549/1662, dismissal), though an alternative absolution is offered which has its origins in those put forward for the revised Roman rite:

Our Lord Jesus Christ, who offered himself to be sacrificed for us to the Father, and who conferred power on his Church to forgive sins, absolve you through my ministry by the grace of the Holy Spirit, and restore you in the perfect peace of the church. Amen.

After the absolution, the priest adds: 'The Lord has put away all your sins.' The penitent replies, 'Thanks be to God.'

The second, fuller form is described by Marion Hatchett as 'particularly appropriate when a person has turned or returned to the Christian faith, or at other possible "crisis" points in a person's life.' (*Commentary on the American Book of Common Prayer* New York; [Seabury, 1981], p. 453).

The priest and penitent together say Psalm 51, 1–3, concluding with 'Holy God, Holy and Mighty, Holy Immortal One, have mercy upon us.'

Penitent Pray for me, a sinner.
Priest May God in his love enlighten your heart, that you may remember in truth all your sins and his unfailing mercy. Amen.

The priest may then say some verses of Scripture (Matt. 11.28; John 3.16; 1 Tim. 1.15; 1 John 2.1–2. He then continues:

Now, in the presence of Christ, and of me, his minister, confess your sins with a humble and obedient heart to Almighty God, our Creator and our Redeemer.

The Penitent says
Holy God, heavenly Father, you formed me from the dust in your image and likeness, and redeemed me from sin and death by the cross of your Son Jesus Christ. Through the water of baptism you clothed me with the shining garment of his righteousness, and established me among your children in your kingdom. But I have squandered the inheritance of your saints, and have wandered far in a land that is waste.

Especially, I confess to you and to the Church . . .

Here the penitent confesses particular sins.

Therefore, O Lord, from these and all other sins I cannot now remember, I turn to you in sorrow and repentance. Receive me again into the arms of your mercy, and restore me to the blessed company of your faithful people; through him in whom you have redeemed the world, your Son our Saviour Jesus Christ. Amen.

The Priest may then offer words of comfort and counsel.

Priest
Will you turn again to Christ as your Lord?
Penitent I will.

Priest
Do you, then, forgive those who have sinned against you?
*Penitent*I forgive them.

Priest
May Almighty God in mercy receive your confession of sorrow and of faith, strengthen you in all goodness, and by the power of the Holy Spirit keep you in eternal life. Amen.

The Priest then lays a hand upon the penitent's head (or extends a hand over the penitent), saying one of the following

[either the new absolution *Our Lord Jesus Christ* . . . or the 1549/1662 form]

The Priest concludes
Now there is rejoicing in heaven; for you were lost, and are found; you were dead, and are now alive in Christ Jesus. Go (*or* abide) in peace. The Lord has put away all your sins.
Penitent Thanks be to God.

One of the curious features of this rite is the provision for a 'declaration of forgiveness' to be used by a deacon or lay person. The form given is this:

Our Lord Jesus Christ, who offered himself to be sacrificed for us to the Father, forgives your sins by the grace of the Holy Spirit. Amen.

It is not clear theologically what the difference is between 'absolution' and a 'declaration of forgiveness' and, given that two forms of priestly absolution are provided this is even more unclear. The Canadian rite of 1985 (see below) goes a step further by abandoning the 'I absolve you' formula and keeping only the new American prayer. In part we have here the ultimate confusion caused by the Anglican double principle which was so well expressed in the preface to the South African rite. At its centre is the question of why, in theological rather than psychological terms, individual confession and absolution is needed if personal confession to God without absolution or corporate confession in the Christian assembly with absolution forgives sins.

c. *The Church in Wales, 1984 Book of Common Prayer*

The Welsh form appears in the context of the Ministry of Healing. A preface provides a rationale for the rite:

Our Lord Jesus Christ gave power to his Church to forgive sins in his Name. This ministry is exercised by Bishops and Priests. Absolution can be given generally, as in the public services of the Church, or individually and privately. . . Confession is open to all Christians. Those who fail by themselves to find peace of mind can, if penitent, be assured of God's forgiveness through the exercise of this ministry. Here, too, is the opportunity to ask for informed counsel when in doubt or difficulty. The prayers, readings or other devotions which the Priest may ask the penitent to use are suitable expressions of his thankfulness to God and his intention not to sin again.

This form follows the traditional shape (blessing, confession, counsel, giving of 'an appropriate devotion', 1549/1662 absolution). The absolution is received by the penitent with the words 'Amen. Thanks be to God.' The Priest may then bless the penitent and dismiss him, saying: 'The Lord has put away your sin. Go in peace; and pray for me a sinner.'

d. The Anglican Church of Canada, 1985 Book of Alternative Services

The Canadian preface differs from that in the American book in its unequivocal statement about the form of absolution:

> Originally, Christians who sinned gravely were publicly excluded from full fellowship in the Church and publicly restored after suitable penitence. Private penitence and private reconciliation appeared only after centuries of pastoral experimentation. The Reconciliation of a Penitent, although private, is a corporate action of the Church because sin affects the unity of the Body. The absolution is restoration to full fellowship: the priest declares the forgiveness which Christ has invested in his Church. The formula, 'I absolve you', which became common only in the thirteenth century, does not appear in these rites: it tends to individualize and further privatize what remains a corporate action of the Church.

Another interesting variation refers to the counsel given by the priest: 'Those who give counsel should be properly qualified.' This is an important safeguard, for not every priest is, or should be, a counsellor.

The main rite – the other is called a short form – is similar to the second American rite. It begins with a versicle and response:

> *Priest* Bless the Lord who forgives all our sins.
> *Penitent* His mercy endures for ever.

After a brief silence, they say together Psalm 51.1–2, 11–13, 16 or Psalm 103.8–10, 13–14.

> *The priest then says to the penitent*
> Dear friend in Christ, God is steadfast in love and infinite in mercy, healing the sick and forgiving the sinful. May God who enlightens every heart, help you to confess your sins and trust in his mercy.
>
> *The penitent says*
> Most merciful God, have mercy upon me, in your compassion, forgive my sins, both known and unknown, things done and left

undone, (especially . . .) O God, uphold me by your Spirit that I may live and serve you in newness of life, to the honour and glory of your name; through Jesus Christ, our Lord. Amen.

e. 'In Penitence and Faith'

This collection of texts compiled by the Archdeacon of Leicester, David Silk (Mowbrays 1988), includes the form for the reconciliation of a penitent that was rejected by the General Synod of the Church of England in February 1983, the main point of contention at that time being the *Ego te absolvo* form of the absolution. Archdeacon Silk has provided two forms of absolution, the first from the Liturgical Commission's book *Lent, Holy Week, Easter* (CHP-CUP-SPCK 1986), the second being the 1549/1662 form.

The service begins with the reception of the penitent:

The priest welcomes the penitent and they prepare for this ministry. The priest says these or other suitable words.

Grace, mercy and peace be with you. May the Holy Spirit enlighten your heart, and give you confidence to confess your sins, so that you may know the mercy of God.

Then the priest reads a short passage of Scripture. 1 John 1.6–7,9 is suggested, after which the penitent confesses either in the *Confiteor* form provided or without particular form:

I confess to almighty God, and to his whole Church, that I have sinned by my own fault, in my thoughts and in my words, in what I have done and what I have failed to do, especially . . . These are the sins which I remember; for them and for all my other sins I ask God's forgiveness.

The priest may then give advice if he is requested or if he judges it appropriate. He may recommend some prayer or action as a token of repentance.

The penitent should be encouraged to express sorrow and repentance in his/her own words or may say either

Almighty God, heavenly Father, I am truly sorry and repent of all my sins. Forgive me all that is past, and grant that I may serve you in newness of life to the glory of your name, through Jesus Christ our Lord.

or

Lord Jesus Christ, Son of God, have mercy on me, a sinner.

The priest may extend his hand over the penitent. He declares God's forgiveness to the penitent sinner, using these or some other appropriate words.

This is not, of course, an official text and the option of using 'some other appropriate words' provides a freedom that official rites (except the Greek Orthodox) usually lack. This is the *Lent, Holy Week, Easter* form:

God, the Father of all mercies, through his Son Jesus Christ forgives all who truly repent and believe in him: by the ministry of reconciliation which Christ has committed to his Church, and in the power of the Spirit, I declare that you are absolved from your sins, in the name of the Father, and of the Son, and of the Holy Spirit.

The rite concludes with a thanksgiving, in the form of a prayer said by the priest, based on the 1549/1662 'O merciful God', and/or a short litany. The three forms of dismissal include a version of the *Passio*. It should be compared with that used in the Roman Rite, on which it depends.

May the Passion of our Lord Jesus Christ
and his infinite merits,
whatsoever good you have done
and evil you have endured,
heal you of your sins,
help you to grow in holiness
and bring you to eternal life.
Go in peace.

8 THE ROMAN RITE

Three rites of penance were promulgated in 1973, one for the reconciliation of individual penitents, and two for the reconciliation of several penitents, one with individual confession and absolution and the other with general confession and absolution. The first form is, in Pope John Paul II's words 'the only normal and ordinary way of celebrating the Sacrament' (*Reconciliatio et Paenitentia*, section 32) and is, in consequence, the only one that we print here.

Rite for Reconciliation of Individual Penitents

Reception of the Penitent

When the penitent comes to confess his sins, the priest welcomes him warmly and greets him with kindness.

Then the penitent makes the sign of the cross which the priest may make also.

In the name of the Father, and of the Son, and of the Holy Spirit. Amen.

The priest invites the penitent to have trust in God, in these or similar words:

May God, who has enlightened every heart,
help you to know your sins and trust in his mercy.
The penitent answers: Amen.

There are five other forms of reception given from which the priest may choose. For example:

May the Lord Jesus welcome you.
He came to call sinners, not the just.
Have confidence in him.

The reading of the word of God follows, but is optional. The priest may read a text which proclaims God's mercy and calls man to conversion or he may say one from memory. Several suggestions of suitable texts are made; e.g. Isa. 53.4–6, Ezek. 11.19–20, Luke 15.1–7, 1 John 1.6–7,9. The priest and penitent are free to choose other readings.

Confession of Sins and Acceptance of Satisfaction

Where it is the custom, the penitent says a general formula for confession (for example, I confess to almighty God) *before he confesses his sins.*

If necessary, the priest helps the penitent to make an integral confession and gives him suitable counsel. He urges him to be sorry for his faults, reminding him that through the sacrament of penance the Christian dies and rises with Christ and is thus renewed in the paschal mystery. The priest proposes an act of penance which the penitent accepts to make satisfaction for sins and to amend his life. The priest should make sure he adapts his counsel to the penitent's circumstances.

Prayer of the Penitent and Absolution

The priest then asks the penitent to express his sorrow, which the penitent may do in these or similar words:

My God,
I am sorry for my sins with all my heart.
In choosing to do wrong
and failing to do good,
I have sinned against you

whom I should love above all things.
I firmly intend, with your help,
to do penance,
to sin no more,
and to avoid whatever leads me to sin.
Our Saviour Jesus Christ
suffered and died for us.
In his name, my God, have mercy.

Again, other prayers are given; for example:

Father of mercy,
like the prodigal son
I return to you and say:
'I have sinned against you
and am no more worthy to be called your son.'
Christ Jesus, Saviour of the world,
I pray with the repentant thief
to whom you promised paradise:
'Lord, remember me in your kingdom.'
Holy Spirit, fountain of love,
I call on you with trust:
'Purify my heart,
and help me to walk as a child of the light.'

Absolution

Then the priest extends his hands over the penitent's head (or at least extends his right hand) and says:

God, the Father of mercies,
through the death and resurrection of his Son
has reconciled the world to himself
and sent the Holy Spirit among us
for the forgiveness of sins;
through the ministry of the Church
may God give you pardon and peace,
and I absolve you from your sins
in the name of the Father, and of the Son, +
and of the Holy Spirit.

The penitent answers: Amen.

The absolution is followed by a concluding section entitled 'Proclamation of Praise of God and Dismissal'. Surprisingly the texts given here are neither very rich nor very varied. The 'praise' is simply a versicle and response. The priest says: Give thanks to the Lord for he is good. And the penitent replies: His mercy endures for ever.

Then the priest dismisses the penitent who has been reconciled, saying:

The Lord has freed you from your sins. Go in peace.
or:
May the Passion of our Lord Jesus Christ,
the intercession of the Blessed Virgin Mary,
and of all the saints,
whatever good you do and suffering you endure,
heal your sins,
help you to grow in holiness,
and reward you with eternal life.
Go in peace.

Three other forms of dismissal are given.

9 THE LUTHERAN BOOK OF WORSHIP, USA 1978

This books provides a form for individual confession and forgiveness. It begins by affirming the seal of the confessional.

The pastor greets the penitent. When the penitent has knelt, the pastor begins:

Are you prepared to make your confession?
Penitent: I am.

The pastor and penitent say the psalm together. [Psalm 51:16–18,1–2]
Pastor: You have come to make confession before God. In Christ you are free to confess before me, a pastor in his Church, the sins of which you are aware and the sins which trouble you.
Penitent: I confess before God that I am guilty of many sins. Especially I confess before you that . . .

The penitent confesses those sins which are known and those which disturb or grieve him/her.

For all this I am sorry and I pray for forgiveness. I want to do better.

The pastor may then engage the penitent in pastoral conversation, offering admonition and comfort from the Holy Scriptures. Then they say together [Psalm 51.1,11–13].

The pastor stands and faces the penitent or remains seated and turns toward the penitent.

Pastor: Do you believe that the word of forgiveness I speak to you comes from God himself?

Penitent: Yes, I believe.

The pastor lays both hands on the head of the penitent.

Pastor: God is merciful and blesses you. By the command of our Lord Jesus Christ, I, a called and ordained servant of the Word, forgive you your sins in the name of the Father, and of the + Son, and of the Holy Spirit.

Penitent: Amen.

After the absolution the penitent may either give thanks in silent prayer or join with the pastor in Psalm 103.8–13. This is followed by the dismissal, after which the penitent stands and may exchange the peace with the pastor.

10 UNITED CHURCH OF CHRIST, USA 1987

Formed in 1957 by the union of the Evangelical and Reformed Church with the Congregational Christian Churches, the United Church is of particular interest because of its large membership and its combination of widely different styles of churchmanship. Something of this is reflected in the rather heavily doctrinal introduction to the 'Order for Reconciliation of a Penitent Person'. Because of the special nature of this order it is here given in full.

Order for Reconciliation of a Penitent Person

Introduction

Services of reconciliation are one means by which the church expresses the universal priesthood of all believers (1 Peter 2.5,9; Revelation 5.10). Christians are called to 'bear one another's burdens and so fulfill the law of Christ' (Galatians 6.2). Priesthood, by definition, is a ministry exercised in behalf of others. It is the privilege and responsibility of Christians to intercede for one another, share mutual concerns, forgive one another's sins with God's help, and assure one another of God's forgiveness when Christians are alienated from God and neighbours. This order offers the freeing power of confession and absolution.

This order may be adapted to the particular circumstance in which it is to be used. It is absolutely essential that great care be taken to protect the confidentiality of the conversation with the penitent person. A pastor or another representative of the church may lead the service. It is recommended that this order be used only after the one leading it has had adequate opportunity to establish a relationship with the person seeking reconciliation.

For full participation, the person seeking reconciliation must have a copy of the order. A careful review of the order may provide a way of interpreting the meaning and purpose of personal confession.

Greeting

When the person seeking reconciliation arrives, the pastor or another representative of the church may greet the person informally and establish an atmosphere of openness.

LEADER

____________,
name
the grace of our Saviour Jesus Christ be with you.

PENITENT PERSON
And also with you.

[A]

LEADER
Hear the words of the psalmist: Have mercy on me, O God, according to your loving-kindness; in your great compassion blot out my offences. Wash me through and through from my wickedness, and cleanse me from my sin. For I know my transgressions, and my sin is ever before me.

[B]

LEADER
Let us say together these words of the psalmist:

ALL
Have mercy on me, O God, according to your loving-kindness; in your great compassion blot out my offences. Wash me through and through from my wickedness and cleanse me from my sin. For I know my transgressions, and my sin is ever before me.

Scripture may be read as a reminder of God's promise of love and forgiveness. The reading may be shared by those present. One or more of the following or other passages may be read.

Isaiah 53.4–6
Ezekiel 11.19–20
Matthew 6.14–15, 9.12–13, 11.28–30
Luke 6.31–38, 11.9–10
John 3.16
Colossians 1.3–14, 3.1–17
1 Timothy 1.5
1 John 1.1–2, 5–10

Confession

A confession may be said by all. After a period of silence, the person seeking reconciliation may be encouraged to make a confession in his or her own words.

General Confession

LEADER
Let us pray.

[A]

ALL
Most merciful God, we confess that we have sinned against you in thought, word, and deed, by what we have done, and by what we have left undone. We have not loved you with our whole heart. We have not loved our neighbours as ourselves. We are truly sorry, and we humbly repent. For the sake of our Saviour Jesus Christ, have mercy on us and forgive us that we may delight in your will and follow in your ways, to the glory of your name. Amen.

[B]

ALL
Gracious God, our sins as too heavy to carry, too real to hide, and too deep to undo. Forgive what our lips tremble to name, what our hearts can no longer bear, and what has become for us a consuming fire of judgment. Set us free from a past that we cannot change; open to us a future in which we can be changed; and grant us grace to grow more and more in your likeness and image; through Jesus Christ our Saviour. Amen.

Individual Confession

The person seeking reconciliation may confess silently and or aloud.

Pastoral Conversation

The pastor or another representative of the church may encourage dialogue with the person and offer understanding, comfort, counsel, and support.

Prayer of the Penitent Person

[A]

PENITENT PERSON
Almighty God, God of strength and mercy, who sent Jesus to save and forgive, I trust you. Forgive my sins. Refresh my spirit. Free me to love myself, my neighbour, and you. Amen.

[B]

PENITENT PERSON
Lord Jesus, have mercy on me, a sinner. Amen.

The petition may be repeated several times.

[C]

PENITENT PERSON
God, be merciful to me, a sinner. Amen.

Assurance of Pardon

The person seeking reconciliation is assured of God's forgiveness with the following or similar words. Agreement about questions to be asked should be reached in advance.

[A]
LEADER
This is a true saying, and worthy of all to be received, that Christ Jesus came into the world to save sinners. This is God's gift to us and to the world, so we can know abundant life.

[B]
LEADER
If we confess our sins, God is faithful and just, and will forgive our sins and cleanse us from all unrighteousness.

[C]
LEADER
I acknowledged my sin to you, and I did not hide my iniquity; I said, 'I will confess my transgressions to God'; then you forgive the guilt of my sin.

AND

A pastor or another representative of the church may ask the following or a similar question, and the person may respond in this or some other way.

LEADER
__________,
name
do you believe the promise of God's forgiveness?
PENITENT PERSON
I believe.

When it seems appropriate, the following question may also be asked.

LEADER
Do you forgive those who have sinned against you?

Time may be given for the one seeking reconciliation to reflect and to respond in this or some other way.

PENITENT PERSON
I do, with God's help.

The leader may give the declaration of pardon in these or similar words.

LEADER
In Christ's name, and as one with you in the church, I declare to you: Your sins are forgiven. Go in peace, in the knowledge of God's mercy.

THANKSGIVING

A pastor or another representative of the church may offer a prayer in her or his own words or may use the brief prayer and/or the acclamation.

A

LEADER

Creator and Saviour, giver and forgiver of life, we give you thanks for ___, your *son/daughter* in faith, who, feeling your presence and trusting your grace, has thrown off the anxiety of sin to receive the hope of your love. We offer our thanks to you, our good and gracious god, in the name of Jesus Christ by whom all sins are forgiven.

PENITENT PERSON

Amen.

11 EASTERN ORTHODOX RITES

As in the Latin Church, true repentance is necessary for the remission of sins in the Greek Church. This must be both inward, contrition and a determination to amend, and outward, participation in the rite of penance with confession of sins, the laying on of hands by the priest, and the prayer of absolution. The following account uses translations of the Greek and Slav rites, together with material from Casimir Kucharek, *The Sacramental Mysteries: A Byzantine Approach* (Allendale, New Jersey, Alleluia Press, 1976). ch. XX, with extensive references.

In Orthodoxy confessions are heard in any convenient part of the church, this may be immediately in front of the iconostasis or behind a screen or in a special room set apart for the purpose. Both priest and penitent stand or sit. The penitent faces a desk on which are placed the Cross and an icon of the Saviour or the book of Gospels. The service is attributed to the ascetical sixth-century Patriarch of Constantinople, John the Faster. Though parts of it originate in the eighth or ninth century, the whole probably dates from the eleventh or twelfth century, when it seems that everything connected with penitence was attributed to John! After the standard opening prayers, Psalm 51 is recited and then three penitential *troparia* (hymns). Then follow these two prayers asking for forgiveness:

> O God our Saviour, who through thy Prophet Nathan didst grant to penitent David forgiveness of his sins and didst receive Manasseh's prayers of repentance, do thou thyself in thy wonted loving-kindness receive thy servant *N.*, who repenteth of the sins he hath committed, overlooking all that he hath done, O thou who forgivest offences and passeth over transgressions. For thou, O Lord, hast said, I desire not the death of a sinner but rather that he should turn from his wickedness and live, and that sins should be forgiven even unto seventy times seven. How beyond compare is thy greatness, and thy mercy is without measure, for if thou shouldest regard iniquity, who should stand? For thou art the God of the penitent

and to thee we ascribe glory, to the Father, the Son, and the Holy Ghost, both now and ever, and unto the ages. Amen.

O Lord Jesus Christ, Son of the living God, both shepherd and lamb, who takest away the sins of the world; who didst remit the loan unto the two debtors, and didst vouchsafe to the woman who was a sinner the remission of her sins; do thou, the same Lord, loose, remit, forgive the sins, transgressions and iniquities, whether voluntary or involuntary, whether of wilfulness or of ignorance, which have been committed unto guilt and disobedience by these thy servants. And if they, bearing flesh and dwelling in the world, in that they are men, have in any way been beguiled of the devil; if in word or deed, whether wittingly or unwittingly, they have sinned, either contemning the word of a priest, or falling under his anathema, or have broken their vow, do thou, the same Master, in that thou art good and cherishest not ill-will, graciously grant unto these thy servants the word of absolution, remitting unto them their anathema and curse, according to thy great mercy. Yea, O Lord and Master, who lovest mankind, hear thou us who make our petitions unto thy goodness on behalf of these thy servants, and disregard thou all their errors, inasmuch as thou art exceedingly merciful; and loose them from punishment eternal. For thou hast said, O Master: Whatsoever ye shall bind on earth shall be bound in heaven, and whatsoever ye shall loose on earth shall be loosed in heaven. For thou alone art without sin, and unto thee do we ascribe glory, Father, Son, and Holy Ghost, both now and ever, and unto the ages of ages. Amen.

An admonition follows which may be in a set form, as in the Slavonic use, or may be extemporaneous.

> Behold, my child, Christ standeth here invisibly and receiveth thy confession: wherefore, be not ashamed, neither be afraid, and conceal thou nothing from me; but tell me without hesitation all things which thou hast done; and so shalt thou have pardon from our Lord Jesus Christ. Lo, his holy image is before us: and I am but a witness, bearing testimony before him of all things which thou hast to say to me. But if thou shalt conceal anything from me, thou shalt have the greater sin. Take heed therefore, lest, having come to a physician, thou depart unhealed.

The confession follows. It may be made spontaneously or in question-and-answer form. Lists of questions are found in the *Kanonaria*, a vestige of the older system of public penance, but the priest would usually use his own questions. An exhortation follows the confession:

> In all these points thou must henceforth be upon thy guard. For thou hast received a second Baptism, according to the Christian Mystery. And thou must see to it that, God helping, thou make a good beginning. But, above all, thou must bear thyself lightly towards these things, lest thou become a cause of scorn to men; for these things do not befit a Christian. But may God, by his grace, aid thee to live honourably, uprightly and devoutly.

Absolution is then given. The older Rituals, both Greek and Slav, give a variety of forms. All are deprecative. Greek Orthodox confessors are free to compose their own formula, though this one, dating from at least the eleventh century is generally used:

> May God who pardoned David through Nathan the prophet when he confessed his sins, and Peter weeping bitterly for his denial, and the sinful woman weeping at his feet, and the publican and the prodigal son, may that same God forgive thee all things, through me a sinner, both in this world and in the world to come, and set thee uncondemned before his terrible judgement seat. Have no further care for the sins which thou hast confessed, depart in peace.

The Slav rites follow a different form. First, this prayer is said:

> O Lord God, the salvation of thy servants, gracious, bountiful, and long-suffering, who repentest thee concerning our evil deeds, and desireth not the death of a sinner, but rather that he should turn from his wickedness and live: Show thy mercy upon thy servant *N.*, and grant unto him an image of repentance, forgiveness of sins, and deliverance, pardoning his every transgression, whether voluntary or involuntary. Reconcile and unite him unto thy Holy Church, through Jesus Christ our Lord, to whom also, with thee, are due dominion and majesty, both now and ever, and unto ages of ages. Amen.

And then this formula of absolution, composed by Peter of Mogila, Metropolitan of Kiev, in the seventeenth century, probably under the influence of Latin theologians:

> May our Lord and God, Jesus Christ, through the grace and bounties of his love towards mankind, forgive thee, my child *N.*, all thy transgressions. And I, an unworthy priest, through the power given unto me, do forgive and absolve thee from all thy sins. In the

name of the Father, and of the Son, and of the Holy Spirit. Amen.

The priest makes the sign of the cross over the penitent and then pronounces a blessing. He may also lay the end of his stoke (*epitrakhil*) on the head of the penitent while pronouncing the absolution.

A Guide to Further Reading

The literature on penance is very substantial. There is a useful bibliography for the entry 'Penance' in *The Oxford Dictionary of the Christian Church* (London, OUP, 2nd edn 1974), pp.1059–60. Fuller bibliographies, especially good for recent articles, may be found in James Dallen, *The Reconciling Community: The Rite of Penance*, New York, Pueblo, 1986; and in Joseph A. Favazza, *The Order of Penitents: Historical Roots and Pastoral Future*, Collegeville, The Liturgical Press, 1988. Bibliographies covering publications in numerous languages are provided in A. G. Martimort, *The Church at Prayer*, vol. iii The Sacraments (London, Geoffrey Chapman 1987), and in volume 3/1 (*I Sacramenti*) of the Italian multi-volume liturgical encyclopedia *Anàmnesis*, Genoa, Marietti, 1986.

The older standard works in English are still useful, especially Paul F. Palmer SJ, *Sources of Christian Theology II: Sacraments and Forgiveness*, London, Darton, Longman & Todd, 1960; and Bernhard Poschmann, *Penance and the Anointing of the Sick*, London, Burns & Oates, 1964. The latter is now superseded by Vorgrimler's 1978 revision, in German: *Buße und Krankensalbung*, Bd. IV.3, in the *Handbuch der Dogmengeschichte*, Freiburg-Basel-Wien, Herder, 1978. Also still of value is William Telfer, *The Forgiveness of Sins*, (London, SCM, 1959); and Paul Anciaux, *The Sacrament of Penance*, London, Sheed & Ward, 1962.

The entry 'Penance' in *Sacramentum Mundi* (London, Burns & Oates, 1969), written by Karl Rahner, provides a useful review of the history and theology of penance. So does the chapter on penance in Joseph Martos, *Doors to the Sacred* London, SCM, 1981. Greater detail and further references are to be found in Monika K. Hellwig, *Sign of Reconciliation and Conversion*, Wilmington, Dl, Michael Glazier, 1982. More recently, the eleventh congress of Societas Liturgica dealt with the theme, 'A Worshipping Church, Penitent and Reconciling', and the wide-ranging and ecumenical papers were published in *Studia Liturgica*, vol. 18, No. 1, 1988. Of particular value are those by Robert Taft SJ, Georg Kretschmar, Karl-Heinrich Bierritz, and Paul De Clerck.

Karl Rahner made a major contribution to the study of penance. In addition to the *Sacramentum Mundi* article, his most important writings are in *Theological Investigations* London, Darton, Longman

& Todd, vol. 1: 'Forgotten truths concerning the Sacrament of Penance', 'Guilt and its remission: the borderland between theology and psychotherapy'; vol. 3: 'Problems concerning confession'; and vol. 15, which is entirely devoted to the history of penance, together with 'Allow Yourself to be Forgiven', in Rahner's *Meditations on the Sacraments*, London, Burns & Oates, 1977.

Modern Roman Catholic teaching on both sin and reconciliation is well represented by the Post-Synodal Apostolic Exhortation of Pope John Paul II, *Reconciliatio et Paenitentia*, London, Catholic Truth Society, 1984. Piet Schoonenberg's study, *Man and Sin* (London, Sheed & Ward, 1965, 3rd impression 1976), remains a standard work on the subject.

The relation of penance and spiritual direction has only been mentioned in passing in this book and directly relevant material is rather limited. Christopher Bryant SSJE, touched upon this matter in much of his writing and especially, but all too briefly, in Cheslyn Jones, Geoffrey Wainwright and Edward Yarnold SJ, *The Study of Spirituality* (London, SPCK, 1986), pp.569–70, with a useful bibliography. Unfortunately there is no discussion of liturgies of penance in the companion volume, *The Study of Liturgy* (SPCK 1978) and the relevant entries in Gordon S. Wakefield, ed., *A Dictionary of Christian Spirituality* (London, SCM, 1983), i.e. 'Direction, Spiritual', by N. W. Goodacre, and 'Penitence' by Richard Harries, and in Sinclair B. Ferguson and David F. Wright, ed., *New Dictionary of Theology* (Leicester, IVP, 1988), 'Penance', by Colin Buchanan, are of little value. For the confessor, there is Kenneth Ross' slim but helpful volume, *Hearing Confessions* (London, SPCK, 1974), and the penitent could not do better than use Martin L. Smith SSJE, *Reconciliation: Preparing for Confession*, London, Mowbray, 1986.

In addition to the works cited here, reference should be made to those included in the footnotes of the appropriate chapters of this book.

Acknowledgements

We are grateful to the following for permission to reproduce copyright material:

Alleluia Press, Allendale, New Jersey, for extracts from *The Sacramental Mysteries: A Byzantine Approach* by Casimir Kucharek (1976).

The Central Board of Finance of the Church of England for the extracts from *The Prayer Book as Proposed in 1928* and *In Penitence and Faith*, compiled by David Silk (Mowbray 1988). The form for the reconciliation of a penitent from *In Penitence and Faith* on pp. 193–4 below is substantially reproduced from A Form for the Reconciliation of a Penitent (GS 530), © The Central Board of Finance of the Church of England 1982; the first form of absolution provided by David Silk is from *Lent, Holy Week, Easter*, © The Central Board of Finance of the Church of England 1984, 1986.

Church in Wales Publications for the extract from the 1984 Book of Common Prayer (Church in Wales).

J. M. Dent and Sons Ltd for the extract from the Dent/Everyman edition of the First Prayer Book of Edward VI, 1549.

Faber and Faber Ltd and Harcourt Brace Jovanovich Inc, Orlando, Florida, for the extract from *The Cocktail Party* by T. S. Eliot.

Grafton Books for the extracts from *Selected Poems 1946–68* by R. S. Thomas (Bloodaxe Books 1986).

The Indian Society for Promoting Christian Knowledge for the extract from the Prayer Book of the Church of India, Pakistan, Burma and Ceylon.

Oxford University Press for the extract from Peter Abelard's *Ethics*, edited and translated by D. E. Luscombe (1971).

The Service for Individual Confession and Forgiveness is reprinted from *Lutheran Book of Worship*, © 1978, by permission of Augsburg Fortress, Minneapolis.

Extracts from the Book of Common Prayer 1662, the rights of which are vested in the Crown in perpetuity within the United Kingdom, are reproduced by permission of Eyre & Spottiswoode Publishers, Her Majesty's Printers, London.

The extracts from *An Australian Prayer Book*, published by the Anglican Information Office, Sydney, © Anglican Church of Australia Trust Corporation 1978, are reproduced with permission.

The extracts from *The Book of Alternative Services*, © The General Synod of the Anglican Church of Canada 1985, are reproduced with permission.

Excerpts from the English translation of *Rite of Penance*, © International Committee on English in the Liturgy, Inc. All rights reserved.

The Order for Reconciliation of a Penitent Person, on pp. 198–202 below, is reprinted from *Book of Worship*, © 1986 by permission of the United Church of Christ Office for Church Life and Leadership.

Index of Biblical References

Index of Names and Subjects